DRAMAS
AND DISSENT 16

clissold**books**

First published by Clissold Books 2013

ISBN 978-0-9572088-1-0

Designed by Audiografix
Printed and bound in Great Britain by CPI

About *N16* Magazine

A couple of friends and I were sitting in a Stoke Newington bar in late 1998 when an idea occurred to us.

Stoke Newington was and is, despite being part of inner-city London, a small town. Virtually all small towns have their own local newspaper and, unless you include the *Hackney Gazette*, we didn't. For an area steeped in a fascinating history and a radical and dissenting culture, abounding in characters, intellectuals, writers and artists of all descriptions, and forever generating unusual, original events of interest and harmless skulduggery, this seemed a curious state of affairs. So my friends and I began to think of ways of overcoming this anomaly, and we came up with the idea of *N16* Magazine.

Our intention from the beginning was to produce a free, quarterly magazine which would be editorially led and would be entirely funded by advertising. The magazine would act as a sounding board for all the opinions, arguments and disputations which constantly arise in Stoke Newington, provide information on all the goings-on – civic, entertaining, mischievous and otherwise – and act as an informal organ of record for the N16 area. We set to work, calling in favours from other friends, writers, photographers and advertisers, and the magazine began to take shape.

In the first issue of *N16* Magazine, published in April 1999, we described ourselves as 'The Voice of Church Street'. From Issue 2 onwards, we decided that, given the diversity of the Stoke Newington area, we would broaden our coverage to include all aspects of living around here, and not simply concentrate on one street. So we then became *N16: The magazine at the heart of Stoke Newington*. Although the sub-title altered over the years, and has now disappeared completely, our original aims have not.

The response to our first issue was overwhelmingly positive, and seemed to demonstrate that we were on to something important. The feedback on the street and from advertisers was cheerfully congratulatory, and the following letters and emails are a small selection of those many positive comments which appeared in Issue 2.

Hi, I used to live in Carysfort Road until Feb 1954 when my father decided to move our family to Los Angeles, a move which I have never been happy about. I often think about my old stomping grounds and how great it was to be able to walk to the Arsenal on game days. It looks like the old area has undergone quite a change since I saw it last during a visit in August 1986.

Today a friend in Stoke Newington sent me the N16 paper. I have read every inch of it with great interest. For a few moments I was back there in my beloved Stoke Newington. I was born in 1947 in Manor Road (no. 111). I went to William Patten School and then to St Mary's just off Church Street. I would walk down Queen Elizabeth's Walk down the little wall at the side of the park. I went to school on the 106 to Clapton Pond and then on to Homerton. When I left school I worked in the Town Hall, and my mum and dad drank in the Jerry (now the Auld Shillelagh) opposite the Old Baths. My mum beat Eric Bristow at darts once when he was 16 years old. In 1971 I came to Suffolk and my two daughters are grown up now. But I just want to say I loved Stoke Newington. It's a very special place. I really enjoyed your paper.

I think N16's great, informative and a wonderful idea for the area. Having lived in the area from childbirth, but moving out due to work commitments, I still have Stokey in my blood and visit Church Street at least once a week (if not more).

I am writing to congratulate N16 on its first issue. The Hackney Labour Group supports this excellent initiative. It's great that the community in Stoke Newington now has such a professional publication. Good luck to everyone involved in producing N16.

I saw your new N16 magazine in a restaurant in Church Street and was amazed. I have seen many free magazines/papers for customers in restaurants but this was exceptional.

Naturally, there were some who disagreed:

PISS OFF BACK TO ISLINGTON OR WHEREVER IT IS THAT YOU CAME FROM — stop trying to create us in your own image and leave our community to the REAL people of Stoke Newington! Like America and Columbus we did actually exist BEFORE being 'discovered'. Now I dare you to print THAT in your pretentious little publication!

Well, we printed it, and we didn't hear from this gentleman again. But the general feeling appeared to be one of staunch support for the magazine, which, as the years have gone by, has become a regular and much-anticipated fixture of local life. We have also extended our editorial reach into adjoining areas, including Clapton, Dalston, Brownswood and down to Haggerston, but our focus remains on Stoke Newington.

Starting with a 20-page, 2-colour magazine in 1999, we are now publishing every three months a full-colour issue, which regularly contains over 50 pages of news, opinion, entertainment, music, cartoons, political views, humorous articles, extended essays, recipes, sport and a good deal more besides. In recent years the magazine has become less news-driven and more feature-led, reflecting the fact that news quickly dates, while comment and opinion have longer reading lives. To complement the diversity of the content, we are continually assessing our design and production values, so that each issue has something fresh to offer, both textually and visually. Our guiding principle, however, remains constant. Although our continuing existence is made possible only by advertising, we remain editorially led. Nobody tells us what to write and we remain proudly independent.

The fact that we reached our 50th issue in December 2011 suggests a serious error of judgement among those who predicted we would struggle to reach three issues, and indicates the loyalty and even affection which we have generated in Stoke Newington and areas beyond the N16 boundary since our meeting in that pub all those years ago.

About This Book

Dramas and Dissent is an edited compilation of twelve years and fifty issues of continuous publication of N16 Magazine. However, the book is emphatically not a self-regarding celebration of the magazine, nor is it a tribute to our sagacity in publishing entertaining, informative and revealing stories (although I think we largely succeeded in doing this). The defining and dominant theme running through this book is Stoke Newington and the surrounding area.

This geographical focus means that rather than trumpeting our achievements, if such they were, I have concentrated on trying to produce a book which will be of interest to, and almost entirely concerned with, all sectors of Stoke Newington life, instead of an inevitably much longer volume aimed at people far beyond our boundaries and reflecting on issues of wider political, philosophical and whimsical import. Therefore, I have forced myself to omit an excellent collection of articles – such as Cal Courtney's theological reflections, most of Richard Boon's entertainingly offbeat columns, Trevor Jones' wider political insights, Matthew Kennard's revealing interview with Noam Chomsky, Susie Snyder's thoughtful views from St Mary's, Nick Webb's cleverly erudite spoofs (except for one which I have retained) and Penny Rimbaud's impassioned and articulate political arguments, among others –

which, while they in many cases provoked widespread discussion and debate amongst our readers, would not look out of place in national publications or more general debating chambers. So, worthy and interesting as these articles are, their focus is not sufficiently local to secure a place in this book (although they can all be found in their entirety on the Back Issues page of our website).

Again, in the following pages you will find scant attention paid to the numerous restaurant and bar reviews which we have published, as these quickly become out of date, and are often in a constant state of flux, which is how things should be in such an energetic and vibrant community. The same criteria of omission apply to our regular football reports (dated as they swiftly become), music and arts listings, shopping reviews, and more general features such as cookery, recipes and gardening which, splendid as they were, tended not to be specific to the Stoke Newington area. My several interviews with Hackney's Mayor Jules Pipe again fall into this category, as they related to specific issues, since resolved, and were of their time. But many thanks anyway to all the above, and I hope you will continue to keep the magazine in mind when wishing to share your informative and often trenchant views with our readership. Also, the requirements of the market place and the cost of printing have both placed constraints on my editorial scope. Indeed, in several places, and mainly for reasons of space, I have had to edit individual articles without, I hope, altering the thrust, meaning or emphasis of each piece.

I interpreted my role as editor of the magazine as being one of making suggestions, where necessary, following up progress and helping to present the articles in a more or less grammatically correct form, without diluting the message. I certainly did not see myself as being a censor or a ruthless pen-wielder. If the piece was longer than requested, but was written with force and clarity, then I would find a way of getting it in the mag. There were occasions, however, when significant work was required. But these occasions were few and far between. Mainly, I discovered to my enormous pleasure how well people could write, particularly if they felt strongly about an issue. People who often appeared diffident and nervous about their writing ability proved themselves more than capable of producing interesting and entertaining articles. I believe their writing talent is evident in this book, and is one of the main reasons the magazine is still in its flourishing existence. I have generally left the articles in the context of the period in which they were written without updating the text. The book is intended to reveal the issues and discussions over a period of time, rather than to present the situation which exists today. However, I have updated the text in italics either in or at the end of some articles where I feel this may be of benefit to the reader.

I have structured the book into two main sections. Part 1 is a series of articles and illustrations in a continuous, almost narrative format. By 'narrative' I do not mean gradually combining the disparate threads of a story into one thrilling denouement. Rather, the three themes – History, People and Music – which comprise this section are more or less chronologically organised (although I jump about a bit), as well as each sub-section being significantly longer in extent than those themes in Part 2 which follows.

Part 2 is a series of illustrated single- or double-page spreads, each concerned with specific aspects of Stoke Newington life and our contributors' reactions to these. Thus, subjects include the 73 bus, education, the various Festivals, the Clissold Leisure Centre saga, arts, theatre, poetry, property, homelessness, the surrounding areas, media comments, international travel and so on. Interspersed throughout are edited

FREE | April 2004 | Issue Twenty One

the magazine at the heart of Stoke Newington

highlights from In Brief and Your Letters, again arranged chronologically. An astonishing panorama of Stoke Newington life is here, albeit in a mildly haphazard, scrapbook format, which seems to me to be appropriate to both the magazine and the area.

In any event, I hope I have managed to distil the essence of Stoke Newington life – its achievements, disputes, celebrations, spirited and often cantankerous mutterings – into a book which will be read, enjoyed and referred to for some while to come by everyone interested in the affairs and foibles of this eccentric little parish, as it has stumbled its way from a down-at-heel, ramshackle outpost of civility to today's buzzing, sought-after and often achingly trendy heart of North London life.

Inevitably, disagreements will arise over my selection, but as editor and publisher of N16 Magazine over the last few years, I believe my judgement in these matters is as good as anyone else's. I'm happy with the result, anyway. If you enjoy reading this book, as I hope you will, you can find all our back issues on the website www.n16mag.com.

Read on, and discover a lot of things you maybe didn't know about Stoke Newington. Well, where else would you live?

Rab MacWilliam, October, 2012

Contents

The Way We Were

It would be difficult to find another area in London with as enthralling and as varied a history as that of Stoke Newington. From its early days as a sleepy hamlet in the forest of Middlesex, through its incarnation as a leafy and generally prosperous home for Congregationalists, Quakers and other religious dissenters, to its current revival as a trendy little magnet for shoppers, diners, drinkers, club goers, yummy mummies and a home to almost 30,000 Hasidic Jews and many other races and cultures, the history of the area is a fascinating and unique one. Here is a selection from the magazine of some of the many different aspects of our history, beginning with a young lad from Stoke Newington Common who became a worldwide rock star. Slightly more conventional, although equally interesting, contributions then follow.

Young Bolan

By Robert Webb, Summer 2000 (6)

Marc Bolan was the first pop star of the '70s: an electric warrior in silver buckles and corkscrew hair. His run of classic hits with T Rex, including 'Get it On' and '20th Century Boy', established him as a teen idol for the post-Beatles generation. Although he died 23 years ago, Bolan is still very much a local hero. One of his top hats is on loan to Hackney Museum, and the Stoke Newington house where he spent his childhood is now marked with a plaque to its famous resident.

Bolan was born at Hackney General Hospital on 30 September 1947, the second son of Simeon and Phyllis Feld, a working-class Jewish couple. Simeon, known as Sid, was a van driver and sometime cosmetics salesman; Phyllis sold fruit and veg on Berwick Street market. Their new son was named Mark, after one of Sid's brothers who had died the previous year. The Felds lived at 25 Stoke Newington Common where they occupied four rooms. Mark shared a bedroom with his brother Harry.

Mark Feld (the name change would come in the '60s) attended Northwood Junior School from September 1952. 'I remember wearin brown corduroy shorts (real hip kid I was) & a blue n white Snow White T-shirt', he later wrote. His style was more than matched by his determination. 'I always had trouble in school. I wanted to find out about things that you couldn't just look up in books.' He discovered his parents' record collection and began avidly soaking up the latest American popular music. At eight his favourite song was 'The Ballad of Davy Crockett' by Bill Hayes. Keen to encourage his son's interest, Sid stopped off at a music store one day in 1956 to pick up a recording by Mark's much-loved songwriter. But by mistake the 78 he brought back to Stoke Newington wasn't by Bill Hayes. It was by Bill Haley. Unwittingly Sid had changed his son's life.

Rock and roll was Mark's call up. 'He used to sit upstairs in his room and play records on his radiogram at full blast', remembers the Feld's landlady, Frances Perrone. Before long he was on tea-chest bass in a school band, Susie and the Hoola Hoops, with fellow Northwood pupil Helen Shapiro. 'Mark was very into the look and the whole rock n roll thing, even back in 1957 when we played the Hackney cafes', she later recalled. The chubby kid with the quiff would sometimes help his mother on the Soho market and seek inspiration at the nearby 2is coffee bar, home of the new British rock and rollers such as Cliff Richard.

The Hoola Hoops soon lost momentum. Helen moved on to senior school at Clapton Park and in 1958 Mark started at William Wordsworth Secondary Modern in Shacklewell. He hung out at the Stamford Hill Jewish Youth Club and for a while fell in with a bunch of lads known as the Sharks, whose principal pastime was fighting rival gangs. 'Stoke Newington ... was a very potent place to be', according to Malcolm McLaren, born in Carysfort Road near Clissold Park in 1946, also into a Jewish family. 'It sported some of the first Teddy Boys ... I was always terrified.' For Mark and the other streetwise Jewish kids, the look was Levis and Italian suits, in opposition to the Teds' retro fashion. His friend Keith Reid shared an obsession with records and clothes. 'They'd just sit together and write music, morning to night at our house', remembered Phyllis. The songwriting stuck: Keith would later co-found Procol Harum, penning such classics as the ethereal 'A Whiter Shade of Pale'.

Stokey's musical youth congregated at the Hackney Empire, where the TV show 'Oh Boy!' was filmed. In April 1960 Mark saw his new American hero Eddie

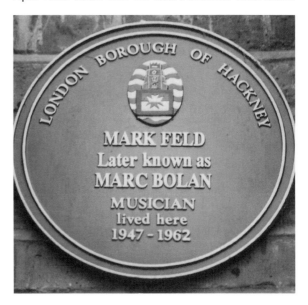

Cochran play there. The story goes that after the concert Cochran let the adoring young fan carry his guitar to a waiting limo. Tragically, only days later, on his way to the airport, the star was killed as his taxi slammed into a lamppost. Throughout his life Bolan was convinced of the mystical significance of that evening when he was handed Eddie's guitar. Cochran's demise was also an unsettling premonition of Bolan's own death in a car crash in 1977.

Within months of leaving school at 14, Helen Shapiro was touring the UK with the Beatles and topping the charts with hits such as 'Walking Back to Happiness'. Perhaps her success spurred Mark on. The Felds moved from Stoke Newington to Wimbledon in 1962, but by then the slimmed-down, sharp-suited Mark was on the verge of fame. At 15 he was featured in *Town* magazine as a face on London's emerging Mod scene. He became proto-hippy Marc Bolan in 1965 and formed Tyrannosaurus Rex a couple of years later. The glamour of T. Rexstacy was just a corkscrew curl away.

The Growth of Stoke Newington
By Rab MacWilliam, Autumn 1999 (3)

Stoke Newington's history goes back a long way. Although there is archaeological evidence that Stone Age people from the Paleolithic period hunted and camped along the 'Hackney Brook', Stoke Newington is not thought to have been continuously occupied until the late Saxon period of 600 AD.

The Romans had built 'Ermine Street' (now the A10, Stoke Newington High Street and Stamford Hill) in 47 AD, which formed the eastern boundary of what became Stoke Newington, with the western end defined by the old Green Lanes. The earliest written reference to 'Neutone', land which had been given by the 9th-century Saxon king Athelbert to St Paul's cathedral, is in the 1086 Domesday Book. It was then a small farming community with 4 farmers, 37 labourers and was part of the Middlesex (Middle Saxon) Forest, the population being around 100.

The prefix 'Stoke', loosely meaning 'timber' or 'tree stump', was in use by the late 13th century and, by the 1460s, the Church was leasing their 'demesne' (land) to 'Lords of the Manor'. The Stoke Newington manor house and grounds covered an area along the north side of Church Street, from the old church of St Mary's to just beyond today's Edward's Lane.

By 1613, the 'New River', a man-made canal to bring fresh water from Hertfordshire to Islington, had been dug out and, as there were no pumps, it had to follow the contours of the land. It snaked in and out of Stoke Newington, where a small part remains in Clissold Park. The need for water purification led to the development of the complex of reservoirs, filter beds and pumping stations to the north of Lordship Park. The old castle

pumping station is now a climbing centre, and a housing development, Myddleton Grange, has recently been built over the filter beds.

The parish's proximity to the City of London attracted rich merchants to the area from the 16th century onwards. By the early 18th century, a group of large mansions had been built at the eastern end of Church Street and in the High Street. Fleetwood House (built c 1634, demolished 1872), on the site of today's Fleetwood Street, was the grandest of them all; Abney House (built 1700, demolished 1843) stood on the western half of today's cemetery; Defoe's House (built c 1700, demolished 1865) was on today's Defoe Road, the grounds stretching back to Kynaston Road; the Manor House School (built c 1700, demolished 1880) replaced the Lord of the Manor's house and was later a school, famous for having Edgar Allan Poe as a pupil, on the site now occupied by The Fox Reformed; and Halstead House (built 1705, demolished 1930) was on the site of today's Rose & Crown.

At this time, groups of slightly smaller houses were also being built on Church Street. Church Row was a group of nine houses built in 1700 and demolished in 1936 to make way for the Town Hall; Sisters Place, the oldest existing building in Church Street, was built in 1715; and Paradise Row, a group of houses on the south side of Church Street facing Clissold Park, was erected between 1723 and 1764 and became the heartland of Stoke Newington's early Quaker community, with some of the re-fronted houses still standing today.

Maps of 1745 and 1800 show the parish as mainly farmland, with the only built-up areas being Church Street and Newington Green. Other roads, such as Lordship Road, Green Lanes, Matthias Road and Boleyn Road, existed simply as country lanes and

cattle tracks with little or no housing. The population at the time of the 1801 Census was slightly under 2,000. However, by 1821, to cope with the pressure of London's fast expanding population, the Pulteney Estate, which covered 60 acres of farmland on the south side of Church Street, was auctioned off in small building lots. Many of these were purchased by the renowned builder Thomas Cubitt, who proceeded to construct Albion Road and form Clissold Crescent.

With a regular horse bus service into central London, the pressure for more housing in Stoke Newington grew, although space was retained for the formation in 1840 of Abney Park Cemetery from the Abney and Fleetwood estates. Between 1840 and 1860 many acres of meadowland south of Church Street were used for the manufacture of bricks for house building. What was then South Hornsey had now been built, with the roads named after poets, eg Cowper and Milton, and Park Crescent on Church Street and Clissold Road had been erected on the Rector's land. By 1868, the land north of Church Street was also being developed, and Bouverie, Lordship and Yoakley Road now boasted fine houses.

By the 1891 Census the population was 47,988. This huge increase in population was caused by several factors. The revolution in transport made Stoke Newington even more accessible and desirable; the GER Stoke Newington railway station was built in 1872 and horse-drawn trams started running on the London Road (High Street) and Green Lanes in the early 1870s; the large brick field to the south of Church Street was built over with dense housing, giving birth to Dynevor, Kynaston, Sandbrook Road, etc and offering homes to the office workers, clerks and the lower middle classes; the demesne (Church) land north of Manor Road had been fully developed but with a bigger and better class of housing for the merchants and grandees; and Brownswood, west of Green Lanes, was being built up.

Stoke Newington's local government also underwent dramatic changes at this time. Originally run by its own vestry, which was instrumental in acquiring Clissold Park for public use in 1889, the area achieved Metropolitan Borough status in 1900, absorbing South Hornsey and its Town Hall in Milton Grove (Town Hall Approach is still evident on Albion Road). After the Great War, during which Stoke Newington lost 852 serving men, many from its own battalion, and suffered London's first Zeppelin bomb attack, Stoke Newington became a separate Parliamentary Borough in 1918, a status it was to retain until the creation of the Hackney and Stoke Newington North constituency in 1948.

Transport, too, was becoming easier and contributing to the area's development. The horse-drawn trams on Green Lanes and the London Road had been replaced by electric trams in the first decade of the century, and by 1936 these were in turn being replaced by trolleybuses. However, it was not until 1952 that the last electric tram (the 33) was taken over by the 171 bus. Although not exactly on Stoke Newington's doorstep, the opening of Manor House tube station in 1932 nonetheless provided another main route in and out of the Borough.

During the 1930s, development proceeded with vigour. In 1930 Clissold Swimming Pool was opened, in 1937 the new Town Hall was inaugurated, and in 1936 the LCC proposed to take over 64 acres of Stoke Newington land at Woodberry Down for housing. The population had now mushroomed to over 50,000, and more housing was urgently required. The LCC's proposal had to remain on ice, however, until after World War Two.

In 1965, to the dismay of many residents, Stoke Newington's independence shrivelled away when it became part of the London Borough of Hackney. Administrative expediency and the ever-increasing centralisation of powers had triumphed over local autonomy, but development and conservation works continued. Clissold Park and part of Church Street was made a conservation area in 1969. A somewhat dilapidated Abney Park Cemetery was sold to Hackney Council for £1 in 1978.

From being a run-down, inner-city street in the early 1980s, Church Street has undergone a cultural and commercial renaissance and is now the vibrant heart of Stoke Newington life, its influence spreading to other parts of the area.

Two Men and a Park

By Rab MacWilliam, Spring 1999 (1)

Clissold Park might now be a housing estate, were it not for the efforts of two men.

Clissold House was commissioned in 1790 by Jonathan Hoare, a Quaker and merchant, whose family were prominent in the anti-slavery movement, and completed in 1793 in what was then Newington Common. However, Hoare got into debt and his mortgage was foreclosed in 1800, the house and estate then transferring to one Thomas Gudgeon. The Crawshay family acquired it from Gudgeon in 1811 and the estate was renamed Newington Park. In 1835, Crawshay died, and his daughter Eliza took it over and married curate Augustus Clissold. Clissold died in 1882 and the estate passed back to the Crawshay family, who sold it in 1886 to the Ecclesiastical Commissioners for the purposes of building and development, to the horror of local people.

However, a newly formed environmental pressure group, the Commons Preservation Society, had other plans for the park. Along with the Metropolitan Public Gardens Association, they argued for the need to conserve the rare trees and local ecology of the park, and their campaign was joined in 1887 by a committee headed by Joseph Beck and John Runtz, both of whom were local residents.

Working day and night, holding public meetings and raising a 12,000-name petition, Beck and Runtz finally persuaded Runtz's employers, the forerunner of the LCC, in the face of stiff opposition from the developers, to accept money from Stoke Newington vestry and three neighbouring local authorities (South Hornsey, Hackney and Islington) to buy the park. The decision was validated by a new Act of Parliament, the Metropolitan Open Spaces Act, which allowed the land to be kept for public use and access. Beck paid a cheque for £96,000 into the Bank of England on the morning of 10 January 1889, and the park was saved.

The park was opened on 24 July 1889 by the Earl of Roseberry, Chairman of the newly established LCC, and was one of the first parks in London to provide animals and rare birds. The newspapers of the day described it as 'the finest of London's open spaces' and concluded that 'for beauty, it cannot be matched for miles around'.

As a mark of respect and gratitude, a public subscription was raised to erect a water fountain in honour of Runtz and Beck. The fountain, on the path from the bridge over the pond to Green Lanes is still there today. The pair were further commemorated by naming two lakes to the north of the park Beckmere and Runtzmere, although the names have fallen into disuse. Thanks to these two men, and the substantial support of the local people, Stoke Newington now had its own public space and one which at least rivalled Victoria Park (the first London park, built in 1845) to the south and Finsbury Park (1860) to the north. And the developers had to look elsewhere.

Daniel Defoe

By Tom Chalmers, Spring 2006 (29)

A pub, a road – there can be no doubting Daniel Defoe's place in Stoke Newington's famous past. But what do people associate with the great writer? For most, it would be that desert island book, or maybe that other story of his which was made into a saucy costume drama a few years ago. Well, what about Defoe the convict, the bankrupt, the spy, the founder of journalism, the disreputable hack, the rebel, the informer, the man who at one point even had his cats taken away from him?

Born the son of a butcher in 1660, Daniel Foe (he added the 'De' later to give his name more of an aristocratic ring) was raised as a dissenter. Unwilling to swear an oath to the Church of England, Oxford and Cambridge were off limits and he was educated at Morton's Academy at Newington Green, a school for dissenters run by the legendary non-conformist Charles Morton. Not one for the quiet life, Defoe decided against the ministry and briefly joined the defeated Monmouth rebellion in 1685 against James II. It was while hiding in a graveyard that he noticed the engraved name of one 'Robinson Crusoe'. Forced into semi-exile for three years, Daniel still refused to let it lie and took to writing pamphlets against the King – a particularly dangerous hobby. However, with a swap of allegiance that became something of a trademark throughout his career, his support of William led to a return to favour, and to London. However, things did not run smoothly for Defoe at home, either. Although a wife, a healthy dowry, seven children and a number of businesses paint a picture of domestic bliss, in 1692 he was declared bankrupt with debts believed to be around £17,000.

While a pamphleteer was considered the lowest form of writer, Defoe continued to produce work at a prolific rate and followed the success of *True Born Englishman* by getting himself straight back into trouble with *The Shortest Way with Dissenters*. When it finally dawned on the Tory government that it was in fact a satirical piece, their laughter quickly turned to embarrassed fury, and poor Daniel was promptly fined, imprisoned and sent to the Charing Cross pillory. Luckily, his pen this time came to his rescue and rather than hurling rotten fruit, the audience toasted to his health as he read out *A Hymn to the Pillory*.

His stay in prison was brought to an end by the help of murky Tory official Robert Harley, and the now-famed writer was working as a spy. During this time he set up *The Review* (a thrice-weekly newspaper and the first of its kind), was sent to Scotland undercover, where he successfully built up support for its union with England, and was taken to court by the Whigs and promptly imprisoned once again. However, when the Tories fell from power, how did he react? Well, unsurprisingly considering his reputation, he swiftly swapped allegiances and started working for the Whigs.

While it's the publication *of Robinson Crusoe* in 1719 and *Moll Flanders* in 1722 that built his reputation as the founder of the modern novel, it is his previous work that has led many to describe him as the founder of British journalism. He also wrote on travel and economics, picked up a few more arrests and hung around on the scaffold to speak to prisoners for novel research – but there is only so much that can be included in one article. Defoe died in 1731 of lethargy but by then he had done more than enough to mark his place in local folklore.

Tom is the founder and managing director of independent book publisher Legend Press (legendpress.co.uk).

A Tale of Two Churches
By Rab MacWilliam, Summer, 1999 (2)

Nestling in the shadow of its neo-Gothic, nineteenth-century offspring, Old St Mary's Church is in appearance more of an old English village church than a typical inner-city place of worship

A church, or at least a chapel, probably existed on the site at the time of the Norman Conquest. Unfortunately, as a large part of the parish was given to St Paul's in 940, the church records were destroyed in the Great Fire of London in 1666, so accurate confirmation of its venerable age must be speculative. What is certain, however, is that the church had a rector in 1313. The oldest recorded burial monument (long since gone) is that of Matilda Elkington, erected in 1473, and the first written evidence of the church's dedication to St Mary appears in 1522. The old stone, flint and pebble medieval building was completely renovated by Lord of the Manor William Patten in 1563, with only the old nave and south porch remaining.

The reconstruction was marked by an inscription above the entrance – '1563 Ab Alto' – the Latin term loosely translated as 'from above', indicating the heavenly inspiration for the enterprise. Various restoration works took place over the next three

centuries, culminating in 1806, when the building was covered with cement to imitate stone, and in 1829 when Sir Charles Barry, architect of the House of Commons, carried out further structural changes and installed gas lighting. By the mid-19th century, the old church was capable of accommodating 700 worshippers.

In 1855 the churchyard was closed to burials in new graves, although it was still possible to bury anyone in brick graves and vaults already built. This right was taken away in 1899, although the last interment was in 1912. Famous residents of the churchyard include the Presbyterian Divine Thomas Manton, the anti-slavery campaigner James Stephen (great-grandfather of Virginia Woolf), Alderman William Picket (Lord Mayor of London in 1789), Lady Mary Abney and Victorian poet and writer Anna Letitia Barbauld.

The renowned architect Sir George Gilbert Scott, whose portfolio included the Albert Memorial, began work in 1853 on the new St Mary's Church on the site of the old rectory, and the building was completed, minus its spire, in 1858. By the time the 250-foot spire was added in 1890, the church could accommodate 1100 people. Although electricity came to Stoke Newington in the 1890s, it was not until 1911 that the old church converted from gas, its more modern neighbour opting for electricity twelve years later.

In 1940 both buildings were severely damaged by bombs, the new church losing, among other things, its roof, and the old church its 18th-century north aisles, but both were back in working order by the mid-1950s. In 1998 the new church became the first London church to be fully floodlit.

In recent years, the Old Church has been used as a community venue and as a setting for musical and dramatic events. Funding and other problems appeared to threaten its essential renovation, and it was in danger of closing. Happily, these issues have now been resolved. The old building will be formally re-opened as St Mary's Old Church Arts Centre in Spring 2013.

A Pint in the Past
By Torquil McTavish, Winter 2000 (4)

They've always liked a drink in Stoke Newington. The oldest recorded inn was Le Bell on the Hoop in 1403, and by 1870 there were no less than twenty-five taverns and beer shops catering to thirsty Stokey dwellers.

Starting with what is now the Bar Lorca (*now The Three Crowns*), its name was changed from the Cock and Harp in the early seventeenth century to The Three Crowns to commemorate the visit of King James I, passing by in 1603 to be crowned king of Scotland, England and Ireland. The name lasted until 1990, when it was rechristened The Samuel Beckett, in an attempt to give the place some Irish intellectual authenticity, and it assumed its present name in 1995. (*The name reverted to The Three Crowns in 2009.*) Famous local resident Daniel Defoe attended his masonic meetings in this pub in the 18th century.

Booth's Cafe Bar (*now Homa*) was once two private houses and, by 1931, both dwellings had been converted into a clothing factory. It was turned into a bar in *1998*. Up the road, we find the imposing Daniel Defoe. Built in the 1860s, it was originally called The Clarence and its exterior was Grade 2 listed in 1975. Its reincarnation as Steptoe's ended recently. (*The Daniel Defoe, a Charles Wells pub, was revamped in 2011.*)

The Auld Shillelagh started life as a dairyman's shop by 1848 and became The Horse and Groom by 1871. It was also Grade 2 listed in 1975 and assumed its present title in 1991. Up the street a bit we find The Stoke Tup (*now the Lion*). An inn called The Red Lion stood on this site in 1697, and behind it used to be the local lock-up and fire station. A gloomy place it was, and an imaginative refurbishment in 1988 saw the pub reborn as The Magpie and Stump, part of the Saxon Inns chain. It's still often known as The Magpie, although it was tupped in 1998.

Not many people know this, but ... there used to be a pub opposite Pronto Pizza, and it predated this fast food establishment by at least 300 years. The Falcon Tavern certainly existed by 1723 and the omnibuses would stop here on their gallop into London in the nineteenth century. It was rebuilt in 1854, and closed its doors for the last time in 1930. The building was demolished in the late 1950s and lay derelict until 1993 when Gujurat House was erected on the site.

The Fox Reformed was built in 1878 on part of the site of Stoke Newington's second official manor house, and was used as a courtroom dispensing local justice. From 1806 until its demolition it was a school (one of whose alumni was Edgar Allan Poe). The building became a wine bar, Fox's, in 1981, and later the Fox Reformed. Over the road is Ryan's. The building and the 19th-century draper's shop extension were listed Grade 2 in 1975 (what was going on in 1975?), and since the late 1980s it has been variously La Mancha, The Vestry and it now seems content with its present title.

Finally on Church Street, the Rose & Crown moved from its original position across the road from the existing building in the 1930s, and the original Truman, Hanbury and Buxton interior has been lovingly preserved.

For up to date information on these Church Street bars and on all the bars in the surrounding area, visit n16mag.com.

Fighting the Flames
By Rab MacWilliam, Spring 2000 (5)

An inscription on an old tombstone in Old St Mary's churchyard commemorates the untimely death of 23-year-old Elizabeth Picket, who died in 1781 from severe burns when her clothes caught fire while ironing. This is the first recorded reference to firefighting in Stoke Newington.

By the 1780s the local parish possessed a pump-powered fire engine, which was probably kept at St Mary's Church. The location of the engine and firefighting equipment was to change several times over the next 200 years, moving in 1806 to the north

side of Church Street, near today's Barn Street, and in 1820 to Red Lion Lane, just behind today's Tup (*now Lion*) public house. By 1858 the station had moved again, this time to Stoke Newington High Street, just opposite Dynevor Road. Within ten years Hackney and Stoke Newington's fire brigade was merged into the new Metropolitan Fire Brigade, and the engine was called out to a house fire in Edwards Lane in 1871. However, it was too late to prevent the death of the occupant 19-year-old Amelia Kennedy.

In 1886 a new, three-storey fire station was built, at the cost of £5,500, in Leswin Road. By the turn of the century, with the service now under the control of the London County Council and renamed the London Fire Brigade, two Fire Escape Stations had been established in the area. These were manned by an Escape Conductor and staffed by volunteers who would manhandle a heavy set of wooden ladders mounted on a two-wheeled cart to the scene of a local fire to save lives. During World War Two, local firefighters were kept busy attending to the numerous conflagrations caused by German bombing. In 1954, a large depository owned by J Hibbard & Sons, situated between Bouverie Road and Abney Park Cemetery, was almost completely destroyed by fire. Over 150 firemen and 30 pumps fought the flames: it was described at the time as 'the biggest catastrophe since the War'.

In 1968, with London now administered by the Greater London Council, the city's 122 fire stations were divided into three commands, Stoke Newington Fire Station No C23 being part of eastern command. The existing fire station on Leswin Road was increasingly outdated and, in 1976, a new, two-storey, two-engine station, with a separate practice tower station, was built on Church Street on the site of the western half of Fleetwood House (*where it remains*). It was immediately in action when a large fire at Whincop's timber yard (*now Whole Foods*) prompted the demolition of houses and shops in Aldam Place. Since then, there have been several substantial fires in the area, notably at the Raleigh Memorial Church in Albion Grove in 1989 and the blaze that gutted St Mary's Church Hall in Defoe Road in 1993.

Newington Green

By Rab MacWilliam, Summer 2000 (6)

Newington Green came into being in the 15th century as a small hamlet, and remained a predominantly rural area until the late 18th century. The early residents were wealthy, as was evidenced by the grand houses and hunting lodges owned by such grandees as Percy, Earl of Northumberland. Henry VIII had a hunting lodge here, as well as several rooms for his mistresses, and the corpulent Tudor monarch took his daily constitutional along the nearby King Henry's Walk. Also of architectural interest are the four houses at numbers 52-55, which were built before the Great Fire of London. This terrace is one of the oldest in London.

Attracted by the area's rural charm, relative seclusion and a sympathetic Lord of the Manor, the non-conformists arrived in the mid-17th century and established various 'academies' on the Green. Chief among these seats of dissenting learning was Charles Morton's Academy, which flourished between 1667 and 1696.

The Unitarian Chapel was built in 1708 (the date is still clearly visible on the building to the north of the square) and enlarged in 1865. It is today the oldest non-conforming place of worship in London. The Reverend Dr Richard Price became minister in 1758. Price was a philosopher, mathematician and friend of Benjamin Franklin, Thomas Jefferson, David Hume and Tom Paine, and his writings in favour of the French Revolution prompted a counter-attack from Edmund Burke in his *Reflections on the Revolution in France*.

Intellectually lofty the area may have been, but baser instincts were also represented not too far away, principally at John Ball's entertainment house, which encouraged bull-baiting, drinking and general lechery, while the local duck hunters enjoyed their sport at the Ball's Pond. Footpads, cutpurses and assorted villains lay in wait between the villages, and care had to be taken when travelling along the path to Stoke Newington half a mile to the north.

Other notable residents of the Green were Mary Wollstonecraft, author of *A Vindication of the Rights of Women* and mother of Mary Shelley, the author of *Frankenstein*, who ran a girls' school with her sister Eliza from 1784 to 1786, and the poet Ann Letitia Barbauld. Andrew Rutherford, an eminent 19th-century researcher on microscopy and microorganisms, and the poet and banker Samuel Rogers were also local inhabitants and members of the Chapel.

By the mid-19th century, however, the surrounding farmland had been largely replaced by buildings and brickworks, and the charming haven of Newington Green was rapidly becoming part of inner London. Mildmay Park railway station was built in 1850 (and closed in the 1930s) and Canonbury Station was opened in 1870. Trams from the bustling Manor House depot came down Green Lanes, round the Green and transported the local clerks and office workers into the City. To serve the growing population, several public houses were opened. The Weavers Arms was opened in 1827 with the Alma following in 1866.

The religious impulse in Newington Green, however, remained strong, and several Christian Missions, including the Mildmay and South Indian, were established in the mid-19th century. The China Inland Mission, on the west side of the Green, was founded in 1872 by missionary James Hudson Taylor, and was transformed into the Alliance Club in 1964 (*it is now a student hall of residence*). Schools were also being built in the area, with St Jude's Primary School opening in 1865 and Newington Green School shortly afterwards. World War Two brought serious destruction to the area – with 22 people killed in a bomb attack on one house in Poet's Road – and there were mass evacuations to the safer countryside. After the War, new developments sprang up, and the social composition of the area underwent changes.

Angry of Stoke Newington
By Anne Beech, Winter 2001 (8)

On 20 August 1971, just after four in the afternoon, eight of the Met's finest burst through the door of a 'dingy first floor flat' *(Daily Express*: although, according to other sources, it was the top-floor flat) at 395 Amhurst Road, arrested the four occupants – Anna Mendelson, Jim Greenfield, John Barker and Hilary Creek – and took away, amongst other things, quantities of gelignite, a sten gun, a Beretta, detonators, a duplicator and a John Bull printing set. The Stoke Newington Four, otherwise known as the Angry Brigade, had been nicked. Yet again, Stoke Newington was in the news – and yet again, it seemed, for all the wrong reasons.

Some nine months later, in May 1972, the four – now joined by four others and collectively if somewhat unimaginatively known as the Stoke Newington Eight (at one stage, in an almost Malthusian expansion, the total had risen to ten) – were charged with conspiring to commit 25 bomb attacks throughout Britain over a period of nearly four years. One target had been local: a branch of Barclay's Bank in Stoke Newington High Street, now more familiar as the Stoke Newington Book Shop, was bombed on 26 October 1970. Inconveniently for the police, the bombings continued even after the trial was underway.

The trial itself lasted 109 days, and involved over 200 witnesses for the prosecution, 688 exhibits and more than 1000 pages of evidence: Britain's biggest ever conspiracy trial. At the end of the trial, in which the prosecution's charges were met with defence counterclaims that the Amhurst Road evidence had been planted by the police, that the forensic evidence offered

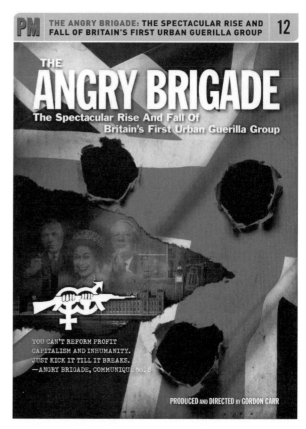

PM   THE ANGRY BRIGADE: THE SPECTACULAR RISE AND   12
FALL OF BRITAIN'S FIRST URBAN GUERILLA GROUP

THE ANGRY BRIGADE
The Spectacular Rise And Fall Of Britain's First Urban Guerilla Group

YOU CAN'T REFORM PROFIT CAPITALISM AND INHUMANITY. JUST KICK IT TILL IT BREAKS. —ANGRY BRIGADE, COMMUNIQUE No. 8

PRODUCED AND DIRECTED BY GORDON CARR

in support of a conspiracy was inconclusive – if not fundamentally flawed or possibly even fabricated – and that no incontrovertible proof had been offered of any real conspiracy, charges against four of the defendants were dropped. In a majority verdict, the jury found the original Amhurst Four guilty of both conspiracy and possession. Creek, Mendelson, Barker and Greenfield were sentenced to ten-year jail terms for conspiracy, to run concurrently with fifteen-year sentences for possession. In his summing up, the judge observed that political trials did not happen in Britain, and reminded the jurors that the Crown case did not have to prove that any of the defendants had actually bombed anything, only that they had conspired to do so.

Who or what were the Angry Brigade? Who did they represent? And why were they considered so important at the time? Opinions and theories differ – now and then. For many on the left, they were the innocent victims of an explicitly political show trial: genuine class warriors fighting heavy-handed state oppression. To others, they were misguided, self-styled 'urban guerrillas', the 'big-head brigade' of university dropouts with no agenda and no legitimate revolutionary credentials. In the eyes of the prosecution, they were but the tip of a post-68 revolutionary iceberg that threatened to destabilise and ultimately overthrow the democratically elected government of the day – a government, it should be remembered, that was facing concerted opposition to plans for a new Industrial Relations Bill, and more than a little discontent.

A Stokey Murder

By Lee Jackson, Spring 2007 (33)

I have gutted a clergyman in Stoke Newington, as well as burying an infamous actress, and disinterring a fraudster – fortunately, all in my fiction. However, despite being fairly steeped in Victorian vice, it was only recently that I discovered that N16 can boast (if that is the word) a genuine Victorian tragedy –'The Stoke Newington Murder' – a case that gripped the capital in the first few days of 1884.

The details of the crime were sketchy at first: a young man had simply gone missing in the early hours of New Year's Day, his coat, hat and shirt collar found on a patch of waste ground between Queen Elizabeth's Walk and the western reservoir of the New River Company. The water was swiftly dragged – the Company being all too familiar with finding bodies, due to either suicide or accident – and a corpse was recovered. But what had actually happened?

Suicide seemed unlikely: the deceased, one John Broom Tower, a lodger at 109 Dynevor Road, was an insurance underwriter, 'a young man of quiet and steady habits', who had done nothing more on New Year's Eve than attend a church service in Highbury with his fiancée and her family. A drunken mishap was an impossibility: a fence surrounded the reservoir's grounds, and the nineteen year old had imbibed only a single glass of claret to usher in the New Year.

In fact, there was every indication of a mugging gone wrong: a ring, watch, and money had been taken, with the young man's clothing lost or torn in the process. Moreover, the place where Broom's hat and coat were first found (other items were found by the reservoir) was a dead-end, obscured by trees, the neighbourhood being described as a 'lonely one ... undergoing the change from country to town'. Queen Elizabeth's Walk was, in fact, a building site, with houses on the western side of the road still under construction. Thus, newspapers speculated that Broom had been lured to the spot by his attackers. The discovery of an earring nearby even prompted rather spurious reports that a prostitute might be involved.

The Coroner's verdict was 'wilful and malicious murder by persons unknown'. Minute examination of footprints by Scotland Yard detectives suggested that Broom was assaulted by two men, then ran towards the reservoir, in a desperate bid to escape, only to be caught, strangled and dumped in the water.

What I find fascinating about this case is the light it throws on London life in the 1880s. It caused something of a panic ... was no-one safe in these new 'lonely suburbs'? A *Times* editorial felt obliged to urge calm and contemplate comforting statistics: 'For one slain by the garrotter or burglar there are dozens killed

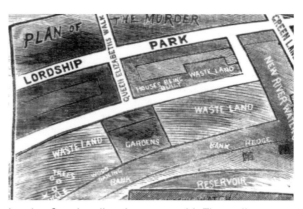

by the fast bowling hansom cab'. The police even offered a £200 reward – twice the young man's annual wage (or, indeed, twice the wage of a police inspector).

But what happened next, you may ask? The murderers were never caught. This is fact, not fiction, after all. There were, however, complaints, on hygienic grounds, that the New River Company refused to drain its reservoir. And, two years later, a lunatic confessed to Broom's murder. Police did not believe him and concluded his (limited) knowledge of the facts was because he was 'among the thousands of visitors who came to inspect the scene of the crime'.

The White Russians of N16

By Leonora Collins, Spring 2001 (9)

There were a number of White Russian (anti-Communist) families in exile in Stoke Newington after the Russian Revolution. Many were Jewish. They were like characters from Chekhov and often spoke amongst themselves, in Russian, of the old times before the revolution. Some went to the Egerton Road synagogue but most were fairly secular.

They lived well, as they had managed to leave Russia with quite a supply of valuables. One large house in Amhurst Park had a ballroom, and all had a drawing room, a breakfast room, a nursery, a maid's bedroom and all the other things necessary for life in Stamford Hill. The women were very smart and had more sophisticated tastes than local people. They were the first to wear the latest fashion: hats large or small, lipstick light or dark, hair blonde or auburn. Like most White Russians they had relatives in Paris, many of whom worked in small exclusive shops or large hotels. This provided an excellent excuse to visit Paris and they all spoke French better than English — at least at first. A fashion-conscious lady would sometimes buy one garment from Chanel or another famous designer and, when it was out of date, carefully detach the label and sew it into something with less prestige.

The White Russians smoked a lot, ate in restaurants in town (there were none suitable in Stoke Newington), played bridge and enjoyed music. They were flamboyant. One woman called Sonya had red spectacle frames shaped like a heart and a letter of her name painted in silver on each of her darkly varnished finger nails. Violent arguments and dramatic reconciliations were so normal as to be almost unnoticed. These domestic dramas were embarrassing for visitors, but an audience didn't inhibit the actors. Sometimes the lady of the house would seize a reluctant dog, cat or child and declare that this was her only friend. Her husband would settle down with a newspaper, muttering, before deciding to take action by storming from the room. A few minutes later both of them would be playing some strange two-handed card game and purring at each other in Russian. The original dispute would be forgotten, of course.

Paradise Regained

By Rab MacWilliam, Spring 2001 (9)

'The gates of the abode of the mortal part of man'
(Inscription at High Street entrance to Abney Cemetery)

Abney Park Cemetery, established in 1840, was from the outset designed to continue the distinctively Stoke Newington tradition of non-conformity and a healthy disrespect for established authority.

Laid out on the grounds of the Abney and Fleetwood estates (the railings on the Church Street entrance were the main gates for Abney House), the thirty-one acre cemetery was, like its contemporaries at Kensal Green and Norwood, an enlightened Victorian attempt to move on from the overcrowded churchyards which were then prevalent. However, unlike the other London cemeteries, Abney Park was unconsecrated and non-denominational, reflecting an area populated by Jewish and Huguenot refugees, anti-slavery and religious tolerance campaigners, and Dissenters, Congregationalists, Quakers and political and religious mavericks of all descriptions.

William Hosking, Professor of Architecture at King's College, London, was responsible for the building and landscaping. He created not simply a burial ground but also a public botanical garden and nature reserve, designed to offer peaceful, leisurely surroundings to the local inhabitants. An arboretum was laid out by the famous horticultural nursery of Loddiges of Hackney, which at the time was the largest arboretum in Europe. George Loddiges planted and tended 2500 different varieties of shrubs, over 1000 varieties of rose bushes and grew a wide range of trees, including American oak and tulip trees.

Variety was also present in the graves, tombs and occupations of the deceased. The earlier, modest tombstones of the sober-minded dissenters were soon outnumbered by the grandiose, ornate constructions of the later Victorians, and the brooding, now decaying Gothic chapel at the centre of the cemetery overlooks a fascinating, if melancholic, jumble of religiosity, piety and hope for the life eternal. A life-size statue of Dr Isaac Watts (author of 'O God, our help in ages past' and who is himself buried in Bunhill Fields) keeps a watchful eye on the inhabitants, who include Salvation Army founder William Booth and his son Bramwell, leading Chartist James Bronterre O'Brian, PC William Tyler (murdered in Tottenham in 1909) and Frank Bostock (local zoo keeper, whose tomb is guarded by a sleeping lion).

The cemetery quickly became popular, and within fifteen years of its opening the ground was described as 'a mass of corruption underneath'. By the beginning of the 20th century over 100,000 people had been buried within its walls, and the practice of infilling – building new plots between existing graves – was beginning to squeeze an already cramped cemetery. In 1896 an observer noted, 'The tombstones are crowded together as closely knit as seems possible and yet they are constantly being added to.' The Abney Park Cemetery Company was running out of money, vandalism was becoming rife and, by the mid-20th century, maintenance was virtually non-existent. The once magnificent botanical garden had turned into an unkempt, dangerous urban jungle.

When the Company finally went bust in 1974, however, the Save Abney Park Cemetery Association persuaded the London Borough of Hackney to buy the space for £1. The years of neglect and decay were finally tackled, and the Abney Park Cemetery Trust was given a 21-year lease in 1992. The site was officially declared Hackney's first local Nature Reserve in 1993, and improvements continue to be made to this unique ecological habitat.

The cemetery is now being increasingly used for theatrical, children's, educational and musical events, and as a backdrop for video and TV programmes.

www.abney-park.org.uk.

The Mysterious Edgar Allan Poe

By Tom Chalmers, Autumn 2006 (31)

A resident of Stoke Newington early in his life, Edgar Allan Poe remains one of literature's most heralded names.

There have been numerous books offering theories on Poe's mysterious early death (alcoholism, drug abuse, cholera, rabies, kidnap, violent assault, drugging and involvement in an election scam have all been put forward to date), and his start to life was also marked by tragedy. His father deserted the family in 1810 when Poe was one year old, and in 1811 his English mother died of tuberculosis. His previously wealthy grandfather had by this time been reduced to poverty and could only take on the oldest sibling. So, as a result, Poe and his sister were adopted, young Edgar going to the family of John Allan, a successful tobacco merchant.

When Poe was just six years old, the Allan family moved to England and Poe began his education in Chelsea. Then, in 1817, he moved to the Manor House School in Stoke Newington, which was situated where Edwards Lane meets Church Street, the current home of The Fox Reformed Wine Bar.

In his short story *William Wilson*, Poe describes this period of his life and calls Stoke Newington 'a misty-looking village of England', noting the resounding sound of the church bell (from Old St Mary's).

Although the landmarks and road remain, this was a very different place to the hustle and bustle of today, and Church Street was lined with grand old residences – Poe describing his school as a 'huge old house'. It is strange now to imagine Stoke Newington as a picturesque village far detached from the urban sprawl of London. The school was run by Rev John Bransby who was, by all accounts (with the exception of Poe's), very popular with the students. In his reports of Poe, Bransby said that he 'liked the boy' though he was concerned that he was spoiled by his parents through excess pocket money: the child was 'intelligent, wayward and wilful'.

The fact that Poe was spoiled in his formative years is interesting when considering his increasingly fractious relationship with his adoptive father, who was a tough disciplinarian and became infuriated with Poe's wayward behaviour. It culminated with Allan refusing to pay a gambling debt, and the two severed all contact until a deathbed wish to Poe from his adoptive mother pushed them to attempt reconciliation. However, following Allan's remarriage, their relationship deteriorated again and they didn't speak until Allan lay on his own deathbed.

This relationship is something that clearly affected Poe greatly. There was to be a final sting in the tail when news arrived that no will could be found. As a result, Poe inherited nothing, having gone through his education in the belief that he would inherit a fortune. In fact, the writer suffered from poverty for most of his life. In 1831, he returned to Baltimore and moved in with his aunt, a home he returned to throughout the remainder of his turbulent life. It was here that he met his aunt's daughter, Virginia, whom he married in 1836, when she was just 13 years old. He had published his first poetry in 1830 and followed this up with five short stories in 1832. Though often producing disturbingly macabre work, he went on to become the best-known US poet at the time, although reportedly it was for his short fiction that he wanted to be recognised.

From the age of 25, Poe became increasingly troubled and sought refuge in destructive alcohol and opium binges. However, this didn't affect his prodigious literary output, and he also held a series of editorial positions, being one of the first to recognise the potential of periodical publishing as a popular medium. Tragedy struck again in 1842, when Virginia burst a blood vessel while singing and was diagnosed with tuberculosis. Years of fluctuating ill health followed, and she eventually died in 1847. This hit Poe extremely hard and, while he still achieved literary success, his life spiralled further out of control, despite his late engagement to childhood sweetheart Sarah Elmira Royster. Then, in 1849, after getting on a train to New York and disappearing for several days, he was found in the street in an incoherent state. Four days later he died in hospital.

Up and Down the Ermine Road

By Mike Roberts, Winter 2001 (12)

As you walk along the High Street today, you still can gain faint glimpses of the long history of the road. Your eye catches old advertising signs like that of Dysons, a long gone grocer's store, and the diverse mix of buildings, spanning several centuries, now clad with the plastic signage and metal/glass frontages of the late 20th century.

During the Roman occupation of Britain, the army built a network of long straight roads to connect its military outposts. What we now know as the High Street formed a small part of what was Ermine Street, connecting London and Cambridge. After the departure of the Romans the road fell into neglect, and it wasn't until the middle of the 18th century that a concerted effort was made to maintain this main thoroughfare.

Because of the strict laws of the City, the good and the great would come out to Stoke Newington, and the area around, to enjoy the taverns and inns and to seek amusement. On the High Street in the 16th century the Earl of Oxford had a residence. He lived for part of the year in Stoke Newington because it was an easy journey to 'The Theatre' in Shoreditch: the first theatre in the country. It is believed by some that the Earl was the author of much of Shakespeare's work. He later moved to Brooke House in Hackney where he died of 'ye plague' in 1604.

In 1603, King James Sixth of Scotland and First of England, who had travelled down from Scotland to claim his new crown, gained his first view of his new capital at the top of Stamford Hill. The royal party stopped for refreshments at the Cock and Hoop on the corner of Church Street. The landlord, spotting a great marketing opportunity, changed the name to The Three Crowns in honour of the event – the three crowns being England, Scotland and Ireland.

Besides the pleasure seekers, who brought money in to the local economy, for the most part the area was given over to farming, and the High Street would see a constant stream of farm animals being driven along the road for slaughter in the City. Big carts carrying grain, vegetables and fruit also took a huge toll of the often-flooded road. In an effort to fund work on the road, The Stamford Hill Turnpike Trust was formed in 1713 and was in charge of the road from Enfield to Shoreditch. The Turnpike Trust erected tollgates at the top end of Kingsland Road and at Stamford Hill. They were supposed to maintain the road and the drainage of the area. However, in 1776 a commission was informed: 'the waters are frequently out in the said road so as to prevent passengers from travelling and have continued so for some hours; that the mail has been stopped several times ... (and) that no money has ever been laid out or method taken by the Trust to carry off the said waters.'

The bad road was not the only hazard faced by travellers along the road. Highwaymen and robbers, most famously Dick Turpin, operated along Stamford Hill. Having held up a coach, they would quickly retreat to the Hackney marshes only a short distance to the east. Things became so bad that in 1774 an application was made to Parliament for an act to establish a proper watch, and to water the parish in the summer season. Tollgates were abolished in 1864. The local residents, however, fought to save the income from the gates, claiming that it was grossly unfair that the upkeep of the road should be placed on the local rates. They argued that the road offered 'benefit merely of great carrying companies, and other persons keeping vehicles'. And, having been one of the first tollgates, Stamford Hill's was not removed for a further six years, becoming one of the last in the country to disappear.

Up until the 1850s Stoke Newington was very much an up-market country village with many fine houses for both the gentry and literary classes. For centuries the church owned the surrounding land, and the right to build new houses was strictly controlled. One of the few exceptions is the small group of large 18th-century houses at 187-191 High Street. With the growth in population, the wealthy residents moved further afield. And in 1830 an invalid asylum founded by Mary Lister 'for respectable females' moved into

number 187. In 1864 The Stamford Hill and Stoke Newington dispensary moved into number 189 and survived until 1952. The third house was used for a period as an orphanage, then returned to use as a private house. In 1884 it was taken over by the London Female Penitentiary 'for the rescue and reclamation of betrayed and fallen women'. This survived until 1939. The three houses fell into disrepair before being modernised and used as Council offices (*one now houses Yum Yum restaurant and flats, while the other two are in use as offices*).

The High Street was the main road from the City to East Anglia, the Northeast and Scotland, with very little building along it except for pubs, inns and blacksmiths serving the passing trade. In 1812, an Act of Parliament allowed the leaseholders of the land to build property. During the next 60 years growth was steady but slow. This, however, was all to change. It wasn't until about 1852, when land values increased, that you could get a better income by building than by farming. And so Stoke Newington slowly took on a prosperous suburban outlook, although not everyone was happy about it. In 1864 Shirley Hibbard, a major Victorian garden writer who lived in Lordship Terrace, noted with worry that new building works was 'a cordon of bricks' around the old heart of the village and was threatening the local nightingales.

The great explosion in building and the development of the High Street came about because of the development of the railway. In 1872 the Great Eastern Railway opened Stoke Newington Station allowing rapid access to the City and, as today with the Underground, the opening of a new station meant that adjacent house prices and the value of land shot up. At about the same time the North Metropolitan Tramways Company began to lay tracks along the course of the High Street through Dalston and into the City. These were electrified in 1907. With the huge influx of people, disease became an ever-increasing worry. As early as 1831 a severe case of cholera stuck the area and yet, as building work increased, very little was done in the way of safeguarding health. The Hackney Brook, which crossed the High Street very near to the entrance to Abney Park Cemetery, was described as the 'receptacle of everything offensive'. It wasn't until 1856 that the ancient Brook was culverted. The Brook still exists as a major drain to this day (*and passes along under Northwold Road beside Stoke Newington Common*). With the boom in housing, shops and entertainments opened up to serve the new community. By the end of the 19th century the local press described Stoke Newington as 'chock full'. At the southern end of the High Street, near to Princess May School, Stoke Newington's own theatre was opened in 1897. The Alexandra at 65-67 Stoke Newington Road was designed by Frank Matcham and seated 1,700 people. After struggling for many years it finally closed in 1950 and was pulled down to create new housing. During the 20th century the popularity of the movies saw a number of cinemas open along the street down to Dalston: such as The Vogue and The Coliseum.

However, it is shopping that has dominated the High Street since the late 19th century and which provides us with clues to its past. By the Edwardian era, the High Street had reached its prime:

'Stoke Newington is one of the brightest and pleasantest of the London boroughs, and from a residential standpoint its attractiveness is enhanced by its excellent shops. These, for variety and the useful services they render, are second to none in any London suburb. The moneyed members of the community, to whom price is not a primary consideration, seldom find it necessary to go to the West End to satisfy the most exacting requirements; while for those who are content with the best quality and reasonable charges there is a wide choice of shops, equal to every demand and covering the whole field of temporal necessities.'

In recent years, the High Street has experienced renewed development, with new and renovated restaurants, cafes and bars opening, alongside other retail outlets. The Turkish and Kurdish communities have been integral to its commercial rebirth.

The Clapton Messiah
By Anne Beech, Summer 2002 (14)

Probably not many people know that a century ago, a certain John Hugh Smyth-Pigott declared himself the messiah. And it's almost certain that no one knows he did so in neighbouring Clapton, at what was then known as the Church of the Ark of the Covenant, which had been built by members of the Agapemonite sect some ten years earlier, in 1892.

The Agapemonites (from Agapemone, literally 'the abode of love') were founded in Brighton in the 1840s by a disaffected Anglican priest, Henry James Prince, whose passionate evangelical preaching proved irresistibly attractive to the wealthy and the gullible – particularly wealthy, gullible women, preferably recently widowed. In 1849, Prince and his followers – and their money – moved to the village of Spaxton, in Somerset, where they purchased a 200-acre plot of land and set about creating what was intended to be a self-supporting community of some 60 disciples, all of them dedicated to the sect's eccentric views on marriage, the messiah, immortality and the sect leader's 'unconventional' views on the role of women, his specially chosen spiritual 'brides', in the newly established order.

The community prospered, so much so that they were able to fund the construction of the church in Clapton, while their spiritual leader wrestled with the demands of his many brides, but in 1899, seven years after they had built the church, the unthinkable happened. The immortal Prince died. Like the rest of the Agapemonites, he was buried standing up, in readiness for the resurrection. But a successor – another messiah – was urgently required.

John Hugh Smyth-Pigott fitted the bill to perfection. A charming, feckless womaniser, he travelled from Dublin to the Clapton church on the corner of Rookwood Road and Clapton Common to announce to an astonished and largely unprepared world that he was the new messiah: 'God not man'. In the ensuing riots, and unable to provide proof of his claim that he could walk across Clapton Pond, he left Hackney swiftly, travelling to the quieter and less hostile environs of Somerset, where he 'modernised' the order and committed himself to an even more vigorous and demanding succession of 'brides' than had his predecessor: seven a week, according to one report. What his long-suffering wife, Catherine, thought of this arrangement is not known.

After one particularly careless 'bride' produced three children, Smyth-Pigott was finally defrocked by the Anglican Church and, regrettably for an immortal, shuffled off this mortal coil in March 1927. To have lost not just one immortal messiah but two, in succession, was too much for the surviving community, which fell into decline and eventually disbanded.

The Agapemonite Church in Clapton, abandoned by the sect in the 1920s, was eventually acquired by the Ancient Catholic Church in 1956, and stands as an architectural footnote to one of the more bizarre English cults of recent years – and two of the greatest religious charlatans of the last 150 years.

What's in a Name?
By Mike Roberts, Autumn 2002 (15)

We all tend to take street names for granted but each in its own way marks a particular person or an event in time. Here are a few local examples.

Abney Gardens and *Abney Park Terrace*:
> Sir Thomas Abney who became Lord of the Manor of Stoke Newington in 1700.

Albion Road:
> The use of Albion in naming streets became very popular around the country, and reflected the wave of patriotism which followed Napoleon's threat to invade Britain.

Barbauld Road:
> Anna Letitia Barbauld was a well-known member of the Stoke Newington literary circle in the late 18th / early 19th century.

Burma Road:
> Honours the formation of Burma as a single province within the British Empire in 1886.

Clissold Crescent / Road:
> The Rev. Augustus Clissold, curate of St Mary's. Clissold Crescent was formerly known as Park Lane.

Defoe Road:
> The road runs through what used to be the grounds of Daniel Defoe's house.

Edwards Lane:
> Job Edwards was the 18th-century builder of Church Row. This row of houses was demolished to provide space for Stoke Newington Town Hall.

Manor Road:
> Marks the northern boundary of what was the Manor of Stoke Newington.

Northwold Road:
> Commemorates the village of Northwold in Norfolk, which was the country home of Lady Amhurst of Hackney.

Palatine Road:
> In memory of properties which had housed the Palatine refugees from the Rhineland in 1799.

Queen Elizabeth's Walk:
> It is believed that Queen Elizabeth I visited the Manor House and used to walk through the grounds of the house into the fields beyond.

Town Hall Approach:
> Connects Albion Road to Milton Grove, where the first Stoke Newington Town Hall was built.

Black History Month
By Ryan Clement, Summer 2003 (18)

October 2002 welcomes the 15th Anniversary of Black History Month in Britain. It is a time when the rich diversity of black people and their contributions to British culture and society are celebrated. From its humble beginnings way back in 1987, when it emerged as part of the African jubilee year Marcus Garvey celebrations, it has grown into a much anticipated and enjoyable annual event.

Additionally, BHM is also seen as a way of improving race relations in Britain. It enables all – of all colours – to acknowledge and appreciate the contributions made by black people to the enrichment of British culture and society. Also, like it or not, we are living in a multiracial and, yes, multicultural society. Therefore, a better understanding of these cultures can only help eradicate racial prejudice, discrimination and ignorance.

British culture is dynamic not static. Its history bears testimony to that. Therefore, controversially, what might be deemed part of another culture in our multicultural Britain today may well form an integral part of a British culture tomorrow. Each snapshot in time reveals something new in our culture; be it when migration began with the arrival of Bronze Age migrants from north-west Europe, to the arrival of the Celts to the arrival of the Romans, to the large scale invasions by Angles, Saxons, Jutes, Frisians, people from what is now northern Germany, southern Denmark and the northern parts of the Netherlands. Then we have the Norse influence by the Viking invasions and the French influence by the Norman invasion. And we are only at the year 1066! Is our British way of life static?

Can any one race claim a monopoly on its culture? Obviously not! Surely, much depends on when that snapshot is taken. Furthermore, people tend to focus on the arrival in June 1948 of the four hundred or so people from the Caribbean to the UK on Empire Windrush. However, these were not the first 'significant' number of black people to emigrate to Britain. Lest we forget, albeit against their will, of course, between 1555 and 1883 Britain saw an increase in the number of peoples from Africa as a result of the slave trade.

Why, therefore, the need for BHM? Well, when, for example, the Director of Public Prosecution, announces during a national radio interview that 'it is my firm belief that British society is institutionally racist within the Macpherson definition from the Lawrence inquiry. A great deal has got to be done across the whole spectrum of British society, so I come to this with the idea that the whole of society has a problem', one sits up and takes heed. Putting aside the question of how 'people' can be 'institutionally' anything, there is a serious underlying message. It beggars belief that people, in this day and age, can still be treated less favourably than others due to their race or, as is often the case, the pigmentation of their skin. Is this the product of the 'civilised society' our politicians boast about?

On 8 November 1965, the Bill described by Sir Dingle Foot as 'a landmark in our legislation' received its Royal Assent to become the first race relations legislation in the UK – the Race Relations Act 1965. Since this first Act there has been further Race Relations Acts; each seeking to build on the success of its predecessor. 'It is a pity', said an MP, 'that a Bill of this character should be thought necessary. In a sense, it is a human failure that it should be necessary to proceed by legislation in these matters. Compulsion should not be necessary to ensure that men and women live happily together and treat one another in a decent and civilised manner.' I agree, but sadly such legislation together with occasions such as BHM are necessities we can ill afford to be without at the moment. BHM should be fun, educational and culturally rewarding. Also, as there is no authorised co-ordinating body for it, anyone can organise an event as part of the many festivities being held.

Squatting

By Tim Webb, Spring 2005 (25)

The Radical Dairy (*see following article*) was a high-profile occupation in Kynaston Road in 2002. It was established in an empty shop and operated as a kind of alternative arts centre. The only jarring note was a semi-permanent police presence that hovered nearby, watching, photographing and muttering into two-way radios.

The forces of law and order then launched two raids, but left after local residents and neighbours protested in support of the occupants. Finally, 30 riot police stormed the building using a hydraulic ram. They said they had a warrant to investigate 'the misuse of drugs and abstraction of electricity.' No drugs were found. The real purpose of the raid was to take away the hard drives of the computers that were being used to provide a free internet service. Stoke Newington's finest probably believed they were playing their part in the war on terror.

So what is a typical squat? Most squatted properties have been empty for some time and quite a few belong to the council. A few years ago, some enterprising staff in Hackney housing department ran a profitable scam by selling the keys to unoccupied council flats and pocketing the money. Nowadays, estate safety teams, employed by the council, talk to residents and keep an eye open for any squats that keep legitimate tenants on the housing waiting list.

Although squatting is not illegal, forcing entry is classed as 'trespass', which is against the law. Squatters' organisations advise against the use of crowbars, and suggest that it is best to keep a lookout for properties that seem a little run down and have been empty for two or three months. Evictions cannot take place without a court possession order. This has to be applied for within 28 days of the owner becoming aware of the occupation. If the order is granted, the squatters will be required to leave within 24 hours.

The roots of squatting stretch back a long way. In 1649, after the English Civil War, Gerrard Winstanley and the Diggers occupied St George's Hill in Surrey and declared 'England is not a free people, till the poor that have no land have a free allowance to dig and labour the commons ...' Needless to say, as punishment for their failure to appreciate the rule of the landowners – many of whom had gained their property by force – the Diggers were beaten up, their houses destroyed and their corn burnt.

After the Second World War, in response to the government's slow progress in rehousing families bombed out of their homes, a national squatting campaign resulted in the mass occupation of vacated barracks. In 1946, over 45,000 people moved into disused army camps. The London squatters' movement targeted empty blocks of luxury flats. Hundreds of homeless people carrying bedding turned up in Kensington High Street at Duchess of Bedford House and were let in through the tradesman's entrance by Tubby Rosen, a councillor from Stepney, who had climbed in through a side window. Four communist councillors were arrested and charged with 'conspiracy to incite and direct trespass'.

The '70s were a boom time for squatting and its organisations. About 70 members of the All London Squatters Federation met in the unlikely surroundings of Imperial College in November 1973. The minutes reveal confusion as well as determination: some did not want to be 'organised'; others – spotting an opportunity – wanted to squat a room across the corridor; objections were raised to having a chairman; and, somewhat surprisingly, given that the meeting was being held in the university's electrical engineering department, the lights flickered on and off. Reports were provided from the various squats. Herne Hill said that although they had been evicted, they had made friends with the guard dogs and their handlers and had reoccupied the premises. 'Flying squats' were discussed and the conditional support of the National Front ('housing English people only') was rejected ('tell them to fuck off – housing for all!').

In parts of London, squatting became rather fashionable, but the motives of some of its practitioners were rather different from those of the puritanical Diggers. *New Society* quoted Chris Welby, a Kentish Town squatter: 'I'm really disappointed with the calibre of people in this squat. There's too much of what I'd call the teacher training college radical, not enough of the university radical. In Hampstead, the local paper reported: 'the squatters protested that although they might keep the residents awake at night, the residents woke them at 8am when they went to work'.

There is now a widespread culture of squatting in the UK. One of the driving forces is the lack of affordable accommodation. The sale of council properties made a bad situation worse by reducing the public housing stock and rents are often prohibitively expensive. It's a fair bet that the latter-day Diggers will be around for quite a time. In the words of the slogan on a radical website: 'La Squatta Continua'.

Since this article was written, the law on squatting has changed. Visit www.squatter.org.uk

The Radical Dairy
Summer 2002 (14)

N16 *asked the Radical Dairy to explain what they're about.*

Conceived by a bunch of mates (the Ragged Army!) in January 2002, the Radical Dairy has been operating as N16's Autonomous Social Centre (there are others across the city, country, world) for six months now, a wide range of social, political and cultural activities in a borough that's ... well, we don't need to patronise you about the state of Hackney. Suffice to say that the 'Dairy' is an essential space in this area.

Amongst the events/classes are radical yoga, Spanish, English, cookery, carpentry, gardening, sustainable living, DJ and acoustic music workshops, benefit gigs, parties and spontaneous socials. The library/ bookshop on the top floor is often host to discussions on various topics from GM crops to local rent prices. We are also having three cafe nights a week now. All events are free and based on self-management and mutual aid. We find that people usually make a donation for things, sometimes in cash, other times in kind.

So why did the cops try to shut us down in April? Well, we reckon that they are merely the foot soldiers of the state and capitalism, which don't like it when people organise themselves in a non-hierarchical, not-for-profit way for the good of themselves and the community. So, in they came, all 30 of 'em, fully tooled up with riot gear etc. They sealed off the surrounding area, booted down the door, searched everyone in the place, nicked our computers and chopped us off the national grid! This meant that, up until very recently (we've just got a generator), we've been unable to provide free internet access and DJ workshops for the kidz. But, as usual, the people came out in droves, many we'd never met before, to express their disgust at the police's behaviour, and their support for the project.

Into July now: the owners of the building have been round again, and, again, they see how positive the place is and don't have the heart to evict us. The old bill's backed off (for now), the sun's out, the garden's flourishing, the collective's growing and the place is buzzing with the energies of the universe! Up-and-coming events include a Spanish Civil War night, featuring discussion, film, food and flamenco, clay oven making workshops, mural painting, nature walks and, of course, lots of sunbathing!

We are open all day, every day. So if you ain't been 'round yet, get yerselves here and catch a glimpse of the new world. Better still, come help create it.

The Radical Dairy on Kynaston Road was a popular, young people's collective, supported by many people living in the neighbourhood and beyond. It was short-

lived, and they were evicted after six months of activity. The Dairy brought harmless anarchic educational, musical and cultural events to what was a rather quiet part of Stoke Newington, and it was a shame when they left. I remember passing by on May Day to find the building surrounded by police, our local Hackney plod being accompanied by others from the City of London, in case anyone escaped to join the Mayday revels in the City. Despite my protestations, I was told in no uncertain terms, to shove off. The building has since been converted into accommodation. No surprises there, then.

The Factory
By David Vandevier, Summer 2003 (18)

The Factory Community Project sits at the top of Matthias Road just before it turns into Newington Green by the Mildmay Social Club and the Unitarian Chapel. The Factory was built in the late 19th century and was one of the first of the piano factories which stretched from Newington Green right into Shoreditch, supplying an eager population with their equivalent of today's television.

It was still making pianos into the 1930s and was a lookout point for fires and bombers during the First and Second World Wars. Many families enjoyed 'a knees up around the old joanna' courtesy of the Factory. In 1973, after being an ink factory, a car repairer, a printer and a host of other things, some less salubrious than others, the councils (both Hackney and Islington, as it falls on their border) agreed to renovate the premises into a community centre in response to the various communities' need for somewhere to meet.

Since then, the Factory has gone through peaks and troughs with the slings and arrows of outrageous fortune (and misfortune) to contend with. It has recently undergone a renovation programme to sort out its access problems and to bring it kicking and screaming into the new millennium. Up until a few years ago, the building was heralded by a complete, full-frontal mural of flying doves, ducks and a lot of peace and love.

Anyway, here we are in 2003 and the Factory has complete access for the disabled and is currently raising the funds to expand into the adjacent derelict property and open a new centre called 'The Mary Wollstonecraft Project'. The building is named after the woman who opened the first school for women in Newington Green in 1784 and influenced the members of a local group called the Rational Dissenters. The Factory is an example of how the community can be best served by a service that actually responds to the needs of the community.

Mary Wollstonecraft
By Barbara Taylor, Autumn, 2003 (19)

In 1792 a young woman published a work so controversial that it is still debated two centuries later. *A Vindication of the Rights of Woman* was not the first book to demand equality for women, but it was the first to achieve real public influence. Readers across Britain, Europe and North America discussed its arguments. Within a few years, its author, a hack writer and translator named Mary Wollstonecraft, had become an international celebrity, and 'women's rights' had entered the political lexicon. If modern feminism could be said to have an inventor, it was Mary Wollstonecraft.

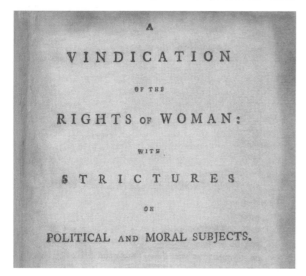

She sought employment, first as a lady's companion and then, in the mid 1780s, as a schoolteacher in Stoke Newington. Stoke Newington in the late 18th century was a hotbed of radicalism. Every Sunday the Unitarian chapel on Newington Green rang with calls for political reform. The chapel's pastor, Richard Price, was a well-known philosopher whose congregation contained many radical celebrities, including the poet Anna Barbauld. Soon after arriving on the Green, Wollstonecraft began attending the chapel (her pew can still be seen there), and joining in political discussions. She and Richard Price became friends. She was an ambitious young writer. He was old and ill, but with a powerful intellect and he made a great impact on her.

These were auspicious times for the radically minded. In 1789 the French Revolution broke out, and soon Wollstonecraft, like many of her Stoke Newington associates, was lending her pen to the revolutionary cause. She wrote a book defending democratic principles and then, even more controversially, women's rights, which the new French government had refused to grant. Liberté and egalité did not apply to women, it seemed. 'When men contend for their freedom...[is it] not unjust to subjugate women?' she demanded of French politicians. 'Who made man the exclusive judge, if woman partake with him of the gift of reason?'

At the end of 1792 Wollstonecraft went to Paris where she met and fell in love with an American radical, Gilbert Imlay, and became pregnant by him. France was rapidly skidding toward war and terrorism, and her position was soon very perilous. Imlay registered her at the American embassy as his wife, which saved Wollstonecraft from possible imprisonment or even death. But after her daughter Fanny was born, her lover began to draw away from her, leaving her heartbroken and suicidal. Alarmed at her misery, Imlay persuaded her to make a business trip to Scandinavia, which revived her spirits. But on returning to London in 1795, Wollstonecraft found him living with a new mistress and tried to drown herself in the Thames, from which she was only narrowly rescued.

By this time Wollstonecraft was Britain's foremost female intellectual. But she was also a single mother, and lonely. Then in the spring of 1796 she fell in love again, this time with the radical philosopher William Godwin. He was a much happier choice than Imlay, and soon the couple had set up house together in Somers Town, near King's Cross. Godwin was a feminist of sorts, and a public opponent of marriage. But when Wollstonecraft became pregnant, they married, to the amusement of friends and enemies alike. She gave birth to a second daughter, the future Mary Shelley, in September 1797, but died ten days later from puerperal fever.

At the time of her death, Wollstonecraft was widely respected in progressive circles. But French wars and fear of homegrown revolution were chilling the political atmosphere in Britain. Six months

after her death, Godwin published a biography that revealed Wollstonecraft's unorthodox sexual history. The reaction was immediate and savage: she was denounced as a 'philosophical wanton', a 'revolutionary whore'. Both her memory and her ideas were cast into a political wilderness where they remained for many decades, scorned even by fellow feminists. But by the end of the 19th century her reputation was on the climb again, and by the late 20th century she had become feminism's foremost heroine, an icon of liberated womanhood.

Today Mary Wollstonecraft is known and celebrated worldwide. A woman whose political career began very modestly, in rural Stoke Newington, is now a global emblem of feminist struggle. It is a status she is likely to retain so long as many women lack equal rights and opportunities or, in some cases, even basic freedoms. Wollstonecraft's feminism still has plenty of mileage left in it.

The Round House
By Jaqi Clayton Church, Spring 2006 (29)

One of Stoke Newington's most distinctive buildings – and one of its oldest – is The Round House in Lordship Road. Prominently situated at the apex of the triangular island just behind Church Street, this local landmark, with its semi-circular frontage and curved roof, attracts all manner of epithets. Likened to a lighthouse, a ship about to cast off down the hill, and even a fondant fancy cake, it is, in fact, the old parish Watch House, which was built in 1824 as part of the vestry's drive to implement better law and order.

As far back as the 1780s there was a sizeable problem in these parts, with ever-increasing numbers of vagabonds, vandals and drunkards. Not so very different from today, then, except for the presence of stocks and a whipping post, which came in for frequent attempts at destruction. Forty-odd years later, the Lord of the Manor, Joseph Eade, granted the parish a lease of land behind the Red Lion public

house on Church Street for a shilling (5p) a year, for a 'cage' or lock-up to be constructed. Three years after, a brand new Watch House was built on the adjacent land for the sum of £107.

1824 was the same year in which the Vagrancy Act was passed, giving more punitive powers to all the parish-run constabularies. In that pre-industrial age, with few dwellings north and south of Church Street, the unimpeded vistas across open marshland and along the ancient drovers' route of Lordship Lane (sic) must have been useful to the duty watchmen looking out for signs of trouble.

When the Metropolitan Police was founded in 1829, individual parishes were no longer responsible for maintaining their own law and order, and the Watch House became a police station until 1870. One occupant was an Irishman called Daniel Leahy, recorded in 1832 as the resident Constable. In a later 19th-century census the house was called Myrtle Cottage and a Mrs Charles was in residence. Her son went on to establish the Lordship Dairy on the premises, and the property remained a dairy for the next 80 years. It has also been a grocer's shop, a squat, an office, an artist's studio and possibly even a mortuary. Fully restored in 1988 by local surveyor/architect Jonathan Shattock, The Round House is now a private residence which has gained Grade II listing and a Hackney brown plaque.

The Kray Twins
By Tom Chalmers, Summer 2006 (30)

The name Kray embodies a sense of dark power, and the twins' story in a unique East End era is chilling yet somehow fascinating. What makes it even more interesting for us is the knowledge that Stoke Newington was very much part of the setting. The Krays' story is long enough ago to depict a very different world, but near enough to make it all the more intriguing. What is certainly true is that the twins quickly built up a portfolio of clubs, which played a major part in their dominance of the East End, in addition to their numerous other protection, fraud and extortion schemes.

One of the clubs which played a major part in their East End stronghold was The Regency on Amhurst Road. This was one of the numerous clubs in which the Krays had 'an interest', i.e. part of their protection income, though it also was the setting for several key moments in their rise and fall. It was at one point run by the father of Frances Shea, whom Reggie Kray had met there while on bail. He went out with her a few times and, on returning to Wandsworth Prison, began to send her letters and poetry every day. She was only sixteen when they met and initially turned down his proposal of marriage, citing her age. However, they did eventually marry, though it was short and tragic rather than sweet.

Popular opinion has it that Frances Shea was unsettled by the constant and unstable influence of Reggie Kray's twin brother, Ronnie, whose state of mind was becoming increasingly alarming. It is also said Reggie Kray was over-possessive and that she felt more and more alienated in their circles. Whatever the reasons, she soon returned to her parents and, despite Reggie Kray's efforts, a happy reunion never occurred. After two failed attempts, Frances Shea committed suicide in 1967. Her death triggered Reggie Kray into a period of destruction that would have been more commonly associated with his pathologically violent brother. Among a number of brutal incidents, he reportedly slashed the face of an ex-boxer in The Regency. There were other incidents in Stoke Newington, and the Krays moved their headquarters for a period to a hotel on Seven Sisters Road. However, Stoke Newington was also going to be the setting for their eventual downfall.

Jack 'The Hat' McVitie was a small-time criminal who had carried out work for the Krays, though, through a number of incidents, he fell out of favour with the twins. Firstly, he allegedly failed to kill Leslie Payne (the mastermind behind many of the early money-making schemes) and he kept part of the money. Then, on one of many drug-induced rampages, he threatened at gunpoint the owners of The Regency, John and Tony Barry – associates of the Krays.

Inevitably, something was going to happen. One night, McVitie was joined by several of the Krays' associates while drinking at The Regency. After staying with him for a while, they persuaded McVitie to go with them to a party. The 'party' was being held at 'Blonde' Carol's house on Evering Road. Little did he know that prior to his arrival, all the partygoers had been ushered out, and McVitie was greeted by the Kray twins along with several of their closest associates. Reggie Kray, long goaded by his brother over the fact that he had never murdered anyone, pointed a gun to McVitie's head and pulled the trigger. However, it misfired. This was only to be a short reprieve as, despite the victim's attempts to escape, Reggie Kray was handed a kitchen knife which he repeatedly plunged into McVitie, eventually putting him out of his misery by stabbing him in the neck.

This, along with Ronnie Kray's killing of George Cornell in The Blind Beggar, were to be the crimes that finally led to the end of the twins' control. A co-ordinated police raid, led by Detective Superintendent Leonard 'Nipper' Read, picked up the twins and a number of their associates. After a lengthy trial, both Krays were sentenced to life imprisonment for murder.

Hammerton Hardware
By Rab MacWilliam, Winter 2006 (32)

Yet another character from Stoke Newington's past is, sadly, no longer with us.

Bob Hammerton, who ran Hammerton's hardware store on Stoke Newington Road for the last 40 years, died at the end of September 2006 at the age of 86. As it is situated close to *N16*'s office, we saw Bob making his way most days to the shop. No matter what you needed, Bob could find it for you, dragging out his old stepladder and making his precarious way to the upper shelves. He would reminisce about his days as a lad in Stoke Newington, when the High Street was a bustling shopping centre, lined with cinemas and shops of all descriptions.

A Book of Condolence was placed beside the door of Bob's shop, eliciting comments such as 'you were the last of old Stoke Newington', 'may you rest in peace in the great hardware shop in the sky' and 'you made the keys to all our houses – they didn't work, but it was a pleasure to come again'. To which we add our own farewell.

A Friendly Society

By Peter Daniels, Autumn 2007 (35)

Quakers have a radically simple religious outlook, based on meeting in silence to discover a deeper sense of God, without elaborate ritual or priestly hierarchy. Women and men participate fully: all people are equal before God, and each person is unique and precious. This belief has led to Quakers (or 'Friends') being much involved in work for peace and social justice. All very modern, but Quakers have been meeting in Stoke Newington for over 300 years.

The movement gathered around George Fox, who travelled in the 1650s preaching the word as the Spirit moved him. He often stayed with Mary Stott in Dalston, to keep away from persecution by the authorities in London. In 1668 he set up a girls' school in Shacklewell, which Mary ran. In 1698 a regular Quaker meeting started in two rooms in Church Street, on the site of the Daniel Defoe pub.

This meeting existed until 1741. Many Quakers then lived around Stamford Hill, and tended to go to Tottenham, a meeting which continued through the 18th century. Meanwhile, some successful city Quakers, like the Hoare family of bankers and the chemist William Allen, started living in quiet rural Stoke Newington but still worshipped at city meetings. Then in 1821 Gracechurch Street Meeting House burned down. This inspired local Quakers to build new premises in what is now Yoakley Road (then Park Street), with a meeting room 44 by 36 feet, plus gallery, and a row of ten almshouses.

Stoke Newington Quakers were very active, especially William Allen who was busy campaigning against slavery, visiting prisons with Elizabeth Fry, and developing allotments for labourers in Lordship Road. Christine Majolier, a young French Quaker, describes William Wilberforce visiting the allotments and being weighed in the scales used for vegetables – he weighed only 76 pounds, including the five pounds of iron stays he wore. Another enterprise was Susanna Corder's girls' school in Fleetwood House, where the Fire Station is now. Its prospectus said 'particular attention should be paid to the state of mind of each child'; the girls learnt astronomy, physics and chemistry as well as classical and modern languages. Susanna also commissioned what seems to be the first school bus, to take pupils to the Gracechurch Street meeting house until the new local one was built.

In 1827, the ageing William Allen married the elderly rich widow Grizzell Birkbeck, which provoked a rash of satirical cartoons including Robert Cruikshank's 'Newington Nunnery in a Pretty Considerable Uproar' suggesting that Susanna Corder had hoped for William's hand herself. In 1860, an Ojibwa woman from Canada called Nahneebahweequay came to petition Queen Victoria about land rights, and stayed in Stoke Newington with Christine Majolier, now Alsop, and her husband Robert who was active in the Aborigines' Protection Society. In the Franco-Prussian War of 1870-71, Friends War Victims Relief Committee included William and Joseph Beck, brothers who also had strong local interests – William as a local historian, and Joseph as one of the people who saved Clissold Park.

At the end of the 19th century Stoke Newington had the highest concentration of Quakers in London, but the meeting declined, while other meetings took on more of the Quaker energy that led to the award of the Nobel Peace Prize in 1947 for unobtrusive 'silent help from the nameless to the nameless' in shattered Europe. By then, few members were left locally, and a much smaller meeting house replaced the old one in 1957. Unfortunately, the almshouses were also demolished, so there was no longer a group of elderly Quakers to keep the meeting going, and the new building was sold to the Seventh Day Adventists in 1966.

By 2000, there were more local Quakers again, and a new meeting started. This currently meets in Room 3, Top Floor, Clissold House, Clissold Park, Church Street, N16. Meetings are held every Sunday at 10am. www.stokenewingtonquakers.org.uk

Historic Tombs

By Graeme Watson, Spring 2008 (37)

One of the things which the 200th anniversary of the Slave Trade brought to light last year was that in Old St Mary's Churchyard are the tombs of two well-known abolitionists: James Stephen and Anna Laetitia Barbauld. Who were they?

James Stephen was William Wilberforce's chief legal adviser in the long campaign to outlaw the slave trade. His legal knowledge and residence in the West Indies brought him first-hand knowledge of the treatment of slaves. On route to Bridgetown St Kitts, where he was to practice law, he witnessed the trial of four slaves accused of a murder which they clearly did not commit. This shaped his beliefs and his subsequent career. He became a member of the so-called 'Clapham Sect', where he met Wilberforce, and his sister, Sarah, who was to become his wife. He was active in the London Abolition Committee, was elected as an MP, and wrote the two-volume text *The Slavery of the British West Indian Colonies*, which became the main source for anti-slavery campaigners. An engraved portrait of him is included in the permanent exhibition 'London, Sugar and Slavery' at the Museum of Docklands, which opened in November 2007.

Anna Laetitia Barbauld, nee Aikin, was born in 1743 at Kibworth Harcourt, Leicestershire. Her father and grandfather were both Presbyterian ministers. An avid reader from the age of two, she began writing poetry on a wide variety of subjects from an early age. Her interests included politics, religion, natural history and science. She published books of poetry, two books on religion and reading lessons for children. In 1773 she married Rochemont Barbauld, a non-conformist minister who became a Unitarian. In 1791 she published a satire, addressed to William Wilberforce, in response to Parliament's failure to abolish slavery. The couple moved to Stoke Newington in 1802, where they associated with a group of radical intellectuals, and here her husband was minister at the Newington Green Unitarian Chapel. After her husband's death, she moved to Church Street, where a blue plaque commemorates her house. She died here in 1825, and was buried with her brother in St Mary's Churchyard. Her brother erected an inscription to her in the Chapel. Barbauld Road is named after her. She is now regarded as one of England's most important Romantic women poets.

St Mary's New Church
By Pippa Crawford, Summer 2008 (38)

If you've walked past the big Victorian Gothic church on Stoke Newington Church Street a thousand times and not given a thought to its history, this year (2008) the church is 150 years old. Compared with Westminster Abbey and St Paul's (and even the Old Church on the opposite side of Church Street) it's an ecclesiastical newcomer. But that's not to say that its history isn't as colourful and varied. In fact, the New Church – as it is officially called – has packed in plenty of drama in its century and a half.

It was commissioned by Thomas Jackson, a charismatic 'high church' preacher who had once set his sights on becoming a bishop. While it's true that the Elizabethan Old Church was bursting at the seams as hundreds of new worshippers settled in an urbanising Stoke Newington, it's also the case that Jackson wanted to meet competition from the area's non-conformists head on. Then, as now, the burghers of Stoke Newington had a taste for dissent born out of the Civil War when Stoke Newington was firmly on the side of the Roundheads. Two hundred years on many were still wedded to Puritan ideals, and anything 'high church', like Jackson's love of choral music and finery, was beyond the pale. Undeterred, Jackson hired a top-name architect called George Gilbert Scott – better known for his work on the Foreign Office – to create a building that fitted his ambitions. Not surprisingly, it was a recipe for local schism. For the next 50 years or so, St Mary's vestry and its rector were often at loggerheads. Not only that, parishioners favouring the low church tradition continued to use the Old Church, thwarting Jackson's plans to demolish it.

Only when he died, did the acrimony subside. By then a building boom was underway. Stoke Newington was growing apace. Enlightened rectors like Leonard Shelford took the helm and the parish flourished. As a result, by the turn of the 20th century St Mary's was enjoying its numerical heyday, with as many as 1200 people attending Sunday mass. The popularity of the Sunday school was staggering: according to the 1903 census, there were 120 teachers serving over 1,000 pupils. What's more, there was a huge range of social groups, from a Girls' Friendly Society and Working Men's Club to the evocatively titled 'Order of St Barnabas for work among the rough lads'.

World War Two saw more dramatic events. Both churches suffered during the 1940s Blitz, with the New Church being particularly badly hit: so much so it was closed for the rest of the war and services moved to the Old Church. After the peace there was much reconstruction work, including the installation of impressive new stained glass windows. It wasn't until 1957 that the New Church was rededicated. Today the congregation numbers around 150 – well short of the 1900 total but vibrant enough to sustain almost as many social interest groups – from historical talks to lively conversation and bible reading.

Park Plans
By Ken Worpole, Autumn 2008 (39)

Although the successful application for lottery funds for Clissold Park was announced in early 2007 (after nearly ten years of local effort and much frustration), park users won't have noticed much has changed so far. That's because, yet again, plans and drawings have had to be drawn up for the refurbishment of the landscape and Clissold Mansion, and then consulted upon. The consultation process is now drawing to a close, and if the Heritage Lottery Fund (and the Big Lottery Fund) approve the final proposals, then work should start next year.

So what might be expected? It is proposed to extend the New River in the direction of the White House pub, as far as the western end of the current bowling green area. A new ornamental bridge will carry people across the river (more like a canal in reality) close to the current deer enclosure. A small majority of the public consulted favoured retaining the aviary, though a smaller, better designed one will replace the present grim compound.

Clissold Mansion – actually a very beautiful house in its aspect and interiors – will be completely refurbished and made open to the public as a series of meeting rooms, extended cafe facilities, interpretation area, and so on. While the café will continue to serve customers on the front lawn overlooking the deer park, a new serving area will be opened up on the ground floor catering for people using the area at the rear and the rose gardens (which of course are more wheelchair accessible). The current toilet blocks will be demolished and improved toilet facilities will be installed in the ground floor of the Mansion.

So far, so uncontroversial. However, arrangements have yet to be agreed with the tennis club based in the park as to where its administrative and changing room functions are to be housed, since there may not be enough room in Clissold Mansion. The tennis club has been one of the gems of the park for some years, providing opportunities for children and young people (including school groups) to take up a sport often denied to them in urban areas. Most noticeable of all probably will be the extension of the play area covering where it is at present and all of the red-surfaced games area, providing equipment for all ages (including a sunken skateboard park), set in a landscaped area with small grassed hills and other landforms. The controversial issues here are why the skateboard area is to be located so close to the flats and houses in Queen Elizabeth Walk, and what is the justification for no longer having dedicated children's toilets in the extended play area.

The paddling pool stays where it is. The One O'Clock Club will continue in its present charmless and frequently-graffitied building, though hopefully with extended opening hours and use at weekends (though the Hackney Learning Trust remains a law unto itself on all such matters). Meanwhile, the former bowling green clubhouse and green will be upgraded to become another dog-free area, with activities for children (though how this will be managed and funded is as yet unclear). The disused and often-squatted park lodge in Queen Elizabeth Walk, was magicked out of the deliberations for legal reasons apparently, though its continuing dereliction has been a major cause of local concern for over five years now, and still seems unresolved – at great cost to Hackney residents.

The current 'fire yard' or recycling area near the deer enclosure will be vacated and re-landscaped, with recycling operations moving – as currently proposed – to the park depot in Greenway Close, if health and safety issues are resolved to the satisfaction of all parties – staff, residents, traffic and environmental health agencies. The two lakes will be drained, cleared and replenished (that will be fun to see – God knows what else, apart from dozens of terrapins and hundreds of rats, lurks on the bottom of them). A major tree-planting programme will be developed to replace dead and dying stock, possibly with other varieties more adaptable to climate change.

All in all, this is an upgrading of the park and its facilities rather than a total makeover. An obvious reason for this is that, even in its current state, it is still an enormously popular and successful park, catering for most interests and uses. The big question which hangs over the whole process is how these changes will be managed and funded in the future – especially if opening hours are extended in the winter, requiring more lighting and greater security. The more people, the heavier the wear and tear on both landscape and buildings, and Hackney Council has often struggled in the past to keep abreast of maintaining play equipment, pathways, fences, tree stock, toilets and so on – though, to their credit, in recent years the gardening staff have done wonders in the park.

Ken is Chair of the Clissold Park User Group but wrote the above in a personal capacity. Clissold Park and House have been thoroughly refurbished since Ken wrote this article.

Springfield Park
By Rab MacWilliam, Spring 2010 (44)

One gloriously sunny, freezing late morning a few weeks ago, my wife suggested that, instead of my usual lazy habit of drifting over to the Rochester Castle, we could visit Springfield Park. What a good call that was.

I'd been to the park on several occasions, but it was usually raining or gloomy, so I'd never really appreciated it. On this particular day, however, the piercingly clear light afforded us a stunning view down the deeply sloping park to the River Lea and across the Springfield Marina (a basin for narrow boats) to the flat wilderness of Walthamstow Marshes nature reserve, complete with longhorn cattle, herons, swans and God knows what else.

It was only the industrial backdrop – the nondescript factories, towering electricity pylons, the railway line snaking towards Stansted Airport and the general seemingly dishevelled urban sprawl disappearing into the distance – that reminded us we were still in the middle of the city.

Opened as a public park in 1905, Springfield was formed from the lands belonging to three private houses, only one of which, Springfield House in the south-west corner of the park, survives to this day. Bounded to the east by the River Lea and to the west by the residential buildings of Upper Clapton, the park comprises around 40 acres which, as you walk from the entrance to the river, moves from woodland through grassland to wetland. All in a five-minute downhill stroll. It was called 'Springfield' for geological reasons. What became the park was formed during the Ice Age, when the River Lea eroded the indigenous London clay and left behind it a sand and gravel floodplain. Any water which permeates this floodplain eventually becomes impeded by the London clay, and gives rise to a series of springs. Hence the name.

The natural ecology is incredibly diverse, and this was recognized in 1997 when it was labelled a Nature Reserve and then in 2002 a Site of Nature Conservation. The trees in the park include sweet chestnut, silver birch, lime, copper beech, mulberry, willow, cedar, and even an olive tree. It is visited by over fifty species of birds, such as kingfisher and great spotted woodpecker, and there are over 230 mature plant species and shrubs, most of which were planted in the Victorian era.

No park should be complete without a bandstand, pavilion and duck pond, and Springfield doesn't disappoint. It also boasts a colourful and at first glance bizarre kids' playground. If you walk along the path past the playground in the direction of Lea Bridge Road you'll quickly come across the Anchor and Hope, a small, oddly shaped but pleasingly comfortable and friendly Fuller's pub, right beside the river. Another refreshment spot is the Grade II listed café – Spark Café – near the top of the park. When I was there, it seemed populated by would-be louche, fashionably turned-out trendy gentry, thumbing through glossy magazines in an languidly bohemian Stoke Newington manner, surrounded by charming and delightfully behaved children, twenty-something, trendy mummies and their banker husbands, dressed 'casual' for the day. So we didn't go in, and there was no room anyway.

Springfield Park is such an invigorating place to be in that I was surprised it wasn't heaving with Upper Clapton life. Perhaps people have been seduced into believing that everything happens in Church Street, and headed west for the day. Church Street and Clissold Park undeniably have their attractions, but Springfield has a special charm and robust identity all of its own.

Shacklewell Village
By Ed Upright, Spring 2010 (44)

From the Middle Ages, Kingsland, Dalston, Newington and Shacklewell, four small villages of west Hackney, were grouped together for assessment purposes. While all have now been subsumed into a modern city, the first three have retained some sort of identity, whereas Shacklewell has been abandoned and squashed to a point of near extinction.

As a whole, Hackney has witnessed greater change than many other parts of London, and it continues to do so. Once a favourite resort for London's wealthiest residents – Samuel Pepys practised archery in the fields of Kingsland, 'ate cream and good cherries' in the village of Hackney, and when he found oranges growing in the garden of Brooke House, 'pulled off a little one by stealth and ate it' – by the 20th century Hackney was a byword for inner-city deprivation. So walking through Shacklewell today is a melancholy experience. While many great merchant houses remain, the prevailing mixture of council estates and light industry gives little clue to the rich history of a once prosperous village.

The village developed around the eponymous Shacklewell Lane, which loops off the main road at the junction with Crossway and Kingsland High Street. From the early 16th century the main building of the village was the Manor House, a mansion first inhabited by Sir John Heron, owner of a large land holdings estate and as Master of the Jewel House the controller of the royal purses of both Henry VII and VIII. His son Giles married Cecilia More, the youngest daughter of famous scholar and Catholic martyr Sir Thomas More, who became a regular visitor to the village. The couple lived in Shacklewell until 1541, when (six years after his father-in-law's beheading) Giles was also executed for treason. According to Iain Sinclair, it was in the Shacklewell Manor House that Thomas More met his political downfall, following unguarded remarks about the whores of the royal court. Ownership of the house then passed through two of the richest families of Hackney, firstly the Rowes (who provided several Lord Mayors of London) and then in 1685 to Francis Tyssen, Lord of the Manor of Hackney.

While the Manor House was demolished in the late 1700s, in its place stands a reminder of a very different age and a distinctive part of remaining Shacklewell. Perch, April, and Seal streets, that lie just off the Green, were a Victorian exercise in the provision of housing for the working classes. Built by Hoxton resident John Grover, these handsome yellow brick terraced houses, which each bear a terracotta plaque with date of completion between 1881 and 1886, remain relatively unchanged.

The transient nature of Hackney's population is also apparent in Shacklewell. Shacklewell Lane synagogue was completed in 1903 and immediately drew complaints that it 'dwarfed' its surroundings. Oswald Mosley stood outside it when targeting the predominantly Jewish area in the 1930s, and it has since been converted into a mosque reflecting changes in the local community. It is the immigrant community that has sustained the 'rag trade', an industry vital to Hackney's economy for many years – in the late 1980s there were over 1,500 clothing factories in the borough. This was no different in the Shacklewell of 1929 when Simpsons of Piccadilly built a large Art Deco factory on Stoke Newington Road, a building that at its peak housed 3,000 workers. The building is now used as the Turkish Halkevi community centre and as all parts of Hackney have seen the influx of luxury offices and flats, other sections of the former factory are now loft apartments.

While the composer Vincent Novello left Shacklewell Green shortly after moving there in 1823, reputedly worried that his children's education may suffer due to the village's seclusion, it is unlikely that those moving into gated communities in the next few years will have the same concerns. Hackney was described by John Betjeman as 'the most interesting and least considered' borough of London, and the intriguing and abandoned microcosm of the borough that is Shacklewell is changing again.

Shacklewell is now trendifying, and has become part of the northward movement of Hoxditch dwellers. It's another example of an area which has come from nowhere to being super-cool in no time and without anyone noticing.

Glory Days

By Rab MacWilliam, Winter 2009 (43)

Finally, after years of ideological disagreement, fevered debate, prevarication and dark threats of selling the thing off, Stoke Newington Town Hall and Assembly Rooms are to re-open in February 2010.

A couple of years ago Hackney Council finally bit the bullet and decided to spend £8 million to restore the historic Grade II listed building, with its Art Deco interior, to its former glory. Standing on the site of the old 15th-century Manor House, the Town Hall was built between 1935 and 1937 by architect J Reginald Truelove in an open competition held by what was then the proud and independent Stoke Newington Metropolitan Borough Council (and there are many round here who wish these grand old days of freedom from the evil barons of Mare Street would return).

After the start of World War Two, the Assembly Rooms staged variety shows and entertainments to boost local morale and also served as, more prosaically, the local gas mask dispensary. If you look closely you can still see the remains of the camouflage paint on the walls. A probably apocryphal story has it that grass was placed on the roof of the building, with a plastic cow innocently grazing on top, to convince German bombers that the building was simply an extension of Clissold Park. From the 1940s to the 1960s, the Assembly Rooms staged classical music concerts, the famed Opera Cabaret and popular dance nights, the Saturday night dance being particularly popular. The question 'Going up to Stokey?' meant the Assembly Rooms.

After 1965, when Hackney, Shoreditch and Stoke Newington became the London Borough of Hackney, the Rooms remained an important and prestigious music venue, playing host to such stars as Eartha Kitt, Barbara Windsor and George Melly, as well as being, after the influx of West Indian immigrants, one of the leading ska venues in London (the other being in Brixton). The Rooms then became a popular choice for weddings and celebrations, particularly for the local Turkish, Orthodox Jewish and Asian communities.

The Town Hall is also retaining its classic features, such as the domed ceiling and vaulted galleries, the Australian walnut timber paneling, the gold cornicing and the majestic Art Deco staircase. Hackney's Emergency Planning and CCTV operations will still operate from the basement, so grim reality and innocent citizen surveillance will continue alongside the brave new world upstairs. There is also a new foyer/entrance with a glass roof, high windows and exposed brickwork from the old Manor House.

The Four Aces

By Bryony Hegarty, Autumn 2011 (49)

Originally from Ghana, Winstan Whitter grew up in Stamford Hill. His film about the Four Aces Club in Dalston, 'Legacy in the Dust' (2008,) has a personal perspective, as Winstan's father was chef and DJ (Scabs) at the club, and his brother worked there for many years. The film is awaiting general release, due to issues around clearances and production investment.

In 1966, Newton Dunbar a Jamaican East Londoner, opened The Four Aces Club on Dalston Lane with three business partners. The doors opened mainly at the weekends, with a mix of Soul and Reggae on the decks and in live performance. An impressive and extensive number of bands played at and visited the club, including Desmond Dekker, Jimmy Cliff, Ann Peebles, Percy Sledge, Ben E King, Billy Ocean, Bob Marley, Chrissie Hynde, The Slits, Sex Pistols, Mick Jagger and Bob Dylan. The Four Aces ran in the theatre foyer of the old Dalston Theatre building; later came the Acid House era when Dunbar initiated the 'Tears' night in the main house which, with other parts of the building, then became home to the Labyrinth. Ravers would queue well down into Kingsland Road to get in for the DJ sets and live shows. They recall the 'anthemic acoustics of the building' with 'tremble your blood-cells low frequencies' and sets where 'the bass lifted you off your feet'. Essex band The Prodigy made their name at the club, and give in-depth interviews during the film.

The importance of the venue as a place for bands to promote recorded music is highlighted by legendary music producer Denis Bovell; with virtually no radio air play for black bands, he recalls the club as expressing 'the critique of the people'. Bovell recalls the significance of Linton Kwesi Johnson's appearances as a freelance journalist on the BBC World Service. The Four Aces was the club that saw an acceptance of Reggae being made in England embodied in Lovers Rock sung by artists such as Louisa Marks and Janet Kay who first performed at the club's 'open mic' night.

This musical history and expression of a generation runs alongside recollections of the frequent use of the SUS law and regular visits to the club from the police. The sense of fear that ran alongside this is expressed in cartoon imagery by illustrator Stacey Bradshaw and cuttings from the press at the time. It is contrasted in the documentary with the later era of the building; when the police raided the Labyrinth the predominantly white ravers had a far more blasé response. Dunbar recalls 'at least 14 court appearances all over minor incidents were endlessly blown up in the media.'

The historical recollection of the police use of SUS resonates painfully with this year's troubled streets of Hackney. Interestingly, club owner Newton Dunbar

noted this summer at Stoke Newington Literary Festival, where he appeared at the town hall for the Ska Panel debate, that the last time he was on stage at the venue was in 1975. This was at the invitation of Hackney Community Relations Council to participate in a panel of eight speakers talking about 'the social pressures and factors contributing towards frustration and violence among certain sections of youths within the borough of Hackney, and to decide upon courses of action which may be undertaken to alleviate this problem'.

Winstan campaigned with the organisation Open Dalston to save the Dalston Theatre building, with its rich performance history of circus, cinema and performers such as Marie Lloyd, and home to the Four Aces. 'Legacy in the Dust' charts the history of the theatre building, centrally during the era of the Four Aces Club, right up to forced closure and the compulsory purchase by Hackney Council when the theatre was allowed to fall into a state of disrepair said to be beyond retrieval. The roof of the building was removed, allowing progressive deterioration of the interior. A prolonged campaign ran, and expert opinion evidence was given in support of preservation of Dalston's grandest historic building for the performing arts, and the oldest circus entrance in the country. Despite a petition of over 25,000 signatures, the demolition of the building made way for a housing development of 550 flats, of which only 28 were social housing.

The Sky is Falling!

By Rab MacWilliam, Summer 2009 (42)

... or so said Chicken Licken in the folktale when an acorn hit her on the head. This is not an entirely inappropriate analogy for the current economic situation in our little parish. I decided to check out, via a series of random conversations with various local businesses, how this area is being affected by the 'biggest economic melt-down since the 1920s', 'the devastating credit crunch', 'the worst recession in living memory', and so on.

The media are having a great time with all this, and the lengthening unemployment lines, number of businesses going to the wall, increasing house repossessions, lack of credit from the greedy, self-serving banks only kept alive by our spineless government (I speak as one who has always voted Labour, but no more) who should have told, not asked, these usurers to pump the money back into the economy and not into their balance sheets, all add fuel to our seeming economic woes.

But what is it really like in the streets of N16? Well, not as bad as the *Daily Mail* tells us. It has been my belief for some while that the 'recession' is overstated and, while I would not agree with some conspiracy theorists that the whole thing was orchestrated in order to take up the slack in the world economy and afford big business and banks an apparently legitimate excuse to offload the dumb, egregious decisions they made to line their own pockets, the fact is that the statistics have been aggregated and ignore the varying impact on specific areas. Like our own neighbourhood.

Stoke Newington is, in my view, something of a bubble. When you consider that we are on the edge of Olympic land, a new tube will shortly be arriving on our doorstep, there is little space available for large-scale, new development, we are less than half an hour away from the West End and the City, the area contains a large number of relatively wealthy, middle class people who are in a financially strong enough position to weather short-term economic storms, and the place is becoming ridiculously trendy, then we have something going for us. Without wishing to be patronizing, we are not exactly Rochdale or Cumbernauld (and, my God, I love them both, except for Cumbernauld).

Just look around Church Street and the High Street at the weekend (OK, it can be pretty quiet during the week), and observe how packed are the bars, shops and restaurants, the number of young wannabe Stokey dwellers milling around outside the estate agents and the three-wheel buggy traffic jams on the pavements loaded with designer babies and carrier bags with strange sounding, exotic names.

And would Sainsbury's and Tesco have moved here if they thought that the Stokey pound was knackered? Also, the Chelsea tractors don't seem to be disappearing. And how many estate agents have shut down? None, and indeed a couple have just opened. So, in a spirit of civic duty, I asked around, with the following results.

'The pubs don't seem as full. However, there is no sign of a downturn, although there is a trend towards buying cheaper wine. We are doing better business than last year.'
Leo, Oddbins

'Demand is as good as a year ago. The downturn in sales is not manifesting itself here.'
Tim, Church Street Bookshop

'There is an actual or perceived lack of availability of funding. We are selling less property (fewer people want to sell while more people want to buy). Credit has to be freed as the demand is certainly there. Although rent prices are down, the level of transactions has been very high.'
Adrian, Bairstow Eaves

'The "credit crunch" didn't prevent us from expanding with Shine on the Green. The so- called "downturn" has had little if no effect on our business.'
Stephanie, Shine Holistic

'People are more careful with money. Commercial sales are very busy and there is a strong demand for commercial property. There has never been a better time to put your property on the market in Stoke Newington.'
Eilish, Michael Naik

'Business is marginally down from last year and people are being more conservative. They are waiting till the end of the month, payday, before buying, and we are seeing more debit card than credit card transactions.'
Guy, Rouge

'The extra pint is out the door, and it's harder to get our customers to spend. But we are holding our own and doing OK. We are optimistic about the future.'
Paul, Ryan's Bar

'Business is steady and Saturdays are really busy. Ironically, our "credit crunch birthday card" is selling well.'
Dominic, Early Bird

'Sales were awful in 2008, but are phenomenal now. There is a huge demand, but a shortage of available stock. It's a price sensitive market. Buyers are aware it's a different playing field and sensible prices sell'.'
Richard, Next Move

'Business is good. Our loyal customers continue to support us.'
Jo, Stoke Newington Bookshop

'I don't believe there is a recession at all. Trading is no different from last year and, if anything, there is a slight increase in trade.'
Eamonn, Daniel Defoe

'Business is better than ever. My sales figures are up and I'm looking forward to the next "recession".'
Danny, The Fishery

To repeat, these comments are entirely random and could well be subject to a number of variables. However, it does seem unlikely that there will soon be a line of desperate local traders queuing up to jump to their doom from the top of St Mary's Church steeple. Business as usual, it would appear, in spite of what we are hearing from elsewhere. Shop local. Keep our businesses alive, healthy and working in everyone's interests. Stoke Newington is a special area and long may that continue.

Times are hard at present, but Stoke Newington survives, and indeed seems to be in fairly good economic shape. To repeat what I wrote here three years ago, I think we live in a relatively protected little bubble. The incoming demographic continues to be a wealthy one and, although it's sad to see old residents being priced out by the rising house values and soaring rents, most local businesses are still in a more or less healthy state.

Speaking Personally

As every Stoke Newington resident knows, there is no shortage of eccentric, assertive and talented people around the area. This selection from the magazine is an attempt to document the variety and singularity of some of the inhabitants whom we have interviewed over the years. This section begins with a discussion I had some years ago with a remarkable woman.

Wrinkled or Wonderful?

By Rab MacWilliam, Spring 2005 (25)

In a small, tidy flat in a road just off Church Street lives an internationally famous model. Irene Sinclair's serene, smiling image gazes from billboards, advertising hoardings, magazines, buses and tube walls across the USA and Europe. She has also been the subject of magazine and newspaper articles throughout the world, and recently she has been featured on 30-metre-high adverts in Times Square, Wall Street and on an external wall of Milan Cathedral.

However, this particular model is not your average, spoilt-brat catwalk queen and could not be more different from the likes of Jodie Kidd or Kate Moss. She is, in fact, a great-grandmother and a 96-year-old woman, who remains both astonished and delighted by her sudden, unexpected global celebrity. Irene (known to her friends as Renee) is an animated, cheerful and vivacious woman who looks at least 20 years younger than her age.

She sits, straight-backed, in her chair and tells me about her experiences. She was born in Guyana in 1908, taught history ('the Elizabethan period was my speciality') in her native country and arrived in Hornsey in 1957 to help look after her daughter's young children. She moved to Stoke Newington on her retirement in 1971 and settled in Filey Road and then Yorkshire Close. 'Stoke Newington was so dull and uninteresting then. I didn't like it at all.' How do you feel about it now? 'Oh, it's a different place. I'm very happy here. Church Street is like a little Paris.'

On to Renee's big adventure. Dove soap – part of Unilever – had dreamt up an advertising campaign designed to challenge stereotyped versions of female beauty. A casting director arrived at Renee's sheltered accommodation in Yoakley Road looking for a suitable woman, between 70 and 80 years old, to illustrate old age. When informed by the block's manager Andy about Renee, she knocked at her door and, confused by Renee's apparent youth, asked her if Renee's mother was in the flat. One thing led to another and she was soon in the studio of top photographer Rankin – co-founder of *Dazed and Confused* and snapper of the Queen – who spent four hours and took 600 pictures to find the perfect image for the ad.

The ad launch was held in September last year in New York, and Renee was selected as the only British model out of the seven in the campaign to attend. Naturally, she was flown over first class by American Airlines, accompanied by a Dove representative, and booked into a suite at the $500 per night Lee Parker Meridien Hotel in Manhattan. She spent four days enjoying photo shoots, television and radio interviews and champagne dinners, and revelling in her sudden change of circumstance. 'It was marvellous. I never felt beautiful in my life but I feel I am now.' The London launch was held in January this year at the Dorchester, and Renee was again guest of honour. Since then, she has flown (again, first class) to other launches in Madrid, Milan and Paris. On her return to Stoke Newington she was contacted by an aide to Oprah Winfrey and asked to appear on the top-rated, coast-to-coast US TV show. A tired Renee declined. The flabbergasted aide told her that no one turns down Oprah. 'Tell her I'm indisposed at the moment', said Renee.

Life has quietened down a bit now, and Renee has had time to reflect on her brush with fame. I asked her if this is the start of a modelling career. 'Well, it's been a good laugh', she replied, 'but my feet are firmly on the ground.

I wouldn't do it again but I'm glad I did it.' Obviously, she was paid by Dove but she has already given some of the money away to charity and intends to do the same with the rest of it, having collected only expenses for her efforts – 'I had to pay for my own clothes and make-up.'

She is now back in her old routine – attending St Mary's Church, collecting her pension at the Post Office, shopping at the supermarket and doing the *Daily Mirror* crossword, a prosaic but probably welcome change from what must now seem a crazy dream. In the Dove ad featuring Renee, the reader has to tick one of two boxes – 'Wrinkled' or 'Wonderful'. The latter has to date vastly exceeded the former, which will come as no surprise to anyone who has had the pleasure of meeting with and talking to someone as charming and remarkable as our own Stoke Newington supermodel.

Rene celebrated her 104th birthday in 2012, and remains as spritely and independent as ever.

One-armed bandit
By Tim Webb, Summer 1999 (2)

The old 'one-armed bandits' were simple. You put your money in the slot, pulled the lever and hoped that the cherries, lemons or oranges would clunk into a winning line. Modern fruit machines involve flashing lights, multiple choices and eye dazzling designs. Someone who understands what goes on inside the money-guzzling devices is Lambert. He services and repairs them and can often be seen fixing machines in Steptoes (*now the Daniel Defoe*) and the Auld Shillelagh.

Lambert came to Stoke Newington from Guyana (via Barbados) with his six sisters and three brothers when he was five years old. Too young to experience real culture shock, the main difference he remembers is that in the West Indies people mostly lived in separate one-storey houses. Leaving Clissold Park School at 17, he undertook a four-year apprenticeship in electronics and electrical engineering at the Central Electricity Generating Board and the LEB.

A bit of freelance ticket touting at Bob Marley concerts got him noticed by the front of house manager at the Rainbow in Finsbury Park, London's leading rock venue in the 1970s. He was offered a job as a bouncer, officially 'security officer'. His main task was to stop over-excited fans jumping onto the stage. A naturally good talker, he found that gentle persuasion backed up with a hint of something stronger usually worked. It was a job well suited to his talents: Lambert is a karate expert. He fought five times for the England national side against some of the world's best. Later he was employed by rock promoters as part of stage security. He went on tour with Paul Weller and The Jam, Dire Straits, Elvis Costello and The Police to a number of countries including Norway, Sweden and Holland. Joe Strummer and The Clash took him to the United States.

On one occasion Sting trod on his toes as he rushed past. Lambert reminded him that even superstars could apologise. He did so and they remained friendly. Marvin Gaye recognised Lambert at a wedding and they shared a drink or three. He remembers that a well-known group were having fun chucking their visitors into a swimming pool. They grabbed one man as he came through the door. Just as he was about to suffer the same fate, someone recognised him. The newcomer was their coke dealer and his pockets were filled with the white stuff.

That phase of Lambert's life ended when his then partner insisted he settle down in England. Lambert is an Arsenal fan and season ticket holder. His sister played for a women's football team called Highbury Ladies and he became their coach. Ian Wright is still his hero and it won't be a short conversation if you disagree with him.

Lambert is still in the electronics business and frequents Stoke Newington on a regular basis. He can often be found in the Auld Shillelagh.

Atique
By Brendan Montague, Autumn 1999 (3)

Restaurateur Atique Choudhury has added spice to the culinary delights of Stoke Newington for well over a decade. Established in 1992, Yum Yum has gained a formidable reputation among Stoke Newington's connoisseurs of cuisine as well as internationally.

As well as running a successful restaurant, Atique promotes Thai cuisine on the national scene. The day we met he received confirmation that the government have granted £550,000 to establish an Asian and Oriental School of Catering. The school will enable experienced chefs to gain formal qualifications as well as providing training facilities for more junior restaurant staff.

Between 200-300 students will cook for and serve the public in a fully functioning restaurant, gaining valuable experience and raising revenue. This will provide young Asians some of whom could face unemployment with training in a field in which they may have family connections. Although the exact location of the school has not been decided, Atique will argue that it should be in Hackney (*it finally settled in Hoxton*).

Locally, Atique pioneered the Stoke Newington Restaurant Watch. The first of its kind in Britain, the scheme was based on the more usual pub watch arrangement that had successfully reduced crime against customers. By coming together and working closely with the police, producing leaflets and posters, restaurant owners were able to tackle an increasing problem.

He does occasionally find time to venture outside the restaurant business. As a business governor at Thomas Abney School, he used his knowledge and experience to help improve educational standards in the area. He told me that he found that the bad reputation of many schools in Hackney is undeserved. Working within the budgets they are allocated and with limited facilities they do very well. The restaurant's advertising budget is also used to make a contribution to the community. Atique makes donations to schools, play groups and charity in many ways. He also played a key role in the Stoke Newington Midsummer Festival.

I asked him why he came to Stoke Newington in 1984. He said it had the right feel in terms of the type of businesses that were already here, the kind of layout and the people who were around. It was a small, low-key area but it had potential.

The original Yum Yum is now Mercado, and Atique now runs the much expanded Yum Yum from a listed Georgian building, 300 years old in 2012, in the High Street. He is also involved in Oiiishi and Punjab 59 on Church Street, and Speakeasy on Stoke Newington Road. Married with a son, he has made the most of his life in Stoke Newington, and he is involved in many business projects, local and otherwise. He has supported N16 magazine from the beginning, was a main sponsor of the N16 Fringe and has helped to sponsor this book.

Porn Again
By Rab MacWilliam, Spring 2006 (29)

When we interviewed local newsagent Hamdy Shahein nearly six years ago (*Issue 6, Summer 2000*), he was engaged in a long-running battle with WH Smith. The struggle continues.

To summarise the story to date, Hamdy – a friendly 54-year-old with an engaging manner – owns Hamdy's newsagent on the High Street. Starting in 1989 he waged a campaign against the corporate wholesaling distributor WH Smith in an attempt to prevent them sending him top-shelf material, which Hamdy considers to be pornography. With the aid of national press and TV coverage, his tenacious efforts to prevent delivery of 'adult' magazines were rewarded in 1996 when WHS agreed to stop sending them to his shop.

However, in 2002 the girlie magazines started arriving again. By December 2003, and by now having returned the offending magazines seventy times and having phoned WHS on 50 occasions without response, Hamdy threatened legal action against the company claiming that they were in breach of contract and 'in breach of Human Rights Articles 8 and 9'. Eventually, WHS's Managing Director apologised and offered Hamdy compensation. As he had already incurred costs amounting to more than this, Hamdy was in no mood to accept this 'insulting' offer and he took his case to an industry regulatory body, the Industry Standard Service Agreement. Although the agency found against WHS, they told Hamdy he should accept the compensation offer, on condition of his agreeing to confidentiality on the matter. Hamdy refused to accept this judgement.

As WHS has a monopoly over newspaper and magazine deliveries in Stoke Newington ('there is no choice but to remain with WHS'), he approached the Monopolies Commission and the Office of Fair Trading but received little joy. In February this year, he was incensed to receive seven copies of the *Sunday Sport* (not what I would describe as 'pornography', but Hamdy sees things differently) and once again contacted the WHS head office, which he describes as 'incompetent and unprofessional'. WHS refused to increase their compensation. Hamdy is fighting this, and he insists that the matter is now about 'justice', as he will donate any money he receives to charity.

The issue now appears to have become as much a moral crusade as a business dispute, with Hamdy recently having meetings at the House of Commons with local MP Diane Abbott and others about introducing legislation to make it illegal to sell adult magazines to under-18s. Surprisingly, unlike alcohol and cigarettes it is not illegal to sell such material to minors, and he told me he has Diane's backing on this. Clearly there will be problems with this complex issue, such as the age of consent being sixteen, who decides what constitutes 'pornography', and so on, but Hamdy is determined to push this as hard as he can.

I asked him why he took such a firm line on adult material and if he agreed that, unless the magazines involved physical or mental coercion or were clearly illegal, that adults should be allowed to read what they wish. 'Reading pornography is entirely up to individuals, so long as it cannot be accessed by children', he replied. 'It's my choice not to sell pornography. If other shops want to sell them, it's down to them. I will not sell under any circumstances any top-shelf material.' Well, if WHS started sending him, say, gun magazines, would he react in a similar manner? 'If I think personally that a magazine is a particular danger to the area and the community in general, I will not accept it', said Hamdy. Indeed, in the past he has sent back the legendary punk fanzine *Sniffin' Glue*, and he has refused to accept deliveries of Tippex thinner (think sniffing glue) and the Class A receptacles, plastic 'button' bags. He stocks 'lads'' mags such as *Loaded* and *Nutz* and reads them closely before putting them on his shelves, and he deplores the violence of some games in computer mags, although he also sells them.

If he had the power, would he ban pornography? 'I'll be stupid. I'll tell you the truth. I don't think so. It's been around for centuries. It's only natural.' But it's certainly banned from his shop. 'We've lost a lot of money', he concluded, 'but gained respect. I have to be responsible as a retailer.' Respect he certainly seems to have, given that the majority of his customers appears to support his stand, and his shop could hardly be any busier. And, whether or not you agree with Hamdy's definition of 'pornography', he deserves respect for his dogged and principled refusal to accept the seemingly intransigent and dismissive demands of corporate capitalism.

An Unofficial War Artist
By Tim Webb, Spring 2001 (9)

The idea that art can make a political point has been accepted for a long time. Picasso's 'Guernica', depicting the bombing of civilians in a small town by the German allies of General Franco during the Spanish Civil War is one of the world's most famous paintings. The war that artist Peter Kennard describes is not one of military slaughter but the economic war waged by global capitalism against the poor and powerless. There is no soft focus in his work: the images are stark and, appropriately, many of them are in black and white. He is recognised as Britain's leading political artist.

Peter and his partner, Judy Barker – she works in the health service in Hackney as a child protection adviser – live in Stoke Newington. Their sons Matthew, 17 and Daniel, 21 are studying at college. Born in 1949 in Maida Vale, the young Kennard went to Marylebone Grammar School and later to the Byam School of Art, moving on to the Slade in 1965. Like many students at the time, he became politicised by the Vietnam War. As he points out, the Labour government of that day, led by Harold Wilson, backed American military adventures uncritically as does Tony Blair over 30 years later. A man of the left, he is not a great fan of Labour leaders.

He gave up painting to concentrate on photomontage, the art form for which he is probably best known. This he describes as the merging of one picture with another so as to create a third and critical image. It cannot be termed propaganda, as Peter's work allows people to draw their own conclusions from what they see. Not one for half measures, Peter joined the Socialist Labour League, the forerunner of the Workers Revolutionary Party. He freelanced for their paper the *Workers Press* and says he learnt a lot about production processes as, after the editorial meeting in the morning, he would have to produce an illustration for publication the same evening. Comrade Kennard found that the Party was not really his thing – he has a keen sense of humour despite his serious objectives (he's also an Arsenal supporter) – and left after about two years. His commitment to the Campaign for Nuclear Disarmament has remained firm over the years, and much of his work has been used by CND in their publications.

One of his best-known photomontages is 'Germany Shakes', commissioned by the *Guardian* at the time of the fall of the Berlin Wall in 1989. The bricks in the foreground are from Cazenove Road, Stoke Newington. Over a period of time, Peter has moved from photomontage into 'installations', which depict a theme through physical objects, not all of them immediately identifiable. People can move among them in order to see the whole from different perspectives. One of these was 'Welcome to Britain', held at the Royal Festival Hall in 1994. It included a star performer, Ken Livingstone, who Peter describes, 'standing on pallets in the middle of placards, an apparent shipwreck of debris, he appeared to be arguing with the materials around him. He was lit by a portable traffic-light set on red.' Some might say that not much has changed since, but Ken and Peter became good friends.

Peter certainly repaid the compliment in 2000 when he organised 'London Calling', an auction of works by well-known artists to raise money for Ken's campaign for London Mayor. Tracey Emin, Sir Anthony Caro, Damien Hirst, Sarah Lucas and others contributed. Over £105,000 was raised in three weeks. He would hate to be described as having become almost respectable but after many years of part-time teaching, he is now a senior lecturer in photography at the Royal College of Art.

To understand what motivates Peter Kennard, it's necessary to read his most recent illustrated book, *Dispatches from an Unofficial War Artist*. Described as 'a thematic rather than a chronological journey through his artistic, political and personal development' it is also very honest, funny and self-revealing. It was not easy to write and he admits to a disturbing feeling of emptiness afterwards. In the book he says: 'The peoples of the world are here now in London. In Stoke Newington, where I live, I hear fragments of countless languages when I wander the streets. What is most important to me about London is that its population is composed of a mix of people from across the world. It is a multi-racial and multi-cultural city. This is the key to the spirit of London, and it is this world culture that is at the root of my work.'

Peter continues to work on his art, exhibitions and publishing; Judy is as busy as ever; Matthew is a highly regarded political journalist and author; and Daniel has just returned from 18 months on the Asian sub-continent.

Mr Sunstone
By Sue Heal, Summer 2001 (10)

Small, dark, wiry and intense, with a remarkably unlined face belying his 53 years, Michael Sinclair, founder of Sunstone gym, watches my every scribbling like a hawk. He is a man by his own admittance who likes to be in control. 'It is over eight years since we opened the gym', he says, 'but I was a solicitor for some seventeen years before, and therefore face to face with the public. I tended to be impatient and do not suffer fools gladly.'

Michael saw a niche in the burgeoning fitness market, a perfect location and potential clientele, found the premises in Northwold Road and characteristically rolled his sleeves up with relish. 'To me Sunstone was all about challenge', he says acknowledging his favourite word. 'The building was a complete wreck. I'd done my research carefully but there were numerous unexpected pitfalls along the way. I love things being like that. I work best in a crisis. I am very proud of the place now.'

Sunstone, recently extensively refurbished, is a local health spa exclusively for women, a concept Michael believes is vital to its success. 'We have white, black, orthodox Jewish, Muslim, Christians, non-believers – women of every ethnic background, shape, size and appearance. A mini United Nations. Everyone has space to be totally relaxed.'

'As we are promoting the absence of men, I never wander around the club. My presence is always announced, it's taken me time to get used to having this invisibility and all that it entails', he says thoughtfully, 'to straddle the line between friendly and polite and being non-intrusive.' The result has been that the people-orientated Sinclair has had to confine himself to a back office, the firm hand on the tiller, and he's now looking for a new, as yet undefined, business venture which will put him more in the limelight again. His appears to be a life split between conformity, typical successful North London family, good schools, high achieving siblings *et al* and an itchy desire to risk and test himself.

In January this year Michael, who was never particularly interested in sport or fitness activities until he set up Sunstone, was easily persuaded by friends to climb the highest peak in Africa (19,340 feet), Mount Kilimanjaro in Tanzania: a trek not for the faint-hearted. He becomes animated when talking of his nine days enduring rib-busting high altitudes and freezing nights under canvas. 'It was wonderful. No picnic mind you, one Briton a month dies on that mountain, a fact I discovered after I'd come down!' he laughs, 'but testing yourself in that way teaches you a great deal about how you and your fellow humans actually tick. Everyone who goes on a journey like that comes down changed in some way. Me? Less

of a worrier perhaps but certainly it showed me that I want to do more of it. I had to stop just 200 metres short of the summit because of an old knee injury, so I need to do it again, this time to the top.' An almost schoolboy mixture of annoyance and disappointment crosses his face at this apparent 'failure' to complete a project. Michael chose to climb in aid of a charity close to the mountain which takes in local street children. He raised £4,500 and is maintaining contact with the scheme. 'Most of the people on my climb were doing it for UK national charities but I wanted to give something back to the local area, not just take away my own personal experience', he says quietly, eyeing me carefully to gauge if he sounded trite or mawkish. He didn't. Sinclair is acutely aware of what you may be thinking of him and this produces an urge for his words, and therefore the man, to be properly understood.

As we talked, the phone on his ultra-tidy desk rang constantly. Sinclair crisply dealt with business and returned to our chat without breaking stride. He obviously enjoys juggling several balls in the air at once and it must be frustrating for him to sit in that office for most of the day excluded from the camaraderie of the club. 'Yes it is', he admits, 'but I suppose I get frustrated rather easily. I'm having to learn that you can't bulldoze your way through life though. Sometimes the calmer, more reflective, way of dealing with change can be more effective.'

Solicitor, entrepreneur, intrinsically a businessman but also a man fizzing with energy and a wish to explore himself more closely before time runs out, Sinclair is undoubtedly proud of his past and present achievements. 'We've got a great team here at Sunstone', he says, but his personal philosophy is etched with the word Onwards. He's certainly not a man to rest on his laurels. Michael Sinclair is a man carrying a label reading 'Watch This Space'.

Michael and Sunstone continue to be one of the fixtures of Stoke Newington. The club has now been trading for twenty years, and looks set for twenty more.

Drama in Dalston
By Avis Fenner, Autumn 2001 (11)

You may not have clocked it yet, but down in Dalston there's a new venture underway in the shape of the Arcola Theatre.

Before it opened at the beginning of the year, some might have been a little sceptical about how a small army of volunteers would transform a spacious but derelict clothing factory into a viable theatrical venue. Eight months on, with two substantial studios, a cafe/bar, and foyer-cum-art space, the Arcola theatre is definitely a site with great potential. Many of its productions, particularly those in this summer's 'Vintage Shakespeare' season, have received glowing reviews and got bums on seats. How has this been achieved in such a short space of time? In addition to the volunteers, quite a lot of it is down to the energy and optimism of artistic director, Mehmet Ergen.

Born and bred in Istanbul, Mehmet studied drama and came to London in his early twenties thinking he would 'do some acting here' but laughingly recounts 'I forgot that I couldn't speak English.' Undaunted, he took drama classes. This facilitated his skill in English and gave him 'the courage to start dealing with actors and directors'. Before long he was encouraged to set up a theatre company, No Wall Theatre, and was directing plays for fringe and pub venues. 'Everything always turned into a production as soon as I was involved', he says, and it was a pub theatre production of a Kurt Weill opera that led to the establishment of the Southwark Playhouse in 1993. Of this formative period, he remembers: 'I worked very hard and directed over fifty plays in so many different levels, operas, musicals, serious European plays, Shakespeare, American repertoire.' Running a small theatre on a very tight budget, however, led to divisions within the management. Mehmet felt artistic quality was being compromised for financial reasons, and that a little bit of 'risk taking' was in order and. After five and half years, he left.

By this time he was back in Dalston, teaching play writing and directing in community centres. He knew the area needed a good repertory theatre, noticed the closure of many local factories, and started looking at potential spaces. 'I wasn't looking for something as big as this', he says with raised eyebrow and smile. Once the lease was secured he, and friends, set about rejuvenating it. The furniture, props and costumes have come from wherever they can be found. The chairs, for example, were a typical bit of good fortune. Mehmet was in Upper Street and passed a bankrupt Indian restaurant with chairs stacked outside and a sign saying 'free for a good home'.

The theatre is run with three full-time and a slew of part-time workers. Everybody, from front of house to actors, directors, and technicians, works for free. The cafe/bar and box office receipts not only have to cover the rent but all the other bills – a tough target. There's a high hope that some core funding will be secured in the next year. Mehmet believes people have supported the theatre because of the production possibilities the space offers and the quality of work. The theatre has a strong commitment to both Turkish and Afro-Caribbean communities in the plays they put on and courses they run. Mehmet says the Turkish community is 'quite laid back ... there's a lot of fun, a lot of chatting' and this is evident in his own calm manner. Unexpectedly, he's not twitching with the nervous energy of a man juggling at least nine balls in the air. He has a quiet, measured way of speaking and an easy laugh.

He feels that to be the 'best', theatres need to be 'ambitious' but at the same time remain conscious of their location. 'This is Dalston/Stoke Newington borders', he says, 'and that border is very distinct. You have a very erudite middle- to upper-middle-class Stoke Newington audience that will expect you to do classics ... and you have Dalston, full of refugees, with nearly 80 languages being spoken. Plus it needs a black theatre initiative.' In the Arcola he wants variety and divides the repertoire into these categories: new contemporary plays; old and new classics; entertainment that fits with the local culture, such as children's plays, musicals, comedies; and lastly that the theatre should be 'open to anyone coming with anything'.

Rightly proud of what they have achieved at the Arcola so far, Mehmet says: 'This is one of the most deprived areas in London and we have really brought a huge lifeblood into it. We are holding on to it by saying we are the biggest opportunity for everyone in Hackney, in North London, as a performance arts space.' With an assured calm he adds, 'We will get money and if we don't, well, we will have to find ways of raising it.'

The Arcola is now an internationally respected theatre and, over the last ten years, Mehmet has certainly fulfilled his aspirations. It has recently moved to a new, enlarged space further down in Dalston.

Alex Norton
By Sue Heal, Autumn 2002 (15)

I approached Alex Norton's Stokey front door with some trepidation. Anyone who's seen his sterling performance as DCI Mike Burke in ITV's 'Taggart' knows that this is an actor who can curdle milk by simply staring at it.

Norton, or rather Burke, is the kind of copper they used to say 'could go either way', ie psychotic armed bank robber or ... a DCI. The man himself was described by the *Scotsman* as having a 'bog scouring scowl'. Norton, 'just say I'm in my forties', laughs at the reminder. 'Burke and I do share certain characteristics', he says as we drink tea and munch biccies at the kitchen pine table surrounded by the various detritus of family life. Norton and actress wife Sally have three sons at local Stokey schools. 'Burke is a perfectionist and so am I. I like a job to be well done and I'm always working away at my lines. And I've got myself into hot water when I was younger by opening my mouth when it maybe should have stayed shut.' I can imagine. Norton, small, stocky and quietly brooding, is a curious mixture of thinly disguised sternness, quick wit and mind, overlaid with great bursts of sunshine when he relaxes enough to smile.

'The older I get, the more I realise there is quite a bit of my father in me', he says talking of the Glasgow plumber and fervent trade unionist with whom he had a highly complex relationship. 'My dad had a thing about discipline and I suppose so do I. Sometimes I catch myself saying things to the kids which sound just like him.' If this makes Norton appear scary or, heaven forbid, unloving, then nothing could be further from the truth. He obviously adores his sons and wife and speaks with enormous pride of his good fortune with them. 'I was pretty chaotic when I was much younger but now there is nothing which can hold a candle in significance to my family', he says without a hint of sentimentality.

Norton was brought up in Glasgow, 'outside lavvy, that sort of thing, but no violins, we never went hungry', and discovered acting at the age of 14 through an out-of-school drama group which led to a surprise part in 'Dr Finlay's Casebook'. He was a grammar school boy, 'too embarrassed to have my classmates back to my place', whose strongly opinionated father had mapped him out for a good apprenticeship. He made his disapproval of his son's acting ambitions very clear. Norton decided against the traditional RADA type route, 'didn't think I'd fit in ... it's one of my regret', and opted instead for entering the business immediately, steadily moving from part to part. He has an impressive CV littered with radical film, television and theatre work.

He was part of John McGrath's seminal 7:84 company – his face wreathes in smiles at the mention – *Gregory's Girl* with Bill Forsyth, the award-winning *Beautiful Creatures, Little Voice, Orphans* and some good old blockbuster Hollywood hokum like *Patriot Games* with Harrison Ford. Norton's won two screenwriting awards. 'I love writing but hate doing it, if you see what I mean. The lone scribbler in the garret isn't really for me. I'd like to do more but I'm more interested in directing at present', he says.

At the moment, life is of necessity built around DCI Burke and a grinding shooting schedule in Glasgow. 'I'm away most of the week. We discussed moving to Scotland but we're very happy in Stokey and the kids didn't want to', he says. 'We've been here about 14 years now and it suits us just fine. I like the Bohemian feel." His sons, Jock 13 and Rory 11, are at Stokey Comp, and Jamie 5, is at Grasmere. They seem to have penchant for The Biz themselves with Jock reaching the last three for a major role in *Harry Potter*. 'Absolutely no pushing from us or telling them not to come to that', says Norton hastily, 'although I was dead proud. He was very professional.' The highest of accolades coming from Alex Norton.

Norton definitely loosens up the longer you're with him and I eventually caught glimmers of the good fun guy, great company, fund of sharp stories his friends talk about. As for the future, like most thesps he's dependent on the phone ringing but says sanguinely, 'when and if it does stop then maybe we'll go to France and I'll sup a glass of red or two'. His home now, though, is most decidedly Stokey: he's not a Scot who hankers for the Highlands. 'I'll tell you how I know', he says. 'I was making a movie in Nova Scotia and it kept running over. I got very homesick. But I wasn't wishing for Scotland. I dreamt about Stoke Newington.'

Foot in the Town Hall?
By Tim Webb, Autumn 2002 (15)

Paul Foot has been described by Geoffrey Goodman, editor of the *British Journalism Review*, as 'one of the outstanding reporters of his generation'. This is due to 'his fearless honesty, intellectual courage, exceptional persistence and integrity in pursuit of social justice and the fight for decency in our society.' Whew. So why does a man possessing all those high-minded virtues want to be Mayor of Hackney?

Issues such as the bin collection, unpaid council tax, parking zones, hit squads in schools, library closures and the animals in Clissold Park hardly seem the stuff of heroic principle, although some might say that he would need all his qualities and a few more besides if he won the top post. His columns in the *Guardian* and *Private Eye* don't pull any punches. Fat cats, Blairites, privatisers, tax evaders, right-wing trade unionists, arms traders and assorted dodgy dealers in business and government regularly get a good thumping from a man who rejected his privileged background to use his journalistic skills to promote what he believes to be the interests of those at the bottom of the pile.

Paul Foot spent his early years in Jamaica where his father Sir Hugh Foot was Governor. His education in Britain was expensive: he attended Ludgrove, the exclusive prep school where Prince Harry was groomed for the royal merry-go-round. At Shrewsbury public school, he met Richard Ingrams, Willie Rushton and Christopher Booker, with whom he worked on *Private Eye* some years later. The King's Shropshire Light Infantry was the local regiment for his national service and as a well-bred young man he was sent to Officer Cadet School where, far from seeing himself as a future military leader, he was, in his own words, 'completely useless'. However, in the fine tradition of the British Army, incompetence was no barrier to becoming an officer and he was posted to the Jamaica Regiment on the island where his father still represented Britain's imperial interests.

At Oxford he was President of the Liberal Club. He then became 'a sort of socialist'. There was no blinding conversion but he says he was 'instinctively a Red' when he worked for the *Daily Record* in Glasgow from 1961. He became involved with the Labour Party Young Socialists when that part of Scotland was a ferment of left-wing debate. The two main strands were those supporting the Communist Party with Jimmy Reid and Jimmy Airlie, who were the leaders of the Clyde Shipbuilders occupation, and the Trotskyist tendency which claimed people like Gus (now Lord) MacDonald amongst its adherents. Foot sided with the latter. He couldn't entirely escape his background – his uncle is Michael Foot – and he was twice offered the candidacy of seats for the Labour Party but rejected the proposals. He finally left the party in 1967, after canvassing for

Ben Whitaker, the successful Labour parliamentary candidate in Hampstead. He recalls knocking on doors for the subsequent GLC election to be told by the same voters that Labour had let them down. Foot believes Blair's lack of firmly rooted principles and control freakery has worsened the situation and this is reflected in the rapidly falling party membership and voting figures. He says 'people want to be represented, not managed.'

So, why Hackney Mayor? Well, he's been a resident of N16, in Stamford Hill for the past 15 years. He's highly critical of Hackney councils – past and present. Apart from their general lack of competence, he believes that they've been too easily led into disastrous privatisation ventures. The profit motive, he says, does not sit easily with the provision of public services. He deeply regrets the end of the Stoke Newington Festival and is critical of the council for withdrawing funding. Again, he says private companies are unwilling to provide sponsorship for public events unless they can see a financial advantage for themselves.

Education is his number one priority and he states that two new secular schools are urgently needed in Hackney. He quotes the example of his own child. Both he and his partner Clare would like their daughter to have a comprehensive, secular education at a mixed secondary school. However, there's only one in the whole borough and it's a long way from where they live. Councils and government should not be pushing so-called 'faith' schools and creating social segregation. If elected, he will open talks with the police on why so many black people seem to be stopped and questioned. In keeping with his stated support for the workers, he opposes council redundancies. Library closures 'are a disgrace' as is any proposal to shut the deer enclosures in Clissold Park. He widens his view from Hackney to oppose any attack on Iraq.

In 1999, he had a close brush with death when an artery started leaking, then burst. Thanks, he says,

to the NHS staff at the Homerton and London Chest Hospitals, he has partly recovered, although he finds difficulty in walking far or standing for long periods. I was about ask him whether he would be up to the stress of a high-pressure job when he started to explain strongly that his partial disability has given him a new insight into the problems faced by disabled people. Not only could he do the job, backed by the right staff, but he would also ensure better facilities in Hackney for people with disabilities.

As we talked, I wondered if I could detect traces of wishful thinking and perhaps not a full appreciation of the depth of the financial mire that has bogged Hackney down and led to the tight grip by the government on the council. Also, his idea that better-off Stoke Newington residents readily identify with the people in the high-rise blocks at the other end of Hackney might be something of an illusion. However, if it is an illusion, at least it's not a dangerous one.

Jules Pipe won the Mayoral election. Paul Foot died in July 2004.

Islam in Stoke Newington
By Rab MacWilliam, Winter 2001 (12)

An affable, smiling 24-year-old, Ismail Amaan has a big job for such a relatively young man. Ismail is Director of the North London Muslim Community Centre on Cazenove Road, which occupies two four-storied buildings set back from the road next door to the mosque and is the only single source for advice, education and guidance for Hackney's 40,000 Muslim population.

Born in Lancashire, he came south to live in Stoke Newington as a child when his Gujurati father, like many of today's local Muslim residents, moved away from the north of England's declining textile industries to find work in London. He attended state school in Stoke Newington and Homerton, and graduated from Queen Mary's College with an honours degree in English. Did this loquacious and articulate man experience any discrimination or racial prejudice in his formative years in the area? 'None at all. In fact my friends, including white and Afro-Caribbean, were fascinated by Islam and we used to discuss the faith at length.' His devotion to Islam, and his strong desire to benefit his community, saw him take up a position at the Council of British Muslims and then, in 2000, he became Director of the Centre.

The Community Centre was founded in the crypt of St Thomas's Church on Clapton Common in 1978, and its original aim was to involve the Muslim youth in the area in sporting activities. Its cricket team, the Young Muslim Cricket Club, soon became feared throughout London. The organisation outgrew these cramped premises and moved to its present location in 1982, where its operations expanded to include, among other services, an advice centre, mental health centre, luncheon clubs, careers advice and education courses, the last in conjunction with Hackney Community College, offering expertise in subjects as diverse as child care and IT. In 1999 the Centre took over the freehold from Hackney Council for ninety years, in return for a peppercorn rent so long as the Centre was used for community purposes, and the building is now being refurbished and expanded.

The Centre is a focus for the many different nationalities in Stoke Newington – principally Turkish, Bangladeshi, Indian and Pakistani, but also whites, Afro-Caribbeans and others who have converted to the faith – who comprise the Muslim community in the area. Indeed, a few days ago in the well-equipped reading room (which, incidentally, stocks several Asian newspapers and magazines unavailable anywhere else in the UK) Ismail observed six nationals from different countries quietly scrutinising the reading materials. The building also operates an open door policy, and Sikhs and Hindus are welcome, as are followers of other religions and faiths. Since the mosque was established in 1972 the first mosque to be opened in Hackney, two other mosques, both Turkish, have followed in Stoke Newington. The most recently built mosque in the borough is the Suleymani on the Kingsland Road, one of the biggest mosques in Europe and a splendid example of contemporary Muslim architecture. Despite the ethnic diversity of the Muslim community, followers of Islam are welcome at all the centres of worship, as Ismail stated that Islam transcends nationhood.

I asked Ismail, therefore, whether local Muslims view themselves as primarily British or as Muslims who happen to live in Britain. Is assimilation in the wider society a desirable objective or has it the potential to weaken the core of the faith? He replied that Muslims welcome the opportunity to live in this country but also have their own ethical and religious standards. Perhaps from time to time these are not compatible with the prevailing view in British society but they emphasise tolerance and respect for the rights of others.

We discuss the perception of Islamic youth, recently the focus of media attention. Why were the disturbances and violence in the North of England not replicated in Stoke Newington? Ismail's view is that the social situation in the North is one of polarisation, with whites and Asians exhibiting mutual suspicion and the Muslims living in what are virtual ghettos. In Stoke Newington, the multi-ethnic diversity of the area militates against such stark confrontation. Although there are poorer and wealthier areas here, for historical reasons we do not have the ethnic bundling and social stigmatisation of, say, Oldham and Bradford. He has also noted the tendency for young males to rebel against the strictures of Islam, only to return to the faith in later years with renewed vigour and enthusiasm.

And women? Ismail dismisses what he considers to be the preconceived western notion of the female sex as the oppressed partners in Muslim society. He describes the 7th century Koran as not only the first bill of rights but also as the first charter of the equal, if segregated, rights of women. He mentions the increasing tendency of Muslim women to adopt the veil, and cites a trip to a local market with a friend and her husband. 'Why do you have to make your wife wear that veil?' asked a trader. 'You tell her to take it off – I can't', the husband replied.

Our discussion concludes, inevitably, with world events post-11 September. Ismail describes the attack on the World Trade Center as 'an evil atrocity. The murder of innocent people is against the teachings of the Koran.' However, the bombing of Afghanistan is 'just as bad. No justice has been demonstrated and the rule of law has been ignored. There has been a complete lack of concern for the innocent people of Afghanistan. The US did not pursue all the avenues available and the west are bullies.' What about the widely reported press stories of young men going to fight with the Taliban? 'I know of no one from Stoke Newington who has gone to Afghanistan. Perhaps a few from Britain but no one from round here.'

What has been the impact of these events on local Muslims? Although relations with other communities in Stoke Newington have been, and generally remain, harmonious, there have been some anti-Islamic incidents. A youth leader was stopped on his way into the Centre and asked 'Are you happy, now?' Comments such as 'effin Muslims' and 'there's Osama Bin Laden' have been overheard, beer bottles have been thrown at Muslims and women have been spat at, leaving many afraid to

leave their homes. Regrettable though such unthinking bigotry is, Ismail feels that this anti-Islamic sentiment has now largely died away. To prevent these incidents from recurring what is needed is 'more understanding of Islam from other ethnic groups. We have been misrepresented and this causes a lot of damage.'

In spite of the importance of the Community Centre to local Muslims, it is in danger of having its range of activities cut back by Hackney Council. This will have a serious negative impact on many of the more vulnerable in the Muslim community, particularly on the homeless, elderly and those who may have difficulties with the English language. The Centre has raised petitions, organised protests and appealed to local and central government to re-consider the cuts. It would be a step backwards in multi-ethnic integration and understanding in Stoke Newington if such an essential resource was to suffer because of financial constraints.

The Community Centre is flourishing. Ismail is currently involved in a number of Islamic projects, as well as running Foster Care Link, the only foster agency catering exclusively for Muslims.

Hasidim of Stamford Hill
By Rab MacWilliam, Winter 2002 (16)

'A marooned Jew was discovered on a desert island after years of isolation. His rescuers were impressed by his survival and by the buildings he had erected, particularly the two synagogues. "But why two?" they asked, puzzled. The Jew looked at them fiercely. "That's the one I use", he replied, "and that's the one I refuse to use".'

Rabbi Herschel Gluck, of the Independent Synagogue in Walford Road, is a man of good humour and laughs easily. A deep chuckle rose from beneath his bushy, patriarchal beard when he finished the story. Clearly, he sees the joke as a metaphor for the self-reliance, determination and, when occasion demands, obduracy of the Jewish people. He settled back into the deep leather sofa in his study in Fountayne Road and we resumed our conversation about the Hasidim of Stamford Hill.

For an outsider, it is impossible not to be intrigued by this enigmatic and obviously devout community, some 25,000 strong, whose presence rarely impinges on the wider area of Stoke Newington but is such a feature of the leafy confines of Stamford Hill. How did these closely-knit Judaic people end up in N16? What are their beliefs? How do they structure their community? Why do the men dress as if they are in 19th century Cracow? Why do they seem to isolate themselves from the wider world?

The Rabbi is Hackney born and bred, although his heavy Yiddish accent belies this. A much respected figure in the borough and beyond, Rabbi Gluck studied for four years with the leader of the world Lubavitch community in Brooklyn where he was 'inspired and influenced' by the Hasidic movement, a profoundly orthodox body of Jewish teaching. The Hasidics believe in total devotion to the Torah – the Hebrew Scriptures (or Old Testament) – and enjoy a mystical, almost cabalistic, tradition of 'joyful worship'. The movement remained resistant to the pogroms of the 19th century and the genocide of the 20th, and spread to New York, Israel, Paris and London, among other places. In the words of the Rabbi, 'Hasidic thought has permeated every aspect of Jewish life and is at the very core of Judaism'.

The community moved to Stamford Hill from the East End in the 1930s and were joined by others fleeing from the Nazis. After World War Two, many Jewish survivors, wishing to leave behind them the ghosts of the blood-soaked continent, also arrived, and the community was reinforced by Hasidim leaving Hungary after the 1956 Soviet invasion. Stamford Hill is now home to the third largest Hasidic population in the world after Israel and New York City. There are a wide number of different groupings within the Stamford Hill community: Satmar (Hungary, Romania), Ger (Poland), Bobov (Galicia), Belz (Western Ukraine) and Viznitz (Romania) are the most numerous, while curiously the largest of them all – the Lubavitch sect – is sparsely represented. They are all of East European Ashkenazai (the old Hebrew word for Germany) origin and, although they have differences on matters of interpretation of the Torah and the Talmud (the oral law written down during the Roman occupation of Israel) they mix easily together within the community. An umbrella body, the Union of Orthodox Jewish Communities, represents their individual interests collectively.

Although social intercourse is the norm within the community, it seems to many outside observers that they appear unwilling to integrate in any meaningful sense with the wider Stoke Newington community. Does this perceived aloofness stems from a sense of theological or moral superiority? Or maybe their apparent indifference is to do with a concern that the Hasidic culture and beliefs may be eroded by exposure to outside influences? I was quietly but firmly disabused. 'The word "superior" is preconceived. A strong spiritual framework is involved with every aspect of life. Judaism is a full-time requirement with a self-contained tradition. It is very precious to us. We have to serve God and have little free leisure time. Any snubbing is misinterpreted. The community does not want to impose its way of life on others but equally it wants to preserve its own culture and lifestyle.'

Well, what do Hasidic people feel about the other communities in the area? 'We think the relationship is a positive one.' Rabbi Gluck cites as an example the groundbreaking Muslim Jewish Forum (where orthodox Jews and Muslims meet regularly to discuss issues of common concern in Stamford Hill. Where else in the world would this occur?). He uses the distinctively non-Rabbinic but cheerfully contemporary term 'good vibes' to sum up his view of their general relationship with the outside world.

He was at pains to stress throughout our discussion that, although there are cultural differences between our various communities, the internal structure of Hasidic life is little different to other cultures within Stoke Newington. Politics? The Hasidic local councillors are Conservative and Liberal and the community is mixed in terms of support for the major parties. Working life? Yes, there are many of the menfolk who devote their lives to studying the great Hebrew texts and who are not formally employed but other men work across the board from building to accountancy. The women, however, usually look after the large families – Rabbi Gluck has eight children – and tend not to work ('If bringing up and caring for multiple children is not considered work', says the Rabbi).

Education is of crucial importance to the orthodox community. There are 20 schools in Stamford Hill which cater for Hasidic children. Has the community considered a more integrative policy? The Rabbi mentioned that the schools act 'in loco parentis, to preserve the culture and faith and to understand other cultures'. The emphasis is on contemplation and study, which explains why a TV set is a rare item in the Hasidic home. 'A lazy medium', says Rabbi Gluck.

Although crime – mainly white-collar – is not unknown within the orthodox Jews, the Hasidics of Stamford Hill are 'an extremely low-crime community'. I ask if the natural reaction would be to contact the police in the event of a serious crime being discovered. Not necessarily, says Rabbi Gluck, such crime would normally be sorted out within the community. They follow a policy of 'enlightened punishment' where prison is an 'alien term' and the emphasis is on education rather than punishment.

The most obvious physical manifestation of the differences between the Hasidim and other Stoke Newington cultures lies in the clothing worn by the men. From the white stockings, the wide-brimmed fur hats, the elegantly-tailored frock coats and the tasselled skull caps, one can conjure up images of 19th century Polish and East German market squares, a beguiling anachronism in the days of back-to-front baseball hats and FCUK T-shirts. Is there any theological significance in the differing and exotic styles of dress, I ask the Rabbi? 'No', he replies, succinctly. Most Hasidic Jews dress conservatively except for Sabbath and festival days when they, like wearers of any other national dress, like to look their best. The differences between their clothing simply reflect cultural origins. While on the subject of holy days, I enquire about the number of synagogues in Stamford Hill and am surprised that there are over 70, several to be found in people's front rooms, although the main religious building are large, often purpose-built structures scattered around the neighbourhood.

Finally we turn to the question of the Middle East and Israel. It has been widely reported in recent months that the majority of the Hasidic community in Stamford Hill is anti-Zionist and objects to the existence of the state of Israel. 'The Holy Land is a special place and religious Jews love the land and the people. However, Zionism is a secular ideology and has contributed to the secularisation of many Jews. The state of Israel wasn't the best way forward for Jewish people. Today more than ever, both in the land of Israel and around the world, we all feel passionately that we want and need Moshiach (the coming of the Messiah).'

The orthodox Jews see themselves as 'keepers of the faith' and are at best unhappy when the deeply entrenched, spiritual traditions of Judaism are under attack, as they claim they are from many quarters within Israel. The most extreme anti-Zionist group in the area is the Neturei Karta, around 100 families, who provoked outrage from many within London's wider Jewish community when they joined Palestinians in protesting at a recent anti-Israel rally in the West End. I ask the Rabbi, then, if he is sympathetic to the plight of the Palestinians. He smiled and commented 'I am sympathetic to the suffering of any human being'.

Rabbi Gluck travels widely as a consultant on behalf of his community. He is often to be seen strolling along the streets of Stoke Newington, and is constantly engaged in conversation by people of all descriptions and races.

George Alagiah
By Sue Heal, Winter 2002 (16)

Stokey has the odd smattering of famous faces, most along the lines of 'do I know him/her?' or 'were they in the background on 'The Bill' last week?' But Sri Lankan-born broadcaster and journalist George Alagiah is your copper-bottomed 'Blimey it's George Alagiah in the flower shop' variety. We met for a quick cappuccino one morning surrounded by mothers with prams who were all pretending that they'd not noticed George Alagiah (*our photo shows him addressing the Literary Festival*).

George, 47, his wife Frances who works for The Fairtrade Foundation (George is a patron) and their two adolescent sons have lived in Stokey since 1988, and unlike many rising stars have not decamped to tidier climes. 'I like the community feel and mix of people', he says. 'There was a moment a while back when several things had gone wrong, my car had been broken into etc … but that evening some Muslim neighbours came round, it was the end of Ramadan, to give us some sweetmeats. We looked at each other and knew we weren't going anywhere.'

Despite his impeccable liberal credentials, Alagiah, a polite, thoughtful yet obviously highly motivated man, has no truck with knee-jerk political correctness. His sons attended a local primary but are now at a much sought after selective secondary outside the borough. 'I get angry that my children can't have a decent enough education near their home', he says. 'They are commuters. But I'm not ashamed of what we've done.

I'm very proud of them. I think political correctness *per se* is just non-thinking, like those old farts we used to point out when we were young who always thought the same way about everything.'

Alagiah is one of the most famous faces on the BBC, moving from award-winning Africa correspondent, where he first gripped the nation's attention for his seminal reports on the Iraqi Kurds, Burundi and Rwanda, to news presenting. From January he will be the face of the flagship BBC 6 o'clock bulletin. Alagiah won the Royal Television Society's Journalist of The Year award in 1994, and it is his reporting from South Africa which 'earned me my spurs' and gave him clout to push other, more long-term reports, within the BBC. 'I passionately believe that the developed world has to be become more involved in the larger economic questions about our attitudes to places like Africa.'

'For instance, I did a report on traditional herbal medicines: who owns them the big companies who come in to take them or the people who've handed them down over generations? I had to push to do that one', he says. Alagiah becomes animated when talking of his beloved Africa. His Tamil family moved to Ghana when he was six to avoid persecution, and he writes of the vast continent with great vibrancy and concern in his recent book *A Passage To Africa*. 'I love the passion and if anything befalls Africa it hits me in the guts', he says. 'I've had to train myself to be dispassionate, to be a reporter.' During the end of his sojourn as a foreign correspondent Alagiah hints that the necessary dispassion was becoming increasingly difficult. 'I would go to do a report and want to help, pitch in. I found I couldn't just walk away and regard my job as a cathartic process in itself. That's when you know it's best to try something new', he says. The 'something new' was presenting the news instead of reporting on it. 'But I don't regard that as a lesser job, quite the reverse. It brings a huge sense of responsibility, especially as I'm not a traditional white news presenter. It's a very real way of demonstrating that we're not all muggers', he smiles.

Alagiah is in many ways a curious mixture. Bright, forthcoming, someone the Beeb is obviously keen to promote further up the firmament ("but it did take three goes to get in') and yet seemingly not afraid to publicly state his own views. How does he regard himself, British or an immigrant? 'Both', he says quickly and unequivocally. 'I was a migrant from the age of six. I believe strongly that we should look closely at our immigration laws in this country. By that I don't mean "come one come all". And I say this as someone whose family fled to find a "better life". We can no more be so-called politically correct about that as anything else. It's about what can people give and contribute.'

Alagiah is incredibly close to his extended family – they live in Finchley – and obviously regards family as the bedrock of his life. 'This is all me, me, me', he says, 'but my most contented times haven't been "in the field" but here on a rainy Sunday afternoon on with my kids watching a black and white movie.' But does he miss the reporter's field? What was it like to come back to the rain and the bin bags? 'Fantastic', he says with obvious relish. 'I walked straight into my local Stokey newsagent to place my order again and it was "hello, George". Great. I was concerned that the boys might find it difficult. By necessity, they had led privileged lives in South Africa, going everywhere in cars with drivers, for instance. But there was no problem. I like to think we slotted right back in.'

George remains presenter of BBC News at Six and BBC News at Ten. He still lives in Stoke Newington.

Dissent in Newington Green

By Rab MacWilliam, Summer 2003 (18)

A small chapel, sitting anonymously on the north side of Newington Green, has been at the heart of the area's reputation for dissent and non-conformism for almost three hundred years. Built in 1708 by the Rational Dissenters (and designed to look like a dwelling place to prevent persecution by Church and State), it is the oldest surviving non-conformist meeting house in London.

Over the years, several distinguished ministers have preached the Unitarian message to their congregations in its somewhat austere surroundings, with perhaps the most famous being Richard Price, minister from 1758 to 1791. Price was a noted liberal intellectual, mathematician and writer, whose chapel was also visited by Benjamin Franklin, John Adams and David Hume, was a supporter of the American and French Revolutions, and his writings prompted Edmund Burke to compose his *Reflections on the Revolution in France,* a conservative rebuttal of radicalism. In recent years, however, Unitarianism declined in numbers and the chapel was kept going

by the efforts of a small group of local women. When student minister Cal Courtney arrived last year, the number of regular congregation members had fallen to just four.

A 31-year-old, amiable Irishman, Cal has had a remarkable spiritual journey. Born in Drogheda, the Irish Republic's 'bandit country', he joined the Redemptorist order of the Catholic Church when he left school at 17. He believes that growing up against the background of 'the troubles' may well have influenced his abhorrence of violence and his embrace of tolerance. A liberal, missionary wing of the Church, the Redemptorists had a presence in Calcutta, where Cal spent much of his time. He describes this period as a 'life-changing experience'. 'Was it the poverty?' I asked. 'Partly', he replied, 'but it was mainly the profound impact of the universalism of Hinduism, where God is everywhere.' He left the monastic life at the age of 20 – 'they were great about it. I've still got a key for the front door' – and worked for two years before studying for a degree in World Religions at University College, Wales. He then gained an MPhil at Trinity College, Dublin, where his thesis was on sectarianism in Irish education.

A radical spirit who is equally at ease with the French builders currently restoring the old chapel as he is with the more arcane points of Jungian psychotherapy and postmodern philosophy, Cal then found his vocation in the Unitarian Church. After studying at the Church's Wakefield education centre and then at Manchester College, Oxford, he took over at Newington Green 'Why Unitarianism?' I enquired. 'Because it's religion without dogma and based on human experience. We free ourselves from the confinements of creed and believe it's OK not to conform.' All are welcome at the chapel, including pagans and atheists, as well as believers in all the world's major religions. Indeed, he rarely uses the term 'God', believing that most people find it gender-specific, ie male. Curiously, though, he still attends Mass every week, on the grounds that although rational, intellectual inquiry is critical to spiritual understanding, a sense of mystery is also an integral part of religious life.

Does his radicalism express itself politically? Although he made a decision not to engage politically, as the biggest questions are theological and not political, the two do occasionally coincide. The evening before the march against the recent Iraq War, he held a silent vigil from 9pm till 9am at the chapel, protesting against the US-led incursion with, among others, Hindus, Muslims, Buddhists and Jews present. 'A Jewish rabbi gave her family prayer book to a Muslim', he remembers, 'as a symbolic atonement for the Israeli occupation of Palestine.' Cal's charismatic stewardship of the chapel has seen the regular attendance grow to 20, and the main service is held on Sunday evenings. He has also re-instituted the annual Richard Price Memorial Lecture, last given in 1981.

This complex but cheerful man, whose enthusiasm for the Newington Green Jazz Festival and local life generally rests easily alongside his concern for matters pastoral and spiritual, appears to be breathing new life into a venerable tradition. Healthy non-conformism is again alive and well in Newington Green.

Cal resigned as minister in 2006. His replacement is an equally independently minded and friendly American, Andy Pakula.

We received the following response in Issue 19 to the above article

I was born and bred and educated in Stoke Newington, and I still visit there regularly, so I am always pleased to read your magazine. I was very interested in your article 'Dissent in Newington Green', since this area has been the home of dissent for many centuries, hence its particular character and history. I should like to add a couple of comments.

First, you could have added that prominent members of the Unitarian Church included the family of Charles Darwin. Second, I find it inappropriate that an article about a Christian institution should gratuitously smear the Jewish State. You refer to a rabbi who wished to 'make an atonement for the Israeli occupation of Palestine'. In fact no rabbi would make such a statement, unless it was qualified by reminding people that the Jews in Israel are threatened with annihilation and have a right to defend themselves. This is a point that Minister Cal Courtney didn't wish to pursue, maybe because, as you mention, he does not like to engage in politics.

Charles Heller, Toronto, Canada

NI6 asked Cal for his comments on Charles Heller's email. This was his response:

I cannot accept that I or my church attempted to gratuitously smear 'the Jewish State'. Firstly, Israel is not a Jewish State. It is a secular state. Secondly, our record of supporting the Jewish people speaks for itself. Charles Heller can rest assured that all acts of cruelty are challenged in this church, irrespective of the religious adherence of the people involved.

And another letter from a reader in Canada...

I find the comments by Charles Heller about the Jewish state (issue 19) to be most provocative. Like Charles Heller I also come from Stoke Newington, like him I also have a Jewish family, and like him I also live in Canada. The Jewish state does not need to be smeared. It is doing an excellent job of this all on its own. For example, it is inconceivable that the British government would build a wall round parts of the country to keep out whole ethnic groups lest some of them may be suicide bombers. Yet that is what Israel is doing. Finally, contrary to what Charles Heller states, there are many rabbis who make no secret of their disgust with the policies of Israel. (27)

Sweet Soul Music
By Rab MacWilliam, Winter 2003 (20)

An engaging, voluble character, Luddy Samms is nonetheless modest about his 40-year career as a soul singer. This is a man who has worked with the all-time greats.

A Stoke Newington resident since the mid-1970s, Ludwig Samuels (his father was a Beethoven enthusiast) was born in Jamaica in 1946 and moved with his family to Houston, Texas when still a boy. He honed his silky, soulful voice in the local Pentecostal church, his formative influences being Sam Cooke and Brooke Benton, and he developed an affinity with 'raw, harsh-edged gospel'. After a spell in the US military in the mid-1960s (and a tour of Vietnam, about which he is reticent) he moved to England and began singing in London's clubs and bars.

Now with a young family, he moved to Finsbury Park, then to a basement in Stamford Hill and finally to Shakespeare Walk. Since then, his distinctive vocals have taken him across Britain and Europe, singing with the Johnny Moore-era Drifters, backing Wilson Pickett ('a nice guy but crazy'), Eddie Floyd, the Chi-Lites, Rufus Thomas ('a great man'), Sam and Dave and the Blues Brothers, amongst others. He recalls supporting James Brown in Belgium. Brown's manager came into

Luddy's dressing room and scratched out most of his set list, saying 'you can't sing this, you can't sing that'. Luddy retaliated by going on stage and singing an entire Brown set, including 'Papa's Got A Brand New Bag'. He never worked with the Sex Machine again.

He remembers the vitality of the Stoke Newington live music scene in the 1970s, citing such classic venues as the Pegasus on Green Lanes, the Weaver's in Newington Green and the Three Crowns ('man, they used to queue around the block to see me there'). He forged an unlikely alliance with Polly Brown (singer with Picketywitch, a 1970s 'novelty' band, younger readers), carved out a reputation as a nonpareil interpreter of the Atlantic, Stax and Motown catalogue and became a fixture in the London soul and r&b scene.

He remembers some ten years ago singing at the famed Gaz's Rocking Blues Club and spotting a familiar face in the front row. 'Hi, I'm Bruce, meet Demi. Would you mind if I joined you?' Bruce Willis pulled out his harmonica and joined Luddy on stage for a storming blues set. Luddy, who has an endearing habit of singing a song's first line instead of quoting it, continues to be a regular presence across the capital, although in the 1980s he disliked singing in Britain. 'All they offered me were functions where they treated me like a piece of shit.'

He now gigs with his band Back II Basics, comprising his long-time partner Bruce Knapp, a splendid guitarist with a day job as lecturer in music at Chichester College and who has been described as 'Britain's answer to Steve Cropper' (the legendary guitarist and leader of the Stax house band); a tight, four-piece brass section; Brand New Heavies keyboardist Neil Cowley; drummer Toby Barron, currently touring with Ray Davies; and bass player Jonathan Banks. He welcomes the arrival of The Eye (*a venue on the High Street now gone, alas*) but is disenchanted with the contemporary music scene in Stoke Newington. 'They've closed down all the good pubs and turned them into synthetic theme bars,' he complains. Likewise, he is out of touch with contemporary music – 'maybe I'm just locked in a cocoon. There are no singers with range and power. Direction is lacking,' he adds.

What next, then, for Luddy? He is a devotee (as everyone should be) of Otis Redding ('a shy man') and is currently preparing an album entitled 'An Otis Tribute'. He has also written a stage play about Otis's life – called, unsurprisingly, 'Mr Pitiful' – and is keen to see it staged, if he can find out where it is hiding on his computer.

Luddy's performances at the N16 Fringe between 2004 and 2009 have passed into local legend, and he continues to perform with his new band across Europe. He divides his time between Marylebone and Scotland, although he still visits Stoke Newington at the slightest possible excuse.

'Bye, Les
By Rab MacWilliam, Spring 2004, (21)

Having known Les on and off for years, it was no surprise for me to find him in the Rochester Castle one lunchtime.

We got to talking, mainly about his insistence that I should invest in Canadian oil shares, a market about which he seemed surprisingly well informed and I was and am completely ignorant. Suddenly his mood darkened, and this diminutive figure told me about a strapping young barman in a Stoke Newington pub who had annoyed him. He grabbed my jacket lapel and, following a furtive look around the pub, confided 'But what he doesn't know, kid, is that I'm a killing machine'.' 'Well, anyone who sees you would know that, Les', said I. 'And I know at least twelve ways to finish him off', continued Les. 'Well then, I'd better warn him, Les.' At this, he brightened up and we continued our chat about global finance. As I left the bar, Les was sitting in the corner, surreptitiously (as he thought) pouring his quarter-bottle of whisky into his half pint, his hat sliding over his eyes on the perfectly reasonable assumption that, if he couldn't see what he was doing, neither could the barman.

Stoke Newington is not rich enough in characters that it can afford to ignore Les Fenwick's passing. Born in Gateshead 78 years ago, his body was discovered in his council flat in Yoakley Road in December last year, having apparently suffered a heart attack ten days previously. It was only a growing concern at his non-appearance at the Rochester Castle – and a consequent visit to the flat by friend and pub regular Caroline Parker, who spotted the overflowing letter box – which prompted the police to break in and discover his body.

Les had enjoyed a colourful life. Starting his working life as a joiner in the North East, his love of music and his talent as a gifted pianist led him to London where he became a sought-after fixture in Tin Pan Alley in the 1950s and 1960s, playing such prestigious venues as Ronnie Scott's and the original Marquee club. This dapper little Geordie, never without a carnation in his buttonhole, could play any style of music from jazz through honky tonk to the classics and, although he could read music, he normally played by ear. After the West End, he gravitated to Stoke Newington where he became a familiar figure behind the piano at the old Coach and Horses, Rose & Crown and Prince of Wales. In recent years Les became increasingly frail, but he was always up for it (as anyone who saw him zero in on the nearest attractive woman at the Auld Shillelagh Frank Sinatra nights and boogie away to his favourite singer would testify).

To the casual observer, Les could appear a curmudgeonly figure, but a friendly 'Hello, Les' would usually elicit a sly grin and a thumbs-up. Suddenly Les was 25 years old again, a debonair young Geordie tinkling the ivories in a Soho club, his easy charm and deft musical dexterity enthralling the clientele.

To the great credit of the Rochester Castle, the pub organised a whip-round, and the pub's regulars responded with equal generosity, raising several hundred pounds to help commemorate his life. Hackney Council paid for his funeral and the service was held in January at the London Crematorium with around 30 of the regulars attending. A few days later a tree was planted in his name in Abney Park Cemetery and donations were made, from what was left of the money, to Abney Park Trust and St Joseph's Hospice. His wake was held in the Rochester Castle and the bar staff gave up their free time to ensure that everyone was looked after, fed and watered (particularly watered). No one could trace any family but who needs family with friends like these?

The Murphys
By Sue Heal, Spring 2004 (21)

Stoke Newington without Jim Murphy is like, well, Laurel without Hardy, Marks without Spencer, booze

without a ten minute chat about your bunions thrown in. But now he's retired, folks, sort of. Mine Host of Clissold Wines, N16's favourite offie for almost two decades, has stepped down to spend more time with his cat Mulder and his property portfolio. But he'll be on hand to show new owner Murat, of The Blue Legume, what it takes to charm, flatter and run one of Stokey's most successful outlets.

'We've seen some changes, yes we've certainly seen some changes', says Jim, 56, fixing me with that lizard-like gaze, and not so much choosing his words as cherry picking them ultra carefully. He's nobody's fool is Jim. 'It was beer and spirits when we arrived but it's wine now', he says of Stokey's imbibing habits. 'The Islington spill over (not spilt drinks but houses) saw a big change in drinking habits.'

Jim's wife Margaret, 56 (she'll thank him for that), son Steve 30 and occasionally daughter Caroline, 22, knew more about you than you knew about yourself. 'We shall miss the people a great deal', says Jim. 'It's the people that have made it for us. It's a great villagey social atmosphere in Stoke Newington. I like to think we've built up a good rapport with our regulars.' He certainly has. In my time I've asked Jim and Margaret about builders, roofers, electricians, passed the time of day, rushed in and out, and my daughter's usually left with a freebie chocolate bar.

Originally from Cork by way of Dublin and Australia, Jim has fought competition from the likes of Oddbins who would have seen off a lesser off licence in less than six months. 'Business was down by over half after they first opened', says Jim, sanguinely, 'but it came right in the end.' Of course it did. Jim's a man who weighs up the opposition and never panics. Even knockdown fights and shoplifting fail to faze him. 'I've had relatively little trouble here, to tell you the truth', he says. 'Last year someone came in with a gun but I told him to, ah, buzz off.' The Murphys will be missed.

Clissold Wines on Church Street has been under new ownership for several years, but fond memories of Jim and his family remain. He and Margaret now live in modest splendour in Plaistow, but he never passes up an opportunity to visit the USA.

Fight for the Vortex
By Rab MacWilliam, Summer 2004 (22)

Although the last rites of the Vortex in Church Street appeared to be read on 11 June when the lease ran out, it seems that there may be life in the old club yet.

The internationally renowned jazz venue is moving to new premises in Dalston later this year, and everyone thought that was that. However, a local pressure group is determined that, as well as going to Dalston, a version of the Vortex will remain on the Street, albeit perhaps in a somewhat modified form. They have organised a petition, signed by over 2500 local residents, which argues that it would be severely to the cultural and artistic detriment of Stoke Newington if the club was to disappear from the area altogether. Under the slogan 'It's our community, let's fight to save it', they have successfully opposed a planning application to turn the building into three upstairs flats and a change of use from retail premises downstairs to a café/wine bar.

network (he was heavily involved in the 'Stop the City' protests), record label (he produced Bjork's first album with the band Kukl) and arts and community centre, operating mainly out of Dial House. He has also concentrated on writing, poetry and drama, and recently staged an Anti-War multi-media event at the Queen Elizabeth Hall (at the request of the QEH), as well as numerous concerts, poetry performances and gigs across the UK.

But why the Vortex? Penny (among other things, a jazz fan since he was a kid) has been a regular at the venue for the last ten years and has played a monthly gig there for the last two years as part of the 'Crass Collective'. In his view, it is 'the only club in London where musicians can play for themselves. It's such a creative, free environment and one of the last bastions of the old London Bohemianism.' A few weeks ago, he discussed the club's imminent closure with the Vortex's manager and guru David Mossman (like Penny, an enthusiastic mountaineer – a sure sign of a free spirit) and they decided to launch the petition. 'It's a bit like tackling the Eiger', says Penny, 'you can only fall off.' Their aims are simple. They want to remain in the building's upper floor, run the venue as a collective, and serve community interests, promoting local film, poetry, dance theatre and jazz as well as being a focus for local groups and concerns. The situation is complex and who knows what will happen. But, fuelled by all this energy, enthusiasm and commitment, it is clear that the Vortex will not give up without a fight.

Other protests were made, an occupation took place, but eventually owner Richard Midda sold the lease on, and the Vortex had to move to Gillett Square in Dalston. It was a sad end to what was a Church Street institution. Penny continues to sing and perform, and he has written several articles for N16 – see our website.

Good news, indeed, but who originated this this last-minute protest? Step forward, Penny Rimbaud. Penny (born Jeremy Ratter) is an activist of many years' standing. One of the co-founders of the Stonehenge Free Festival in the early 1970s, Penny divides his time between his anarchist/pacifist 'open house' Dial House in Essex and Stoke Newington, where lives his partner Eve Libertine. Penny was the founder of anarcho-punk band Crass in 1977, and the band remains today a massive underground influence on younger anarchists, anti-authoritarian protestors, anti-globalisation campaigners and all attracted by its 'laissez-faire existentialism' stance.

Constantly in conflict with the police and the DPP during its existence, Crass became notorious in the popular press during its seven-year existence (its dissolution in 1984 was deliberately chosen to coincide with Orwell's nightmare vision of the totalitarian state). The band has sold millions of albums, although workers at an Irish printing press objected to the lyrics of a song, 'Reality Asylum', on their first record. The band dropped the song and substituted three minutes of silence, which they called 'Sound of Free Speech'. They were visited by the Vice Squad when they reissued the song – now titled 'Christ's Reality Asylum' – as a single on their own label but charges were eventually dropped. They again fell foul of the authorities when their anti-Falklands War song 'How does it feel to be mother of 1000 dead', containing classified information passed to them by soldiers in the Falklands, was quoted by a Labour MP to Margaret Thatcher in the House of Commons. Penny's reasoning for why they were never prosecuted is that the State had too much to lose by putting the band on open trial. Penny's credentials as a free-thinking activist are obvious. Since then, he has continued to help run Crass as a political information

Ever Since I Was A Young Boy
By Rab MacWilliam, Autumn 2004 (23)

As soon as I walked in the front door I could tell that I was in the home of a cheerfully eclectic obsessive. The cosy flat in Gibson Gardens was crammed with a staggering collection of distinctly classy objèts – vintage pinball machines, an old juke box, mechanical curiosities, robots, toys, wooden animals (a particularly fetching penguin), old pictures, memorabilia, books, albums, drums, a fish tank, and that was only the front room. The bathroom looked like an exhibit from the London Dungeon. I sat down in the only chair, narrowly missing the cats, and was offered tea by Pinball Geoff.

Geoff (real name Geoffrey Roland Harvey) – an amiable, engaging fella and an entertaining raconteur – fell in love with pinball machines on a trip to Jersey when he was 14. Thirty-four years later, the affair remains a passionate one. He had just returned from a holiday in Spain and, passing through Perpignan station, Geoff whiled the time away by rattling up, in front of a couple of goggle-eyed French school kids, the highest score ever recorded on the station's pinball machine.

By the time Geoff was 15, he had ten wooden pinball machines in his bedroom and, with no room for a bed, he slept under these, to him, iconic creations. To pay for this unfolding romance, he left Highgate School in the afternoons to hustle pinball at the Golden Goose in Leicester Square, parting tourists from their money. After walking out of school one day never to return ('I couldn't stand it'), he took a succession of pinball related jobs, but a 'real' day job beckoned. Armed with a CQSW in Social Work, he became a psychiatric social worker at a drug unit in City Road, then at a needle exchange. Out of the blue, he received a call from Madame Tussaud's and left the world of social work to become probably the world's first full-time 'pinball consultant' at the company's Rock n' Roll Circus. 'I was interviewed in front of full-size robotic models of the Beatles', recalls Geoff. 'They couldn't find Ringo's head so they stuck on Winston Churchill's instead. Then they started playing, Winston's head and cigar jerking in time to "Please Please Me". It was bizarre.'

After Tussaud's, he set up a company, Full Tilt, renting and selling pinball machines, and then he established The Pinball Machine Company. He bought a 1958 Austin Princess Van der Plas hearse to ferry around the machines – 'It was perfect. You could slide them in the back door and they wouldn't move about.' Flashed down by a following car early one morning, Geoff feared the worst. It turned out to be a producer of a Channel 4 series on British eccentrics. Geoff became a TV star.

Business was good, until the popularity of video games and computers saw the pinball market enter a decline in the mid-1990s. 'My partner and I used to

draw a downward, 45-degree straight line on our profit margins', says Geoff, and they closed the company down. Geoff then went into business for himself. Currently, he owns 180 machines, with 100 stored in a farm building near Billericay Cricket Club (don't ask) and 80 in his workshop off Stoke Newington High Street. The machines at the workshop have to compete for space with an assortment of drum kits and motorbikes, including a 1968 Harley, a Moto Guzzi and a classic BSA. He now makes a living repairing, hiring out, restoring and customising pinball machines.

"Where do you find them?' I ask. 'They find me', he replies, explaining that when he sells them – a typical machine from the 1960s and 1970s starts at £700 – he'll often find himself buying the same ones back a few years later. However, he admits that 'I can't bear to sell them, really. I have to like someone first. I have a sliding price scale depending on how much I like them.' Reluctant vendor he may be, but he has an impressive client list, including recent commissions from, among others, Bacardi and 'comedian' Frank Skinner. He was also asked by the BBC's 'On the Record' programme to illustrate the differing Tory and Labour views on Europe, a pinball machine serving as a streetwise swingometer.

As one would expect from a self-defined 'creative psychotic', Geoff has other interests in his life, chief among which is drumming. He can often be found sitting in local venues with famed Stokey funsters The Bikini Beach Band ('I'm the oldest surviving member. I used to dress up as a gay biker when we played Madame Jo Jo's'), rock n'rollers The Witchdoktors, Luxury Condo and Ruby Throat.

A long-time resident of Stoke Newington, he finds the area has become increasingly conformist and complacent over the last few years but, nonetheless, there remains 'a diversity of delightfully eccentric people here'. With free spirits like Pinball Geoff around the place, this state of affairs will happily continue.

Hackney's Hospice
By Anne Beech, Summer 2005 (26)

Hackney in the second half of the 19th century was for the most part a place of dire poverty, its overcrowded tenements a breeding ground for infection and disease – the dark and largely obscured underbelly of one of the most prosperous cities in the world.

For the malnourished, poorly housed inhabitants of the area, there was no safety net, and apparently no hope: no welfare state, no health service, no prospect of care or relief, and certainly no dignity in the manner of their dying. They were, to the larger world, expendable.

A small army of philanthropists, charitable organisations and compassionate clergy did what they could to attend to the suffering and deprivation of local people. One such

was Kerry-born Father Gallwey, who for thirty years was the Rector of the Farm Street Jesuit Mission in Hackney, and whose determination was to be instrumental in the establishment of what has become one of Hackney's most enduring and remarkable organisations: St Joseph's Hospice, in Mare Street, popularly and rightly known today as 'the people's hospice'.

Established by the Irish Sisters of Mercy, with the aid of their benefactor Grace Goldschmid, the hospice first opened its doors in Hackney in 1905. In the hospice's centenary year, *N16* visited St Joseph's to talk to Sister Monica Donaher, one of the many dedicated staff who continue to 'give to the poor what the rich could buy for money' – in an institution that enjoys a worldwide reputation for its expertise in what is now known as palliative care for the terminally ill.

Sister Donaher – a veteran of the NHS who joined St Joseph's eight years ago – spoke to us in the newly opened Centenary Wing at St Joseph's, a brand new 61-bed building that is obviously (and justifiably) a source of great pride to everyone who works there. As she showed us round the immaculate ward, with its spacious bedrooms, guest rooms for relatives who wish to stay overnight, children's play area (set carefully to one side to avoid mishap) and even its tiny hairdressing salon, it was clear that she felt that her staff and patients deserved no less – that at last they had a setting that matched the quality of the care provided. The atmosphere is astonishingly informal (more so than most other hospices, apparently), and there's an unmistakable atmosphere of warmth and calmness pervading the place. It is, says Sister Donaher, like nowhere else she's ever worked.

Sister Donaher's team of nursing staff, carers, support staff and volunteers would, she admits, be the envy of most NHS wards in terms of staff/patient ratios, but, as she emphasised, the needs of St Joseph's patients are clearly very different – as is their model of care.

In conventional nursing, the focus is on 'getting well and going home'. When the hospice movement began, it was in part a response to the fact that the care and treatment of the dying was a contradiction in terms – quite the opposite of what 'modern' 19th-century hospitals were established to deal with. In one respect, not much has changed: the taboo of dealing with the fact of death continues to this day.

The staff at St Joseph's, many of whom have seen at first hand how difficult it is to provide appropriately sensitive care for the dying in a conventional hospital, are focused on very different outcomes, and receive not only specialist training in pain control and mentoring, but also an introduction to the holistic care which is so much a part of St Joseph's model: aromatherapy, massage, reflexology, acupuncture, and even the occasional cigarette, if that's what a patient enjoys. (They have a dedicated smoking room...) If you add to that the range of respite, out-patient and community nursing care offered by the hospice – for patients who might wish to stay at home, but can only do so with the expert care of the hospice staff – you can begin to understand why St Joseph's is so highly regarded world-wide, and why patients, families and friends (including a number of *N16* readers) are so grateful for the care they receive.

The patients themselves are only part of St Joseph's work. Staff must recognise and respect a bewildering variety of different customs and rituals, given St Joseph's East London catchment area (the hospice deals with people of all faiths and none). Relatives may need support or counselling to help them come to terms with the reality of terminal care. In recent years, family complications (divorce, separation, estrangement) have added to an already complex and fraught situation. The staff are required to handle delicate situations with sensitivity, tact, empathy – and sometimes diplomacy. The job would seem to make impossible demands on staff, and yet Sister Donaher spoke of the many ways in which the staff support each other in their work, something she hadn't encountered in her years at an NHS hospital. Staff are given formal help and guidance, too: in talking through cases, in learning how to 'break bad news', in maintaining composure, professionalism and morale.

We'd gone to the hospice a little nervously, but came away inspired. As we left, we asked Sister Donaher what she would wish for the future: 'That the palliative care we offer at St Joseph's should be available to all'. Just for once, Hackney can feel truly blessed: we know we have the best there is.

Hub Caps and Tail Lights

By Laura Howard, Autumn 2005 (27)

Mr T Elford Gerald ('Speedy' to his friends) has been running one of Stoke Newington's most striking shops in Allen Road for 18 years. The shop front festooned with hub caps, radiator grilles and tail lights wouldn't look out of place as an entry for the Turner Prize. Speedy says of his display: 'I just don't think of it. I never rush putting it out and I never rush putting it in.'

Selling all kinds of parts, Elford's opens at 11am till 8.30pm every day winter or summer. Between 7am and 11am he is out on his rounds sourcing parts and acquiring for the business. 'It has to be interesting; nice things ...' Customers may ring with their needs, and Elford will try to source the right part from his suppliers. He says people dismiss second-hand car parts as poor quality, but they don't realise that many parts are nearly new: '85% of my tyres and exhaust systems are like new; I only take the best from the firms I deal with'. He explains that many of the cars reaching the breaker's yard have been wrecked not because they are old or written off, but are picked up by the council or bailiffs and wind up scrapped.

Elford, who came from Monserrat when he was just 13, has seen many changes in Allen Road over the past 18 years; the post office and many of the shops have closed down. 'It's a knock-on from the supermarkets and the major stores; the back streets can't survive the competition – some of my suppliers, the breaker's yards, have closed down. It's getting harder for the small businessman.' As we talk, a couple of kids run up with their bicycles: 'Speedy, can we use your pump?' He keeps a foot pump handy for the local kids to pump their tyres free of charge.

Hackney's small businesses are the treasures of our backstreets. Take a drive down Allen Road to admire the shop front, and remember Elford's when you need a new tail light for your car.

The People's Champion

By Rab MacWilliam, Summer 2006 (30)

When a flurry of punches from Chris Eubank slammed against Michael Watson's head early in the twelfth round at White Hart Lane in September 1991, it deprived Michael not only of his dream of becoming WBO World Super-Middleweight Champion. It also very nearly ended his life.

Stoke Newington-born Michael's determined and courageous fightback from the appalling brain injuries he suffered in the fight has been well documented, as has his physical and spiritual journey since that dreadful night, culminating in his receiving an MBE and his completion of the London Marathon, against all the odds, in 2004. The fact it took him over six days to complete the course is an indication of the physical pain he had to endure and also of his indomitable will. 'It's the fighter's spirit in me', he says.

I meet up with Michael and his friend Lennard Ballack at Dem Café in the High Street to talk about what he's up to now and his plans for the future. The pair are well known in the area and are frequent visitors to Z Bar, where Michael is received with admiration and respect. Although Michael now lives in Chingford, he still considers Stoke Newington his home. Born in Rectory Road in 1965 he spent his early years in the area. 'Why do you spend so much time here?' I ask. 'All things start from home. I don't forget where I'm from', he replies. He sees his role, here and elsewhere, as 'inspiring and encouraging people, helping them to overcome adversity', He talks to the youth in Stoke Newington – 'I'm coming from where they're coming from' – and is a role model for the kids. As if neatly to illustrate this point, a young man interrupts our conversation to ask for Michael's autograph on his bus ticket. 'I'm a boxer, too' he mutters, bashfully. Michael throws a feint right hook in his direction, saying 'no, friend, you're a warrior'. I swear the kid grew six inches in height.

I ask him if he still follows boxing. 'I still love boxing. What happened to me was due to negligence (he won a substantial compensation sum from the British Board of Boxing Control who were found guilty of lax behaviour). I have never blamed Eubank for what happened. I go to boxing matches when invited but I'm generally too busy to attend many fights.' Earlier in his career, he had an acrimonious split from controversial promoter Mickey Duff. Do you still see him? 'I saw him recently. I carry no animosity. I have learnt to forgive people.'

He keeps in touch with old ring rival Nigel Benn, whom he defeated in Finsbury Park in 1989 to win the Commonwealth Middleweight Championship. Benn, like Michael, is now a committed Christian, and Michael recently spent several days at Benn's home in Majorca discussing the old days. Before the White Hart Lane fight Benn had defeated Iran Barkley to win the

late teens) and his Christianity. 'I've always believed but I wasn't committed. Commitment began after the accident. I had to go through darkness to get to the light.' However, he is far from being a typical churchgoer. He believes that, with Lennard nodding vigorously in assent, 'the church is within yourself. If they wished, the churches and mosques could wipe out starvation and poverty overnight.'

'How do you feel when you wake up?' I ask. 'I give thanks every morning. Most people take feeling, speaking and seeing for granted. I don't. The experience has turned me into a better person. I'm still part of the lads but I feel that my mission in life is to help people overcome the odds and help them stay on the straight and narrow.'

Michael remains a regular visitor to Stoke Newington and a champion of a number of charitable causes.

Property Man
By Trevor Jones, Summer 2007 (34)

A cheerful and outgoing character, and clearly an astute businessperson, Lawrence Albonico has been in Stoke Newington since 1987 when he bought Next Move estate agents on Church Street. He was born in Oakwood, near Southgate, and he lived there until he was 12 years old before going to a Hampshire boarding school. Lawrence came back to London to work in the West End for several advertising agencies, including Young and Rubicam, as a TV advertising slot buyer before moving into property development. Although his business is in Stokey he lives with his wife and young son on his farm in Hampshire. Appropriately for Stokey, his farm is both green and self-sufficient. 'We keep animals and we grow and cut hay to feed them. We also chop wood for fuel.' He lives in Hampshire because his partner is Hampshire born and bred, and her roots are there.

World Middleweight Championship. After Michael's accident, he handed the belt to Michael saying, 'it's really yours – you deserve it', a gesture which deeply touched him.

He has also been an Arsenal fan since an early age and used to fight wearing the Arsenal colours, complete with the word 'Gunners' on his vest. He numbered the late 'Rocky' Rocastle and Kevin Campbell among his friends, and he used to play in club testimonials. The club gave him a fund-raising game after the Eubank fight and, having attended the match, I can attest to the deep affection and sincere applause that greeted him as he was wheeled round the stadium. Scandalously, he now seems to be forgotten at Highbury and he has not been invited back since. He says, diplomatically, 'I feel disappointed that they seem to have ignored me', but I sense that the hurt goes much deeper than that. However, he remains a Gooner at heart and a fan of Thierry Henry – 'I really admire him.'

Michael now spends most of his time raising funds for his charity work, helping the Red Cross, the Teenage Cancer Fund ('I try to put a smile on their faces and tell them never to give up') with Roger Daltrey and Eric Clapton, and the Brain and Spine Foundation, which was the beneficiary of his Marathon epic. Although he still suffers, understandably, from bouts of depression, he says 'the more I look to the future, the better I feel. I look forward to the light'. He is helped through this by his family (his mother and two daughters in their

So, what was Stokey like in 1987? 'It had a similar village atmosphere as now, but a lot of the houses were in a poor condition and there was a lot less money around.' In the early 1990s 'you could buy a house for £90K, but now I find it hard to get my head round the huge prices'. How has the area changed? 'The changes are superficial – there is more money spent, smarter houses and better businesses, but the place feels the same.' Lawrence dislikes the 'bloody parking', but feels that 'Stokey people are relaxed, as a whole. There is a good mix of people which is central to what's going on.' He thinks there is a strong sense of belonging and, because he has been in Stokey for 20 years, he feels 'part of the community'.

Lawrence has recently opened an Islington branch of Next Move because, as in Stokey, 'people like independent estate agents'. His Islington business 'draws in high budget people' but he has got a highly visible presence in Stoke Newington and for him this is the 'best of both worlds'. Anyhow, 'there is a lot of movement of people between Islington and Stoke Newington'.

Through Next Move, Lawrence has 'tried to do a lot of things in the community'. He invested in the old, now sadly defunct, Stoke Newington Festival, is one of the principal sponsors of the N16 Fringe Festival, and he is involved in local school activities. 'I have tried to put something back into the community, and I am not trying to have a corporate image.' He says that a lot of his staff 'have been with us for years and live in Stoke Newington'. He would like to think that Next Move is 'laid back and relaxed, but highly professional' and that this mirrors the attitude of many people in the area. It seems clear that, under his stewardship, Next Move will remain part of the local scenery for a long time to come.

Lawrence's two Next Move branches are flourishing, and he is active on the local business scene, as well as a sponsor of the N16 Fringe and this book.

Top of the Pops
By Rab MacWilliam, Summer 2008 (38)

Sadly, yet another Stoke Newington character passed away in June. 'Pops' (real name Donald Campbell), 84 years old at the time of his death, was a regular at the Auld Shillelagh, always sitting at the same table just below the stairs, immaculately turned out in suit, tie and polished shoes and ready for an animated conversation with anyone who sat down beside him.

He had been ill with cancer for some time but bore it all with a fatalistic but never depressive acceptance. 'Ach, I can't live for ever. I've had a good life', he said. He was a cheerful fella, a stranger to melancholy with a quick mind, an easy laugh and an inability to tolerate pomposity. Most days he would take two buses to the Shillelagh from his home in Southgate Road, drink a

couple of pints and a brandy, sometimes more, drop into the next door Ladbroke's and take the buses home again. He had many friends in the area, and he was a genial, intelligent and modest man who inspired great affection. An Irishman, he once confided to me that the main source of sadness to him was that he never found out who his father was. He spent many years on his trail but eventually gave up the quest.

He appeared on the cover of the Autumn 2002 issue of *N16* Magazine, his photograph taken by local resident and internationally respected photographer Seamus Ryan. It's sad to think that he's gone but it was a pleasure, and, indeed, an honour, to have known him.

Cutting Edge
By Richard Boon, Autumn 2007 (35)

It's Grim Up North', Private Eye's regular cartoon strip, featuring the foibles of a group of upmarket newcomers to an unspecified district of North East London, which might just be Stoke Newington, is the work of Knife and Packer.

Knife – real name Duncan McCoshan, a local resident of some seven years – won't be drawn on the subject. After all, it's he who wields the pen, in partnership with Packer – actually, his real name is Jem Packer – who collaborates on the scripts and lives in De Beauvoir. Both well situated to observe the real-life counterparts of regular characters Jez and Quin, Max and Poppy, little Lottie and Gideon ('someone's nephew': Duncan had a memory lapse, here, about the cast). Unlike those of, say, The Simpsons, these cartoon actors age: baby jokes become replaced by those about toddlers, but the adults remain unreconstituted in their affectionate

affectation: rather than fill a van taken to some French hypermarket to stock up with wine, Jez and Quin opt for barrels of Brie.

Duncan met Jem when both were living in adjoining blocks in Islington's Thornhill district, overhearing one another singing from the catalogues of Demis Roussos and Serge Gainsbourg. Jem had been part of the Edinburgh Fringe duo Dallas and Packer, as well as contributing to BBC Radio 4's 'Weekending' satire. Or else it was through a mutual friend (memories are faulty, here, including your reporter's).

As an adolescent, Duncan would send 'stuff' to *Punch*, but gave up cartooning for a while, due to lack of response. Later, he sent some 'toons to *Private Eye*'s Ian Hislop, who did respond one Xmas with a cursory 'I quite like it', then commissioned the strip, allowing Duncan to quit his day job at an antiquarian bookshop in 1991 to live off his wits and with his pen. 'I fell back on something I failed at before', he observes, adding, 'for me drawing is escapism.' Using his favourite pens: Faber Castell PITT, Staedtler pigment liner and occasional Japanese Pilots – there was some militaristic joke, there, when he showed me his kit, but a post-interview mailing told me not to mention it. It's big, though (I mean his pens). And, of course, his favourite colour scheme is black and white.

As evidenced in the other products he and Jem author – six titles in the 'Captain Fact' series of informative books about science for kids and new fiction series featuring Fleabag Monkeyface, a totally gross character who appeals to the toilet humour most parents pretend their kids don't share (first instalment: 'When Fleabags Attack').

Duncan has other favourites, too, being very fond of Americans B Kliban, Gary ('Far Side') Larsen, Sam Gross (that's a real name, not another joke, by the way) and Charles Booth – the latter pair from *New Yorker* magazine. Showing occasionally at Little Russell Street's Cartoon Museum, and with some three years' involvement in the annual Big Draw events, it's sad to note that, local colour aside, a recent show of 'It's Grim...' strips resulted in no sales. Regardless, *N16 Magazine* is pleased to welcome Duncan as a regular contributor from this issue and we recommend the website: www.knifeandpacker.com, with his warning: 'It's animated, but not updated.'

Ska Man
By Rab MacWilliam, Autumn 2007 (35)

So you enjoy weekends in Stoke Newington bars but feel that you're overdosing on DJs playing contemporary hip hop, dance, indie or whatever? Give your ears a rest and visit the Coach and Horses on Sunday nights, when one Harvey Sylvester Roberts, aka DJ Harvey, spins his amazing collection of ska, rocksteady and reggae.

An amiable, laid-back 60-year-old man – and a committed Rastafarian ('it's born in you and manifested in later years') – Harvey was born in Kingston, Jamaica. 'I was a country boy. I was properly brought up.' He arrived in England with one of his four sisters in 1961 and made his home in Cazenove Road with his parents. We hear a lot about racism in that period. Did he experience this? 'When you're young, you don't see it. Perhaps there was racism but I didn't really notice.' Aside from a brief dalliance with Burton-on-Trent ('man, you could smell the beer in the air'), Harvey has spent all his adult life in Stoke Newington, including Kyverton Road, Downs Park Road and, most recently in his flat in Rectory Road, where I visited him.

Sitting in his kitchen in his Bob Marley T-shirt, and with his locks tucked under his leather hat, he described his musical upbringing and influences. Although the first record he bought was 'I Want To Hold Your Hand', and he loved any pop and soul music with a beat and rhythm, he then re-discovered the attractions of ska and reggae. His mum was a ska enthusiast and used to play it all the time. Says Harvey, 'it's in my blood. Ska was everywhere in the 1960s and was the music of the times.' He began collecting Jamaican music in his early 20s, beginning with the Techniques 'I'm in Love' on the Bluebeat label, and he now has at least 2000 7" singles ('I've never got round to counting them'), as well as shelves packed with 12" singles and albums, all concentrating on the period between the early 1960s and the late 1970s. His collection stops when 'the computer came in and music was no longer natural'. There seems hardly space for his sound system, of which he is justifiably proud.

No surprises to discover that his hero is Bob Marley – 'a prophet and a true Rastafarian; reggae died with Marley'. Indeed, the two pictures on his sitting room wall are of Marley and Haile Selassie, late Ethiopian emperor and Rasta's spiritual father. He appears to have little time for contemporary Jamaican music, with its cynical, and often misogynistic and homophobic lyrics and rasping deliveries, preferring instead the mellow innocence and dub beats of bands from that early- to mid-1960s period. As Harvey says, and I can only concur, 'everything was better in the 1960s.' He remembers seeing Stevie Wonder and the Skatalites, among many others, in clubs on Dalston Lane, and naturally he was there for the famous Marley concerts at the old Rainbow in Finsbury Park in 1977.

Harvey is by profession a delivery driver, and has been for 25 years, but his job allows him the time to DJ across the area. 'I've played everywhere: Stoke Newington, Stamford Hill, Tottenham and far beyond.' He started his current gig at the Coach and Horses just before Christmas last year, and it is fast becoming one of Stokey's most popular evenings. He is slightly bemused by this, saying that 'young kids come along and they stay to listen to my music'. That's because it's distinctive, melodic and friendly, unlike so much of what passes today for contemporary music culture.

Dishonesty at the Chapel
By Anne Beech, Winter 2009 (40)

Evan Davis, the distinguished economics correspondent, is probably best known as the avuncular presenter of BBC TV's 'Dragon's Den' and more recently, for radio junkies such as myself, as one of the regular team on Radio 4's flagship news programme, 'Today'.

In the midst of a toxic cocktail of credit crunch, mortgage crisis and global financial meltdown, it was tantalisingly apposite that he should have been invited to deliver this year's Richard Price memorial lecture a few weeks ago as part of the Newington Green Unitarian Chapel's tercentenary celebrations.

N16 seized the opportunity to talk to one of Britain's brightest and best commentators prior to the lecture.

Evan had been to Hackney before: the first few series of 'Dragon's Den' were filmed in a warehouse off Manor Road, before building work on an adjoining site forced the production company to relocate. So why did he accept the invitation from the Chapel? Partly, he explained, because he welcomed the opportunity to celebrate the dissenting voice of the celebrated Unitarian Richard Price at a time when the media's obligation to communicate at almost any price is seen as becoming part of the problem rather than the solution. An alchemical mix of spin and chicanery – in the Faustian pact between the media and the financial world – makes it virtually impossible to distinguish between truths, half-truths and downright dishonesty (the topic of his address). The prospect of honest, accountable journalism – possibly always a delusional objective – is more elusive than ever. In trying to explain the complex origins of the present crisis, for example, he felt that journalists on the whole had done a reasonable job in difficult circumstances, describing complex developments in lay terms that tried not to exaggerate the extent of the crisis or to misrepresent an unfolding and rapidly changing story.

Could journalists have done more to demystify the arcane and convoluted world of sub-primes and financial instruments – a world that even bankers don't appear fully to understand? Probably not, in Evan's view, but they were doing far better than many critics were prepared to accept, given that facts – and agendas – can change even during the course of a thirty-minute news programme.

So would Hackney escape the downturn in house prices, *N16* asked (blind optimism doesn't even begin to cover it ...)? 'No', was Evan's short answer. And his top tip for surviving the recession? 'It doesn't pay to be terribly clever.' So I'm alright there, then ...

Farewell to Mort
By Rab MacWilliam, Winter 2009 (40)

Mortimer Ribbons, who ran the vintage clothing shop Ribbons and Taylor on Church Street, died of cancer in October at the early age of 58. Mort had clearly been ill for some while, although in his own inimitable way he tried to laugh it off. When his condition worsened he entered the estimable St Joseph's Hospice, and he passed away a few days later. Instantly recognisable by his tall, spare frame and a fedora perched rakishly on his head as he strode purposively up and down Church Street, Mort had been a Stamford Hill resident and Stoke Newington businessman for at least 20 years.

Born in Dover and public school educated, he appeared to me to be a natural rebel, perhaps as a reaction to his somewhat privileged background. A dandyish

hippy, blessed with good looks and charm, he dropped out of Bristol University minus a degree, and formed an apparently jaw-droppingly experimental theatre ensemble (well, that's what you did in the 1960s) known as the Crystal Theatre Group. The group stayed and performed for a while in Rotterdam, and after they disbanded Mort set up a performance poetry group, which lasted for ten years before also disbanding. Artistic differences, no doubt. In his later years he performed solo sets which, having attended a couple at Ryan's, I can say were most impressively delivered, if rather scary. He deftly juggled his artistic talents with a canny business sense for the profitable flogging of vintage clothing, beginning at Portobello Market and then setting up a stall at Camden's Electric Ballroom, as well as settling in at Ribbons and Taylor in 1988.

Mort was a man of compassion, warmth and humour, and was no fan of what he perceived as narrow-mindedness, bigotry and injustice, especially if it emanated from Hackney Council, a particular target for Mr Ribbons' ire. Although witty, sociable and amiably erudite, with a wicked grin and a perceptive take on the world, he also seemed to me to be an essentially private, self-effacing and thoughtful person, and none the worse for that.

I asked Mort a few years ago to write for *N16* as a lead columnist and, although I formally acted as his editor, his precisely observed, occasionally splenetic and often hilarious writing style required precious little editing. It was a pleasure knowing you, Mort.

Good Evening, Stoke Newington...

Music – rock, blues, jazz, classical, Turkish, opera, folk, you name it – is everywhere in Stoke Newington. The area has an enviable reputation for performers of all musical tastes and descriptions, and the music scene is constantly growing. Our website n16mag.com is by some distance the area's leading source of information on musical events and venues. Here are some excerpts from our extensive coverage over the years, beginning with the campaign to save the Vortex Jazz Bar. Despite everyone's best efforts, one of Britain's finest jazz venues was forced to move to Gillett Square in Dalston. It continues to thrive just down the A10, but its totemic presence on Church Street meant a great deal to Stoke Newington's sense of musical identity and independence. To find out more about the saga, read our discussion with Penny Rimbaud, co-founder of Crass and one of the leading pro-Vortex activists, on page 51.

Room For Jazz
By Philippa Jones, Autumn 2001 (11)

Tucked away in an alcove of the Pizza Express in Dean Street, we compare two excellent jazz venues - the Pizza Express that attracts international stars to its gently formal setting in Soho, and the Vortex that brings Britain's most creative musicians to the edge of Stoke Newington Church Street. John Fordham is dapper and self-effacing. He embodies his notion of the jazz critic as conduit for the music, not for his or her ego. Writing mainly for the *Guardian*, he offers consistently vivid plaudits to the succession of musicians who appear in venues the length and breadth of Britain.

We are discussing the beleaguered Vortex. Unless its manager David Mossman finds a million quid before March, it will have to close. We agree that its informality provides a natural setting for the creation of jazz, and the intermingling of musicians with a knowing open-minded audience.

Its importance for musicians is inestimable. As Fordham says, it's somewhere that local musicians can play in a sympathetic environment, 'It's a kind of cultural public service to a non-mainstream art form, and so it needs a mixture of subsidy and box office to work, as you'd find

in Holland or France.' Where else over the last ten years could you have found New York's avant-garde finest Tim Berne with a specially assembled British band and Billie Holiday's last piano accompanist Mal Waldron playing with UK's George Haslam?

On David Mossman ... 'He's a hero, there's no other word for it. All adventurous art, not just jazz, has always depended on a chemistry between the artists and the rare people like him who devote their lives to supporting the work.' It's Mossman who organises bands that draw queues and bands that occasionally outnumber the audience, it's Mossman who cleans the windows of his own club, climbing out onto the ledge over the traffic while everyone looks on horrified. And no doubt it's Mossman who maintains the club's only two loos that serve the punters, regardless of gender.

David Mossman, who kept the Vortex afloat for as long as he could, helped organise a gig at the Ocean on Mare Street to raise funds for the jazz bar. Unfortunately, Ocean lasted about as long as the Vortex campaign...

Ocean strains to save the Vortex
By Philipa Jones, Spring 2002 (13)

It's a Thursday evening and the Vortex benefit, hosted by guitarist Deirdre Cartwright and Vortex creator David Mossman, is blowing up a storm at Ocean. Will David, not known for his singing, nevertheless give us a song? Meanwhile a trio of *N16* fans sit scribbling 'post-it' notes with tributes to the musicians.

Slap, slap, slap, on the table for the frenetic Zappatistas who unleash Frank Zappa's manic anthems with astonishing discipline. Keyboards supremo Steve Lodder manfully orchestrates a row of brass stalwarts and John Etheridge on yelping lead guitar. Amidst barks, rattles and squeaks, a percussive virtuosity emanates from the drummer and a congas-pelting Teena Lyle, pieta in black PVC trousers. All quiet on the 'post-it' slapping front as classical guitarist John Williams opens with a solo, exquisitely executed. Zappatista guitarist John Etheridge joins in a Senegalese conversation that complements John Williams's ululating rhythms with bell-like melodies.

Suddenly Bill Clinton, the Pope, and Irving Berlin, ring David Mossman to bid in the auction for a lifetime membership of the Vortex. A dizzying standoff between David's vibrating mobile phone and members of the audience leads to a price of £1,000. An even greater prize (could there be such a thing?) is clinched by us *N16*ers – £150 for yes, you've guessed it, a song from David Mossman – he becomes vocally active on stage, hand in hand with a respectfully silent Carol Grimes.

On with the diva. Ocean's hall gives Sarah-Jane Morris the scale she deserves. Using a curiously repetitive vertical motion with her left arm, it is as if she commands her lymphatic system to express song. She disgorges that most visceral of sounds, the husky and ringing articulation of a woman who can distil whiskey on her breath. Sustained bravura from her band (including Mornington Lockett) provides virile support.

Monkey Business
By Mathew Priest, Winter 2001 (12)

I feel it is my job to inform you of any bands or artists from the area whose star may well be in the ascendant. One such band is Monkey Island. In fact, for me not to focus on a band who have recently received Single of the Week in the *Guardian* and been described as 'the best live band in the country' by the *NME*, would be foolish and *rude*. So I met up with their splendidly un-hirsute drummer and co-lyricist Jan, and we shared a bottle of wine or two, which is something I wouldn't normally do, but he is a rather insistent chap.

Monkey Island are Jan, singer/guitarist Pete Bennett from Blackpool, whom he met at Canterbury Art College, and bassist Darren whom Jan knows from 'the days' when they used to knock about in bands together in West London. They all converged on this area about the same time as the M11 protests: 'you couldn't help but be inspired by all that'. Coincidentally, Jan's great-grandmother is buried in Abney Park Cemetery, something he didn't know until he moved here, and it seems that she, in fact, was the original punk, albeit a righteous one. 'She was arrested for preaching on street corners', says Jan proudly, 'and she was only nineteen.'

She's not the only member of Jan's family who contributed to his 'calling'. 'My dad was in a band called The Joystrings. They got to number 45 in the charts in 1964 with a song called 'It's an Open Secret'.' And if anybody reading this has a copy, then let us know and we'll get Jan senior to sign it for you (*see Letters, p* 118).

Completely and fiercely independent, they recorded their first album, *Mere Pawns to the Monkey God of Rock and Roll* back in 1996 at the infamous Pathway Studio near Newington Green. 'It's the best studio in the world, and probably the smallest. The Damned and Elvis Costello have used it. We went there for a day to record a single and decided to cut the whole album instead.' What, in ONE day! 'Yeah, I wanted to retire after that.' Well, thankfully, that didn't happen, and two albums, six singles and countless tours down the road, Monkey Island are stronger, better and more committed than ever.

The last single – 'Mussolini's Teaspoons' – is a fantastic slice of full-on, spoken-word rock and roll with a twist. Finally, I asked Jan what he thought of Stoke Newington. 'It's a great place to be creative, you know, to be an artist.' Why's that? 'Well there's loads of places to go and get drunk and talk bollocks all night.' Hear, hear!

Mathew, drummer with Dodgy and Church Street ex-resident, was our first music columnist. He was also instrumental in helping get the N16 Fringe off the ground in 2002.

Good Evening, Stoke Newington...
By Robert Webb, Autumn 2000 (7)

The Rochester Castle on Stoke Newington High Street is a natural place to find seasoned Clash fans, nostalgic for the days when you could get a round in, catch a bit of pub-rock, and go home with a kebab and change from a pound.

The Rochester started hosting live music in the mid-70s. When punk came along it became a favourite north London destination for pop's three-minute heroes. Between 1976 and 1979 a host of hopefuls in drainpipes and skinny ties rocked the Rochester. Former musician Pete Tombs, now an author and TV producer, has been a regular since punk's heyday, and even played the pub a few times with his own band. 'It was very rough and ready', he recalls. ' It had been an old man's boozer, with a poolroom at the back. When they started putting on music, Ian Dury, who'd just left his band Kilburn and the High Roads, was the opening act.'

Dury was already well established on the pub-rock circuit, although it would be a couple of years before he would hit his rhythm stick bigtime. But he's by no means the only star to pass through the doors of this cavernous tavern. South Londoners Squeeze played at least twice, in November 1976 and December 1977. The Tom Robinson Band appeared in February 1977, six months before their first hit '24-68 Motorway'.

The Jam played a couple of Saturday nights in March 1977, whilst recording their debut album 'In the City'. The following month XTC played one of their first London dates at the pub and, according to a review in *Sounds*, drew quite a crowd, despite suffering keyboard failure. Once they get that organ working properly they could be going places, the reviewer noted. They did, and XTC, with their psychedelic power-pop, became regulars, appearing every couple of weeks over the summer. In June 1977 the very wonderful Only Ones played. The following week angular minimalists Wire took to the stage (well, carpet), returning four months later for another set. Cambridge's finest, the Soft Boys, featuring Robin Hitchcock, headlined the 1977 Christmas bash.

The outrageous Wayne County and the Electric Chairs were another favourite, appearing several times at the Rochester Castle. In 1977 they toured with the Police as support. Wayne County, a trans-sexual punk act from New York, dismissed Sting and co. as 'the most boring people I have ever met', but by March 1978 the boring Police had gained quite a following and were headlining at the Rochester and on their way to chart success. Wayne County, meanwhile, underwent a sex change to become Jayne County. Also in March 1978, long before they discovered face paint and pantomime costume, an early incarnation of Adam and the Ants played the pub, returning a couple of times that Spring.

While gigs at the Rochester helped break many bands who, in the following months, would be offending your parents on Top of the Pops, others had to settle for cult status, or obscurity. Among the dozens of new groups to burst onto the scene in the late '70s was the aptly named London, featuring Jon Moss, later of Culture Club. They debuted at the Rochester in late 1976. Singer Riff Regan recalled a typical audience: 'There was quite a bit of violence at gigs and a lot of gobbing. Steve and Dave would walk off stage with guitars covered in it and Jon's drum kit almost had to be hosed down!' On 31 December 1976, you would have been able to see in a punky new year to the plangent strains of the Boys and the Maniacs. Does anyone remember the Wasps (played January 1977), the Kicks (May 1977) or Big Girls Blouse (May 1976)? Although admission was invariably free, many would often only get small crowds. 'I was the only paying punter for one band I saw there.' says Pete Tombs. 'Their manager was so pleased he bought me a drink!'

The gigs tailed off towards the end of the decade, once punk had run its course. The Rochester Castle hasn't been a music venue since the early '80s, but no doubt there will be many *NI6* readers with fond memories of seeing their favourite band rattle the glass roof. Hurry up Harry! as Sham 69 once urged, We're going down the pub!'

The Rochester Castle, part of the JD Wetherspoon chain, has a policy of not promoting live music. This is a great pity for such a potentially splendid venue which, ironically, is usually full of off-duty musos.

City Farm
By Richard Boon, Spring 2004 (21)

The joint was jumping. Transformed for one night a couple of months ago into an exemplary small rock venue (backdrop, lights, PA, video crew), St Mary's Old Church had a full congregation, bearing witness to the live premiere of local guitar luminary Mike Gibson's debut solo album *City Farm*.

Perhaps better known in these parts as leader of those titans of twang, The Bikini Beach Band, Mike reveals that under the garish Hawaiian shirts of his cartoon combo beats an aching, breaking heart. Songs of plaintive yearning, regret and the exorcism of personal demons are delivered over superbly executed, deceptively upbeat backing. Some bittersweet country tinges (honourable mention, here – and on the night – to guest lap-steel guitarist Martin Fieber of local Customtones), some plangent rocking ('Wild Heart', 'The Truth'), some poignancy ('Purify', the reflective 'Tear It All Down'). 'Well I'm going down the dark side', sings Mike, 'with my fortune in my bag' and, while unlikely to make his fortune, this CD collection deserves to find its place on the nation's hippest station, Radio 2, in your homes and in your hearts.

Richard is a local librarian, ex-manager of Buzzcocks, ex-record label founder and owner, NI6 Fringe MC and stalwart of the Literary Festival. In short, an esteemed polymath.

Hackney Proms
By John Flower, Winter 2005 (28)

Castrato. In an age of polymorphous perversity, the word retains a curious power to both fascinate and appal. How could a man have his balls cut off just to provide others with entertainment? The unfortunate lad who displayed talent had little choice; the Catholic church, and later opera houses, provided a ready home and an income for a poor family willing to sacrifice a son. And was the result – the clarity of a boy's voice with the strength of a man's body – worth it? Alas, we may never know. The last castrato, Alessandro Moreschi, director of the Sistine chapel choir, died in 1922. What we can do, however, is listen to a counter tenor, a man who sings soprano or alto in falsetto. Baroque opera was written for a castrato, to be a glittering showcase for a virtuoso, who would be idolised, be paid vast sums, and, sometimes, would end in crash-and-burn style (just like a modern film star).

The Hackney Empire proms concert season set out to recreate this 18th century world in music, words and images. Led by Hackney-born George Crawford conducting on violin as done in the period, Battuta are an informal ensemble of the authentic performance movement, playing baroque music as it was intended to be heard. Singing the castrato part was Iestyn Davies, a counter tenor who began as a boy chorister and choral scholar at Cambridge, before an international career that has included singing on the soundtrack of Ridley Scott's crusader epic *Kingdom of Heaven*.

The concert, mainly pieces by Handel and Vivaldi, explored their world, and that of the famous Italian castrato Senesino, with George Crawford giving history and anecdote, and contemporary illustrations projected behind the stage. Handel composed his most outstanding works of opera seria for Senesino, but it was an all-too-brief partnership. The star singer was poached by a rival London company, while the tragic plots were too florid and high-minded for opera house audiences.

The baroque works, and the modest ensemble of instruments, offered an intimate yet stately style that at once harked back to the formality and austerity of Renaissance church worship, while suggesting what was to come in the ease and magnificence of an Enlightenment orchestral performance. Unlike the castrati, whose stature grew with age into tall creatures with barrel-like chests, Iestyn Davies was a slight, boyish figure, in open white shirt, black suit and spikey hair. His singing was delicate, precise and understated. It breathed vocal life and passion into the noble sentiments and agonised feelings of arias such as 'Cara sposa' ('Where are you, my dear beloved') from Handel's 'Rinaldo'. It was a journey back to an age and a music whose enthusiasms and virtues, so different from those of today, should not be forgotten.

Hackney Talent
By Yolanda Daniel, Winter 2005 (28)

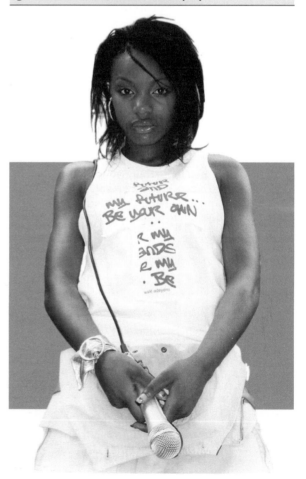

As a young female West African, brought to this country at the age of 10 by my mother and now living in Hackney, I look at life in a different way from what many people may imagine. When I feel down, I listen to music to overcome my problems. Most people like I who grew up and studied in Hackney realise what a great influence the area has had over our lives. Its reputation is often bad: violence, teenage gun crime and pregnancies, drugs and homelessness all seem to be increasing. But the good thing about Hackney is that it has a lot of talent and a bright future for young people who want to achieve their aims in a multi-racial, multi-cultural society. Much of the young musical talent seen on TV is from east London. The most popular form of music, particularly with the kids, is rap. Some people think that it encourages street violence, but it only reflects our experience.

My friend Naila Boss is a good example of Hackney talent. Twenty years old, of Nigerian origin but born and raised in Hackney, she first sang in public in a church choir with her mum and dad before joining a female rap group. Her early influences included Michael Jackson and Aretha Franklin. In the hip-hop field it was Lauren Hill, Missy and Busta. She says leaving the group taught her to become a stronger individual. The production company Rockizm signed her when they first heard her. She warmed up for Blu Cantrell, Ludacris, 112 and DMX and worked with The Pirates and Shola Ama. An upcoming star, she features regularly on MTV Base. Now with La Boss records, she's been working with Chris Patrick from Rockizm, Wayne Beckford, JD (So Solid) and Fingaz (Big Brovaz). Her latest collaboration is with Jayme – another rising star – on 'Blue Jeans.' Her first single was called 'La La' and the second one – to be released shortly – is 'Love is a Crazy Thing.'

She says the strength of her performances and that of other rap artists is that they are singing about what they know and what they've done, not what they've seen or heard about. There's plenty more talent in the area and there are many organisations who can help develop it. If only people are willing to look past the negative side, they could see that there are good things happening in Hackney.

A Fibre torn from the Fringe
By Richard Boon, Autumn 2007 (35)

Friday, August 10: I had my MC Ricky B hat on (*Richard MC'd the N16 Fringe*) and had managed to introduce Kal Lavelle on to the stage at the old St Mary's, doing what we in the trade call 'housekeeping' – indicating fire exits; what to do in case of turbulence; how the oxygen masks work in case of a bumpy landing; discouraging smoking and use of mobile phones. Health and Safety routine. Then I'd intro'd Martin Carthy's first set – routine – and taken my well-deserved drink into the graveyard. Of course, I hadn't

followed my own advice, and my mobile was still on, so I got the news: my old mate Tony Wilson, late of Factory Records and The Hacienda, had just died. Close to him for a couple of decades (less so since – in his proud civic chauvinism – my apparent betrayal of moving here from Manchester), I was more upset by the news than I'd thought I'd be. Expected, after all. Terminal cancer will do just what it says on the packet. So, back-announcing Martin, I became the town crier (surprised myself with tears, actually) and asked the congregation to spare Tone a thought, as someone else who'd done a lot for British music. Deathly silence, natch. Then I said to cheer up – Martin would be back in fifteen. Tony would've approved. But the moral of this story: when the MC says to turn the phone off, do so. It could be bad news. And follow your own advice.

Opera Cabaret
By Richard Boon, Winter 2007 (36)

When the High Street meets high culture, it's the yearly return of a celebrated classy and classic hootenanny in the 'hood. 'There are singers everywhere in the community', asserts Farquhar McKay, organiser of the Stoke Newington Opera Cabaret, which has become a more or less annual event since its beginning as part of the old Stoke Newington Midsummer Festival in 1996, 'and the singers really like it'. Early enthusiasm from performers and an increased and increasingly vocal audience led to the Cabaret becoming a fixture of the Festival, seeing its then regular venue, the Assembly Rooms, transformed with colour-coordinated hangings and matching paper tablecloths. Until the Rooms' closure, when the Cabaret had to become a movable feast.

After a subsequent gap year, the Cabaret was forced to find other venues, and other sponsors. So the feast, indeed, moved. Inspired by the offering of interval strawberries and cream on one year at the Assembly Rooms, the audience began to bring their own, increasingly elaborate, picnics. ('gourmet bollocks, of course', Farquhar asides). As a result, the Cabaret has had to introduce a 40-minute eating interval into its programme, which features ten or so thrilling young singers. The repertoire of popular opera extracts, Farquhar continues, 'gives singers a chance to sing a whole aria, and do ensemble work, which otherwise they would rarely get a chance to perform. We provide a unique opportunity for them to demonstrate the full range of their talents to a highly welcoming and appreciative audience.'

'It belongs to the community, is of the community and is not transferable', Farquhar insists, having spurned offers to restage or relocate it elsewhere. 'Both the performers and audience are determined to have a good time', encouraged by one of the Cabaret's mainstays, its stalwart MC, the witty, contagiously enthusiastic and informative Adey Grummet (a tune's history and context trips off her tongue), herself an opera singer of no mean repute. As well as Adey's annual appearance – and that of Alenka Ponjavic, who has sung in every performance – the Cabaret has established its own traditions. For instance, all bar proceeds go to the Canon Collins Trust, which provides bursaries for Southern African students who otherwise have no access to education. Every show starts with Verdi's 'Libiamo' (better known as 'The Drinking Song' from 'La Traviata') and ends with his 'Va Pensiero' (otherwise 'The Chorus of the Hebrew Slaves' from 'Nabucco').

Top of the Popes
By Rab MacWilliam, Winter 2007 (36)

When you've played live on the David Letterman Show, headlined venues such as Roseland in New York City, Shepherd's Bush Empire and the Filmore East in San Francisco among many other major gigs around the world, why would you want to play in a bar in Stoke Newington Church Street? 'Because we began here and I love Stoke Newington', replied lead guitarist, singer and songwriter of The Popes, Paul McGuinness. Paul, a resident of Church Street in the 1980s, when it was somewhat less salubrious (by some margin) than it is today, is appearing with his band at Maggie's Bar to preview and test reactions to the Popes' new album *Somewhere Between Heaven And Woolworth's*.

Maggie has pulled off a major coup by persuading a band of the magnitude of The Popes to play a gig in the People's Republic. The band was formed after Shane McGowan left (left?) The Pogues – apparently there was some discord at the time between certain band members – in the mid-1990s. Since then, they have become one of the world's most admired exponents of anarchic, punk, Irish folk rock – otherwise known as 'Paddy Beat', although Paul describes the new album as 'The Pogues meet Thin Lizzy'.

Open Tuning
By Nick MacWilliam, Spring 2008 (37)

Keith Richards once told me that playing live is what it's all about. Okay, that's not strictly true but I'm sure this is what he would have said if I'd ever met him. After all, isn't the lure of the gig what inspires people to form bands? Surely no one actually expects to make it big these days? Unfortunately, most of my live performances in recent years have been limited to my living room, much to my neighbours' delight. To give their ears a break from my wailing banshee impressions, I figured it was time to head down to one of the area's numerous open mic nights, acoustic guitar in tow.

The main premise of an open mic night is simple: it offers a chance for people to showcase their talent to a generally appreciative crowd, regardless of their age, gender, religion or, perhaps most remarkably on the music scene, fashion-sense. Anyone can turn up and have a go if they think they're hard enough, and it's not restricted to Lou Reed wannabes and James Blunt impersonators either. Poets, comics and magicians can sometimes be seen treading the boards in N16. You could probably even get away with a striptease if that's your bag (all things being relative, of course).

When I got to the pub, I found a healthy number of people in attendance: not enough to be intimidating but enough to generate an atmosphere, which was one of joviality and support (although I expected this to dissolve pretty sharpish once I started playing). On stage, a couple were duetting what sounded like

early Johnny and June, all tuneful and heartfelt. They were good, and I immediately began to question what I'd let myself in for if this was what I was up against. Thankfully, the following act inflicted a painful version of Angie upon us, and I realised that, whatever happened, I wouldn't be any lower than second worst. Reassured, I largely enjoyed the next few risk-free but able acts. The Beatles, Dylan and original material were the norm. I could delay the moment no longer so, armed with my Tanglewood, I took to the stage.

As a particularly murderous rendition of 'I Shot The Sheriff' drew to an end, I prepared to duck behind my acoustic to shelter from the anticipated deluge of pint glasses and phlegm. I struck the final chord and began cowering, only to be met, not with abuse and fury, but with applause, and I was emboldened to do a second number, 'John Barleycorn', which drew a similar response. It was my first time singing solo in public, and I didn't know why I'd felt nervous beforehand.

The preening, attention-loving ponce in me has now been fully awakened, so I'll be getting in some practice for the next one, as these evenings are a good laugh and about as much fun as you can have round here that doesn't involve petrol bombs and estate agents' windows. If you've always wanted to play live but never had the confidence or the encouragement, not to worry, you'll be fine. One word to the wise, however: anyone playing 'Stairway to Heaven' is likely to be forced to swallow their guitar, strings and all.

On the Beach
By Travis Elbrough, Autumn 2008 (39)

It's half a century since Cliff Richard and the Drifters (soon re-named the Shadows) persuaded British teenagers to 'Move It'. Seemingly overnight we'd never had it so good. Suddenly no new Wimpy burger bar was worth frequenting unless its cheeseburgers sizzled and its coffee machine frothed to the accompaniment of staccato-style electric guitars 'ding a ding ding dinging' from a tranny on the counter. With rapier-sharp instrumental hits such as 'Apache', synchronized stage moves, dapper suits and cheesy grins, the Shadows, especially in the killer line-up that boasted Jet Harris, Tony Meehan, Bruce Welch and the ever-bespectacled Hank Marvin, proved that an emerging generation of Brits, fortunate enough to be spared national service but given free school milk, NHS dentistry and eye tests, could easily best corn-fed American twang-merchants like Duane Eddy, Dick Dale, The Champs and The Ventures.

And in keen-on-a-drink, bad boy bassist Jet Harris, Britain even had its earliest rock casualty. Fleeing the pack to notch-up a vocal-less number one of his own, 'Diamonds' (with Tony Meehan), Harris would lose a wife to Cliff and his marbles somewhere on Brighton seafront in 1963. By then, though, the tide

was already starting to turn on Cliff, The Shadows and the whole scene. The Beatles, whose chief songwriters John Lennon and Paul McCartney had spent hours diligently mastering the guitar intro to 'Move It' in 1958, were off performing a blitzkrieg on the charts. Such an assault would leave few acts unchanged; well before the evangelism and Eurovision, turns in panto and as Gerry Anderson marionettes were beckoning for Cliff and the gang.

You can't help thinking that The Bikini Beach Band, in a sense, exist to right that ignominious fate. Evidently tapping some psycho-geographical ley line on the train track from Cheshunt to Rectory Road station that has so far evaded Iain Sinclair's gaze, this long-established Stoke Newington combo inhabit a parallel pop universe where Hank and his ilk never fell from grace. And, significantly, where wielding your Fenders in unison, and afloat as if casting off with a fishing rod, remains pleasingly mandatory. Always resplendently dressed in matching fezzes, Hawaiian shirts and Elvis shades, the group's sartorial mores actually put one less in mind of the King in *Girls! Girls! Girls!* or Frankie Avalon in *Beach Blanket Bingo*, than Eric Morecombe in any of the comedy duo's big screen capers.

Sour Cream for the Soul is their third album and finds the Bikinis squeezing Gnarls Barkley's 'Crazy', The Artic Monkeys' 'I Bet You Look Good on the Dancefloor' and Amy Winehouse's 'Rehab' through their wang-bar mangle. With so much of this, a kind of reverse ringtone principle is at work – the genuine pleasure is in simply hearing the familiar rendered in an entirely unlikely sonic register. An equine-saluting medley that gleefully processes from Rossini to The Osmonds is a particular delight. While a crammer with Pink Floyd's 'Another Brick in the Wall' that ends with a tipped fez to one-time Shadow Alan Hawkshaw's music for Grange Hill succeeded in summoning up memories of graphitized school desks I'd thought long, lost.

Local author Travis has written books on a number of subjects, including the Routemaster bus and the English seaside.

The Dublo
By Rab MacWilliam, Autumn 2008 (39)

Formed just over a year ago by two 23-year-old local girls, and including a 61-year-old harmonica player and a 40s-something slide guitar player, The Dublo describe themselves as 'an authentic filthy blues boogie band with tingling, suburbia-on sea gospel shanties'. Eclectic, then, but if you like yer blues raw, moody and haunting, The Dublo's your band.

They play a variety of instruments, including the double bass and piano accordion of Rowan Lambourne-Gibbs, with the drums supplied by Davina Pascal, the guitars twanged by renowned local muso Pete Bennett and harp from 'Dr' Jeremy J Ison, with everyone dipping into the vocals. They build their own amps, use old equipment, write their own material, and follow in the illustrious footsteps of main influences Mississippi John Hurt, Sonny Terry and particularly Hound Dog Taylor. Pete says 'we write authentically about our experiences and try to avoid the contemporary pub rock thing. We're like a family. It's serious fun.' Imagine the blues tinged with smokey folk and jazz, with black r'n' b, gospel and early soul music providing a pervasive atmospheric backdrop, and you're getting to the spirit of the band.

They headlined the AMP stage at the 2008 Stokefest, and played Not the Spitz Blues Festival, Gypsy Hotel and many other venues, as well as going down a storm at the White Hart during this year's Fringe. 'Cock Crow Blues', the sultry vocals delivered by Rowan, was their first official release, and is included in the *What's*

Cooking CD. Their first album is forthcoming from local label Falcone Records. There's no band around quite like them, and you shouldn't miss this.

Retro Boogie
By Rab MacWilliam, Autumn 2008 (39)

A cheerful fella, with a wide grin and an easy manner, Andy Butlin is head Redcoat, lead singer and guitarist with 'modernist retro' local band Luxury Condo. Modernist retro? 'It just sums up Stoke Newington', he explains, 'look at Ribbons & Taylor, Cobbled Yard... it's got an amazing radical history with an exciting, contemporary cutting edge to the area'. The four-piece band, including the riveting Pam Donaldson on bass guitar, the eccentric Jim Bishop on keyboards ('move over, Paganini') and Stokey's very own beloved and bowler-hatted Pinball Geoff on the drums, have been delighting the parish and beyond for over five years.

Their list of conquests includes the Lost Vagueness tent at Glastonbury 2007, Shunt at London Bridge and other triumphant appearances across the London area, climaxing in the gig with Tony Wrafter at the Shillelagh on the Sunday afternoon at this year's Fringe, described (by me, to anyone who will listen) as the musical community highlight of the weekend. Indeed, Luxury Condo has been a welcome and hugely popular fixture at the Fringe since the festival began.

Describing himself as a 'wannabilly' and not a 'rockabilly', and noting that the most important component of the band is the tremolo pedal (well, he would say that), Andy writes the songs, and his main influences are Link Wray and 'stripper music from the 1950s', which would explain his desire to write a concerto for strippers. Despite his genuine and long-held enthusiasm for our little village, he is somewhat downbeat about the decreasing availability of music venues around the place. 'It's going downhill and in danger of fragmenting. There is nowhere to play and, given the number of bands and talented musos in Stokey, it's increasingly a frustrating scene.'

From Ryan's to the Empire
By Rab MacWilliam, Winter 2008 (40)

If you've lived in Stoke Newington for a while and you haven't heard of the Brick Lane Boogie Boys, then you really haven't been paying much attention. With their irresistible combination of ragtime, blues, boogie woogie and good ol' rockabilly, the Boys have kept the joints jumping at more than a hundred gigs in the parish over the last ten years or so, as well as spreading their musical message across the country.

The band's leader and singer/ songwriter/guitarist is 48-year-old Stoke Newington resident Charlie Wilson, a cheerful and entertaining character with the finest and most elaborate quiff this side of Memphis. Born in Ontario, Canada, he moved back to the UK at the age of one, and returned to Canada in search of his roots when he was 21. 'I went out for six weeks and stayed for ten years', playing with a number of leading Canadian bands. He married an English woman, had a son (Charlie Junior) and moved back to the UK in 1989 to bring his boy up as a Brit.

A pro musician since 1979, he was walking along Brick Lane in 1997, stopped to listen to pianist Big John Carter busking on the street and spent the day jamming with him. The pair recruited a banjo player Mickey Carrol and double bass player Eddie Edwards,

and the Brick Lane Boogie Boys were born. Their first gig was at the 1998 Street Festival, and since then they have graced the likes of The Prince of Wales, The Eye, White Hart, Red Lion, Hackney Empire, 93 Feet East, Bodrum and Maggie's Bar, to mention just a few. They also have a social conscience, having played for free in the Hackney College recording studio in 2005 so that students could record them for their sound engineering diplomas.

'We are a unique group. We don't have a drummer. You can't shoebox the Boogie Boys', says Charlie, the proud owner of a classic, 1971 Martin D28 acoustic guitar, an instrument of such reverence that I bow respectfully every time I see it. The band's music – tight, rhythmic, melodic and impossible not to dance to – has ensured their reputation as one of the area's most popular bands, with audiences of all ages turning up at their gigs. The future, Charlie? 'We've been packing them in for ten years and it's just getting better.'

Walking Wounded
By Bryony Hegarty, Summer 2009 (42)

Local band the Walking Wounded opened their gig in Biddle Brothers on Lower Clapton Road with the song 'Hackney Central Murder Mile', sending a ripple of amusement across the room.

Front man Hugh Poulton leads his Walking Wounded on a handsome 1962 Hofner Senator guitar which, he tells me, used to be favoured by jazz musicians, for its loud acoustics. From the band's inception 'in the heyday of punk', supporting The Damned 'in a shower of spit', to their latest CD, *Waiting on the Outside*, Poulton has literally travelled through music, gathering on his way rhythms, styles and influences that interest him. He uses them as a backdrop for strong poetic lyrics, juxtaposing melodic, rhythmic tunes with sometimes harsh and often powerful imagery. Having developed their own style from this myriad of inspirations, the Walking Wounded retain the energy of punk. The performance is vibrant and at velocity; the music is arranged into tight and well structured layers of sound.

Poulton lived in Macedonia working as a researcher for Amnesty International in the 1980s where he first encountered Eastern European rhythms. During the rise in the popularity of World Music in the 1990s he adopted this sound and the band now have a distinctive Balkan/Gypsy feel. Poulton sings about the world and the neighbourhood, from gun and knife crime with a Middle Eastern rhythm, to more affectionate personal writing in 'Fallen Angel', lamenting the transition of one's little darlings into opinionated adolescents.

The band move on to play loving renditions of blues numbers, and dance with the crowd to ska and reggae beats. There is a more lofty, poguish feel to 'The Devil went to Tesco'; then their arrangement of 'The Raggle Taggle Gypsy', with subtle strains of the accordion, brings the room to silence. It is evident that the Walking Wounded have a loyal following; finale, 'Home Sweet Hackney', could be described as a band anthem. A tune of grand dimensions which leads you into a deceptively warm embrace of sound and, while the lyrics evoke grime in the streets with lines such as 'the petrol of despair' and the 'lunatics that rant and rage', the crowd of locals joyfully join in the chorus 'home is where the heart is'.

Cesarians

By Richard Fontenoy, Summer 2009 (42)

Something has been brewing on the waters of the River Lea at the fringes of the N16 diaspora where Clapton descends into the valley and the air is cleaner, the atmosphere quieter and more conducive to an artistic bent.

Singer and songwriter Charlie Finke, composer and multi-instrumentalist Justine Armatage and roundhouse drummer Jan Noble have cooked up a sound nurtured on their previous experience with local

stalwarts Penthouse, Gretchen Hofner and Monkey Island respectively. 'We all lived in Stoke Newington donkeys years ago', says Justine. 'We were musicians in bands who never earned any money, so we went where it was cheap.' Pushed out by rising house prices, Justine and Charlie decamped in search of space, silence and the company of a like-minded, tolerant community still within reach of the locality they loved. 'I used to have a woman living upstairs who would bang on the floor if I played the piano after 8pm. When you're writing, you want a bit of space to do it in.' explains Justine.

Bolstered by fellow water dwellers bringing the glamorous biker chic of trombonist Suzi Owen, Alison Beckett's lilting clarinet and Ali Hutchinson's tenor horn, The Cesarians have taken the louche, frayed glamour of Berlin between the wars and transposed it to an equally bohemian London, penning songs which rouse the senses, with Charlie's charismatic stage presence and the band's striking demeanour; four women, two men, one trombonist, a clarinet, piano, tenor horn and those meanly-beaten drums – but no guitars, for now at least, though they remain essentially a rock'n'roll band at heart.

After building a solid reputation for gripping live shows across their home patch and on regular jaunts to Italy, to Spain and France via Austrian festival dates supporting Spiritualized, their début album has finally arrived, after undergoing a traumatic gestation. 'We did a prototype which went very wrong', remembers Justine. 'Everyone had a really rough time – I even cried twice, and I never cry!' Unhappy with what they felt were stilted recordings, they sought out veteran New York producer Craig Leon, who had worked with punk legends such as Suicide and The Ramones. They invited Leon to their self-built rehearsal space (complete with mixing desk recovered from a skip) in a converted storage room in the Earl of Warwick on Beatty Road in October 2008.

'This is where we were born, this is where we make our music', recalls Jan. 'He walked in and he said it was exactly like when he first saw Blondie.' With Suzi recovering from a recent motorcycle accident, and all full of nerves, they played long into the evening. Despite having spent ten years away from recording rock bands in favour of the LSO, Leon agreed to produce the album, but in order to capture their live sound in the studio suggested they record at 'the old EMI place' – which turned out to be Abbey Road studios. Jumping at the chance, The Cesarians plunged into capturing their energetic sound on disc, resulting in one of the freshest first albums to emerge from the teeming Stoke Newington music scene in recent years.

Local shows for them have waned. 'There aren't the gigs', explains Charlie. 'After about twenty shows here, Mike Gibson from City Farmers said "I just want someone from this borough to do well, because so many bands seem to get so far and never break out".' Maybe The Cesarians are the band to just that. 'I'm conscious of Justine driving everyone forward', emphasises Charlie. 'She tells me off when she thinks I've been a bit slack, saying "you've only been half-power on this song-writing; get back to work!"'

Tin-Tone guitars
By Pete Bennett, Autumn 2009 (43)

Taking a stroll down Church Street of late you may have noticed a curious old-fashioned sign above a ground floor window. Drawn closer by its promise of 'Sonic Fascinators', the eye falls upon what appears to be a new breed of musical instrument. I stepped inside to get some facts from the proprietor of Tin-Tone Guitars, John Free. John's pedigree in guitars runs back to the tender age of 13 – when he re-fretted an unplayable birthday present. Since then he hasn't looked back. A few years ago, tired of botched repairs to his own instruments, he studied luthiership and set up Black Guitars – rapidly gaining a reputation for top quality work on vintage semis and excellent affordable repairs to electrics: a trade he continues, offering all services.

However, his love of sonic invention rose to the surface a year ago, and he set about designing something with the tone of the old blues recordings he admires. He began building the Tin-Tone Guitar from recycled furniture and attractive vintage tin boxes. Unusual tonal materials, you may suppose, but the instruments shouldn't be considered as merely eccentric. It's important to point out that the Tin-Tones sound as fantastic as they are beautifully made. As John points

out: 'It makes sense to use good quality chair and table legs for the necks, as it's vintage, seasoned hardwood. All sound craftsman principles. In fact, Gibson started out with the very same.'

With a clientèle growing by the week, and including Sonic Youth, Heavy Trash, Seasick Steve and Tom Waits's band, Tin-Tones are in demand. However, they are neither expensive nor difficult to master. 'They're great instruments for a beginner or expert, it's really easy to get a musical sound out of them quickly and I've noticed that everyone rapidly finds their own voice.' Usually tuned open for lap, slide or picking, none of the guitars are quite the same, but a general idea would be an old delta blues feel with the tin body somehow incorporating the sound of the 78 shellac. There are acoustic and electric models, even a tiny tin amp to go with them.

Fest Memories: 'mixed-up confusion'
By Richard Boon, Autumn 2009 (43)

'Man, it's a-killing me,' as Bob Dylan continues on the song of the above title, one of the select few officially-released tracks recorded with an electric backing band way before he mythically 'went electric.' Now, restoration of the complete, equally legendary, full-band takes of the *Freewheelin'* album would be something tasty, wouldn't it? Bob is only about 1 cm tall, at this point.

Which is: recalling the Isle of Wight festival, 1969, where, though I forget much of the set, he didn't perform that tune. Still living in memory, however, is a poignant, lyrical version of traditional 'Wild Mountain Thyme'. By now Bob's maybe 2 cm tall, due to what's being more freely circulated among the crowd than reefers: binoculars. 'Don't bogart those field-glasses, man.' Also notable, those announcements: 'Can Suzie go to the St John's Ambulance tent, she's got Neil's insulin?' Or the celebrated: 'The festival's had its first birth. Suky's had a girl!' Probably called Skylark or Sativa or some such. Picture the tent. Heavily gravid mum-to-be in throes of labour: 'How much longer?' Harassed St John's midwife: 'Just one more push, dear.' Mum: 'No, not this – that bloody drum solo!' That'll have been Jon Hiseman's Coliseum, then, with the solo that lasted about most of the weekend, perhaps in a cunning ploy to curtail the tawdry sets of, in retrospect, over-rated West Coast psychedelic merchants.

Significantly, a dubious bookstall, run by a wild-eyed hippy intent on living-up to tabloid caricature by peddling wares likely to corrupt the nation's youth. Here offering a badly-Roneo'd bootleg of Dylan's also mythical, then unpublished, 'novel' *Tarantula* – a sly speedfreak series of short slapstick surrealist sketches, funny and worth (re)visiting. Stallholder, reaching under makeshift counter: 'Kid, you might dig this', proffers equally patchily printed *Society of the Spectacle* by Guy Debord, which was like starting out on burgundy and soon hitting the harder stuff. Later, led me to Raoul Vaneigem's *Transformation of Everyday Life,* whose admittedly doomed humanitarian approach to Situationism appealed more than Debord's didacticism as they played out hard/soft ideological cop routines, with, Professor John Gray notes in *Straw Dogs,* 'audacious borrowings from a medieval sodality of mystical anarchists, the Brethren of the Free Spirit.' Arch self-propagandist Malcolm McLaren, having turned Situ slogans into fashion statements, remarked that all he knew about them had been learned in Stoke Newington Library.

'What do we want? A free people on a free planet!' That's not Situ, it's Mick Farren and his cartoon version of the White Panthers. They really stuck it to The Man by attacking the fence at the following year's IOW fest, and later hijacked a live David Frost TV show – to do what? Look like naughty schoolkids, pleased with themselves. Storming the Reality Studios? Not. Still, Mick's heart and eye for a chance (like McLaren's) were arguably in the right place and his memoir, *Give The Anarchist A Cigarette,* is an amusing, engaging, ultimately slight read (title, of course, from Dylan in Pennebaker's *Don't Look Back* tour movie). Lightweight compared to Stuart Christie's *Granny Made Me An Anarchist,* which at least features Stoke Newington, where McLaren was raised by his own gran.

Didn't make the '70 IOW, but did Bath, where I failed to meet my (then, future) wife, also there. Can remember even less. Probably still had that fucking drum solo (roadies just pick up Hiseman, still playing, and drop him wherever), or else – you could always swear by – Sam Gopal's Dream or Edgar Broughton endlessly driving-out demons. Hearing that shit, if I were a demon, I'd head for the nearest herd of swine and jump off a cliff: maybe it worked, after all.

Another festival I adolescently failed to attend was the apparently fabulous Bickershaw, up in the Pennines in 1972 (in a feat of extraordinary nihilistic organisation, the coach hired by the Leeds Anarchist Group left early). With Beefheart, his hair gassed back, and, like, really at dawn, with the sun coming up at a crucial moment, like dawn, the Grateful Dead, forgetting both that they were originally a jug band and, endlessly, whatever they were playing, unless it was a kinda guitar-tuning routine trying to equal in length Hiseman's solo. They, of course, went on to record a notoriously bad live album with Dylan.

Later, I did meet my (now) wife, but not at a festival. We mark a notional date, however, as seeing The Clash in Victoria Park, Anti-Nazi League gig; going there last year for its 30th anniversary. Decidedly, not as much fun this time. Too many hectoring Trot speakers between bands being heckled by Trots, laughably. But, boy, did we stick it again to that simpering neo-Nazi BNP! Not. Surely, the best tactic to keep creep Nick Griffin from further TV slots would've been for

absolutely no-one to watch him on 'Question Time' inna first place – like a naughty schoolkid, pleased with himself. Horror at BBC TV mid-management: 'We got zero statistics on this one'.

Yet, the wife and I do fest: Latitude, in particular, sometimes with 'the kids'. It's that kinda thing: you stand in the middle of a field in Suffolk among 30,000 people, yell 'Stoke Newington,' and hands fly up in the air. Neat trick used last year by local stand-up Stewart Lee, introducing his routine about Weight-Watchers Club at Stamford Hill Library to good effect. Mind you, drifting down Church Street yelling 'Latitude' would probably get you sectioned at worst, ignored at best.

My last thrilling episode in this mag, a sardonic, if not ironic, drift down the A10, satirising 'cool' Dalston, was apparently taken seriously in some quarters. Thought we were so over this. My joking conclusion as to where's cool (Deptford) was undermined immediately after publication by the *Guardian Weekend's* 'Let's move to...' item suggesting it was. But it's OK, they were later back on track in the same feature, in Dalston: 'it's come a long way baby.' Let's hope it stays there. Yet other responses provided the following link to a site that is more than equally caustic and well worth exploring: baddalstonshortstories.wordpress. com; full of stories, blogs, whimsy and similar Dalston commentary. Take, for instance, the following haiku by Francis Sandbrook: 'A Dalston bedsit. Full of edgy artists, blud. O look! Pashmina.' Haikus are, naturally, cool. So, to confusedly conclude, some announcements: 'Steer clear of the brown acid', and Bob Dylan is 5'7".

Talkin' Nigel Burch Blues
By Nigel Knapp, Winter 2010 (46)

The first time I met Nigel Burch he hit me. Well I was being a totally drunken arse and trying to get off with his girlfriend. I was a bit wary of him after that. You've seen him around Stokey, always wearing his black pork pie hat – probably in The Rochester. That's where I met up with him for a chat.

Nigel started performing at the age of eight in a band with his brother. 'We called it The Blackouts. I didn't realise then how much that name would relate to my life in the future'. Later he played in various punk bands supporting the likes of The Dammed and Sham 69, but he realised he wasn't going to make it when he was described by the 16-year-old Paul Morley as being too old – at only 22.

During the 1980s – 'I didn't want anything to do with 80s music' – he'd been playing solo in folk, comedy and cabaret clubs. He'd picked up the ukelele wanting to strip his songs back to their bare bones. 'I find guitars a bit macho.' But he found that 'if I played folk clubs I wasn't folky enough and when I played comedy clubs I wasn't funny enough'. So he added

I need an agent or a manager. I've always thought that writing the songs and performing them would be enough. Actually, since 1986 I've had an art dealer (he draws Hogarthian cartoons) "Nigel", he said, "These are fantastic. You could make a living doing this". I've got an exhibition on in Austria at the moment. He's sold something. It's the first thing he's sold since 1986.'

Future plans? 'We released our first album *Bottle Sucker* 10 years ago and recorded a follow-up which is still gathering dust because I can't afford to put it out. But there is supposedly a new record company who might be interested in releasing it. And hopefully there will be lots more gigs to follow'. And about that first meeting: Nigel and Nigel will just have to put it behind them. I think they already have.

That's Me in the Cornershop
By Bryony Hegarty, Spring 2011 (47)

UK band Cornershop have a huge international significance, with a major following in the US and Europe, and a unique place in music. It really is very hard to say that they 'sound like' anyone else at all. Their inclination with each album release has been to move in ever changing directions while bearing a trademark 'electronica' tag.

other instruments, starting with cello and double bass and then Dylan Bates on violin along with Andrew Rankin (from The Pogues) on drums. And so The Flea Pit Orchestra came into being, in about 1998 he thinks. He now plays the banjulele.

So what do you write songs about? 'I write about real life – it's all quite dark but with some humorous aspects. Some of the songs are about drinking. But there's a bit of romance there – well, romance gone wrong'. You don't really write love songs do you? 'Love Letters Down the Toilet' is a love song. It's all about good songs basically.'

The band has played all over London and pretty much every pub and club in Stokey. They have also toured in Germany and Ireland and play in Moscow quite a lot. 'Another thing I did, recently was a dance thing with Lea Anderson of Cholmondeley and Featherstonehaugh fame, 'Dancing On Your Grave.' 'I co- wrote the music and performed, for two years on and off. We went all over the UK, Edinburgh Festival, Glastonbury. Then Singapore, Poland, Australia, New Zealand. To rave reviews.' So you must be making a living doing this now? 'No, not really. I was busking whilst doing all this. The first time we were in Moscow I was taken aside after we'd been there a week and the promoter said "You're not getting paid, and you must tell the rest of the band." They paid for the hotels and the flights but ... they treat us much better in Germany.'

Have you ever felt like giving up? 'No, no. It's just a natural thing to do. I'm too old to stop. It would seem a waste of time if I gave up now. It would be nice to make a living at it. I've always felt slightly out of kilter – in the margins. That's not a bad place to be. It would be alright being a cult figure, as long as somebody has heard of us. I think the material is really strong.

Stoke Newington resident, Tjinder Singh, founder member of Cornershop, cites diverse influences as inspirations for his sounds, including reggae 'a benchmark for experimentation', hip hop, country and traditional. The band have attracted an intriguingly wide spectrum of artists to collaborate on their recordings over the years, including Allan Ginsberg, Brian Eno, Noel Gallagher and, of course, Norman Cook (Fatboy Slim). Tjinder is modest about this, saying it's been a combination of making suggestions to individuals and being approached by other artists. During our conversation we move from discussing autonomy in production, touring America, and musical progression, to the relationship between folk music and agricultural life and whether he's ever been asked to DJ at his children's school disco (come on, this is the man behind 'Brimful of Asha').

From the very outset, coining the band name Cornershop, Tjinder has been playing with his audiences' perceptions to great effect. His take on music is to focus on what interests him and he's skilled at turning concepts slightly on their own head. The recordings are clearly creations of a lateral thinker and music is a means for him to express ever-developing ideas within a bigger picture. He is emphatic that he wouldn't want anyone else to produce the band's music. Everything from the song writing to the artwork on the cover and the experimentation with sound is precisely placed. Their latest album *Double 'O' Groove of* was in production for a significant time and the band raised a significant sum towards completion of the project via 'pledge music' (whereby individuals pre-order the recording in advance of it being released.)

The album features Tjinder, Ben Ayres (co-founder band member) and Bubbley Kaur, a Delhi-born Pujabi folk singer, who grew up in Lancashire. Bubbley first sang with the band in 2004 on the release 'Topknot'. The album conveys a lush and dreamy sound, that focuses strongly on her voice, backed by ornate guitar, and a rhythmic beat. Kaur had never worked as a recording artist prior to this release. Using sounds of Punjabi folk, the mixes of the tracks on *Double O Groove of* are anything but traditional, and Tjinder tells me it really was challenging drawing on such broad musical influences.

With lyrics throughout in Punjabi, song titles in English are key leaders into the themes. Tjinder says whilst it was important to have this suggestive element, the vocals become another instrumental element to the mix. The symptomatic playfulness is intriguing as are the song titles themselves. Single release 'United Provinces of India' is a fun, vibrant mix, featuring distinctive sounds of a single-stringed Tumbi, blended with an electronic dance beat. The quirky 'The 911 Curry' has shades of Miami or LA TV show soundtracks bursting through a screen of dhol drum, and 'Natch' swings back to an intro rooted in military march, before the rhythms and Kaur's rich vocals bring in the distinctive sounds of the Punjab. 'Double Decker Eyelashes' seduces with a teasing mix of vocals, bass and strains of harpsichord. 'Biro Pen' introduces piano and percussive mix, Kaur weaving her reedy sounds into the blend. Brass and a funk beat feature in' Supercomputed'. 'Don't Shake It' the final track is a harmonic fusion of diverse elements.

The ever expansive mix on this recording is key to Cornershop's approach, unrestrained by conventions. If there are any rules in music they are not bound by them. *Double 'O' Groove of* is a seriously eclectic blend of ideas honed into a complete form, fully expressive of Cornershop's composite sound.

My Fantasy Career
By Mike Marqusee, Spring 2011 (47)

In another life, I'd like to have been an ethnomusicologist. It would have been a wonderfully open-ended excuse to discover new music, to travel and imbibe foreign cultures at close range. As an academic discipline, ethnomusicology began as a western study of non-western music, but in recent decades it has come to embrace the study of the musics of the peoples of the world, western and non-western, elite and popular, parochial and cosmopolitan. In particular, ethnomusicology studies the musics of the peoples of the world in their social settings. It hears them as part of, and sometimes a key to, a larger culture.

In trying to explain the complexities between music and its place and time, ethnomusicology faces a host of thorny questions. Each musical style, each performance casts in a new light the ever-shifting relations between audience and performer, tradition and innovation, individual and collective, art and economics. It's a ticket to explore the glorious, border-less mystery of human creativity. Songs, scales and rhythms have been described as 'indefatigable tourists'. They cross geographical, linguistic, political and cultural barriers. As they do so, they are modified. The history of music is fluid, with local and global engaged in a perpetual mutual exchange. So, whatever course it takes, ethnomusicology is always a journey, through both space and time.

Growing up in the '60s and early '70s, I was lucky enough to be introduced to music during an extraordinarily fertile era for Anglo-American rock, soul and pop. There were of course the Beatles and Dylan, and along with them a brilliant array of individual stylists, musical explorers and genre-busters: Van Morrison, Joni Mitchell, Gram Parsons, Aretha Franklin, Marvin Gaye, Captain Beefheart, Randy Newman, Stevie Wonder, to name only a few. Each of these formed part of my musical education. Like many others I followed the contemporary sounds to their sources in blues, folk, jazz and country – the musics of North America's marginalised communities. The '60s/'70s taught me my first lesson in the social context of music: no one could miss, though many misinterpreted, the connection between the era's innovative pop and its political turmoil. A number of those for whom ethnomusicology is not merely a fantasy career embarked on their studies from the same starting point, alerted by personal experience to the richness of the subject.

After that my musical journey has been shaped by travel, politics and accidental connections. When I worked in a north London youth club in the early '80s I listened to a lot of reggae. It's amazing that the music of a small, marginalised island community could be so warmly embraced by such a wide global audience. But then perhaps not so amazing, when you reflect that reggae mixed influences from Africa, North and South America, dancehall and church, local patois and internationalist anti-colonial politics. In other words, it was a distinctively Caribbean contribution to global culture.

As a result of much travelling in India, I fell in love with Carnatic music, which, I learned, was not nearly as conservative and hidebound (or as ancient and unchanging) as it was made out to be. I've heard some bravura celebrity recitals during the annual Chennai season, but nothing more quietly moving than modest restraint of the Bombay Sisters at a sparsely attended Christmas morning kutcheri. One of the things I cherish about Carnatic music is that for all its elaboration, the song remains at its heart. But I've also come to enjoy the more expansive Hindustani school, largely because I've been fortunate enough to hear Hari Prausad Chaurasia, Amjad Ali Khan, Shiv Kumar Sharma and Zakir Hussein live. And on record there's nothing sweeter than the sound of Bismillah Khan's shehnai. I'm also a fan of '50s and '60s Bollywood music, especially the folk inspired

SD Burman and the classically minded Naushad. Bollywood is a delight for the sociologist of music, harnessing folk, classical and western instruments and influences, Urdu poetry and Goan orchestrators. Later visits to Morocco, Portugal and Spain triggered excursions into Andalusian (the plangent, ruminative classical music of the Arabic west), fado (and the heart-shaking voice of Amalia Rodrigues) and especially flamenco, which has become something of an obsession.

An intriguing book by Timothy Brennan called *Secular Devotion: Afro-Latin Music and Imperial Jazz* prompted a detour into the lavish melodies and percussive abundance of salsa, which draws on Cuban sources but was forged entirely in the ghettoes of North America. Salsa is as authentically and completely 'New York' as the Broadway musical, which was itself an amalgam of African-American, Jewish and Western European influences.

So I'm not even a pretend ethnomusicologist. Just a blundering amateur. These days you don't have to spend years in the field to sample the banquet of the world's many musics. It's all recorded, readily accessible and downloadable. That's a great boon, but there's still no substitute for live performance, for being part of an audience, for contact not only with the music but with its context.

Brennan's book includes a chapter titled 'There is no such thing as world music', which made me want to cheer on sight. He's referring to the marketing category launched in the 1980s to bring artists from the developing world to Western notice. While it did succeed in creating new audiences for the likes of Nusrat Fateh Ali Khan and Youssou N'Dour, 'world music' is an amorphous and deeply patronising catch all. If you visit the 'world music' racks in a London emporium, you'll find Indian classical alongside Algerian Rai, Afro- Beat, Berber gnawa, klezmer, qawalli, fado, flamenco and all manner of Latin American styles (which in New York would have a rack to themselves), but not jazz or Western classical.

The only music with anything like a global reach today is the one that's never found in the 'world music' racks – mainstream western pop, whose ubiquity stems from the global distribution of power and wealth. Anyway, what could a truly 'world music' be other than a dismal lowest common denominator? The world muzak of airport lounges and hotel lobbies?

Music is a human universal that exists only in infinitely varied forms. It's in the differences, the variations, that its beauty and meaning resides. And that variety derives from the specifics of historical development. Which is what makes the ethnomusicologist's quest so rewarding – and so endless. It's a reassuringly inexhaustible field. You encounter a new music. Gradually, your ears adjust, your consciousness makes space. What was alien and forbidding becomes familiar and intimate. It's a small miracle but in it there's a portent of something much bigger.

Mike is a local resident, author of several books on subjects as diverse as Dylan and Indian cricket, social and cultural commentator and poet. His most recent book, a collection of poems entitled Street Music, *was published by Clissold Books in April 2012.*

An Old Folkie Writes...
By Rab MacWilliam, Autumn 2011 (49)

My introduction to 'folk' music began with my great-uncle Dave's record collection. Dave, as I never dared call him, was the archetypal Calvinist – bowler hat, which I never saw him remove, stern three-piece dark suit, grim reproving countenance (designed, literally, to put the fear of God into you) – and he had a collection of three LPs.

These vinyl recordings featured the greatest hits of the popular Scottish singers of the period, Kenneth McKellar and Moira Anderson and, as if to demonstrate his grudging tolerance for those of the papist faith, Count John McCormack. The first two were straight out of the 'kilt and railyard' school of tartanry, the heirs to the Ossian heresy. The works of the great Scottish bard Rabbie Burns were to be found in their repertoire, but they inclined more to the Victorian sanitised versions of his works than to the bawdy ballads, *The Merry Muses*, to which the farmer poet gave lecherous birth. But their powerful deliveries and melodies came as a revelation to me. These people sang sweetly and confidently, and the music, much of it based on old bagpipe reels and laments, excited me to the degree that I shared my enthusiasm with Uncle Dave, who grunted approvingly through his pipe.

Then I put on Count John, an Irish operatic tenor with an even more remarkable voice. And a few of the songs – 'Star of the County Down', 'The Garden Where the Praties Grow', 'Rose of Tralee' – sounded like they came from the man's heart, a loving appreciation of the people of misty, oul' Eire, rather than the vision of some Bonny Prince Charlie, mountain-and-glen paradise to which I had previously been listening. There was a dreamy evocation, a rustic almost mystic longing, eloquently expressed, in McCormack's renderings, which, despite my current cynicism, still touch my heart.

So there I was, a wee boy whose voice had not yet broken, already coming under the influence of what seemed to me 'real' music, as opposed to 'How Much Is That Doggie In The Window', 'The Laughing Policeman' and all the rest of the pap to which I was exposed through our radio set. I began to progress through early Cliff and the Shadows (The Young Ones still recalls the first stirrings of my adolescence), Helen Shapiro and the other pre-Beatles, boy-meets-girl pop. These filled a gap, but I had a feeling that there was still something missing in my musical development that would reignite the sense of tradition, people and places that I intuited in Dave's old recordings.

I got hold of my first guitar at age twelve. The abiding memory I have of how music was changing was sparked off, naturally enough, by listening to, and marvelling at, Bob Dylan, whose early albums I revered, and I began to pay serious attention to the leading figures of the emerging 'folk revival'. I became a dedicated novitiate, a more than willing disciple of the folk movement which exploded in that decade of the 1960s.

In the USA, such collectors, singers and enthusiasts as Alan Lomax, Ramblin' Jack Elliot, the Kingston Trio, Pete Seeger and Woody Guthrie had lit the spark, and the new folk music built on the foundations of the blues, experimental jazz, ragtime, the Beats, Appalachian (itself a hybrid of Scottish and Irish immigration) and country music to create a 'folk music' based on the fusion of musical experimentation with the social unrest, civil rights movement, Vietnam and other political upheavals of the times. The scene was electrifyingly and imperiously dominated by Dylan, and the young visionary's intoxicating blend of surrealist imagery, unbridled anger tempered by humour and compassion, and his dazzling recordings and performances. But if for many he was the mouthpiece of the folk generation, he also reflected what had gone on before his startling emergence, and he lived and sang alongside the other dreamers, poets, eccentrics and dissenters – Phil Ochs, Dave van Ronk, Joan Baez, Tom Paxton, Jackson C Frank – who were all vital participants in the embryonic revival movement, which provided the basis for the folk/rock of Buffalo Springfield, The Byrds and Crosby, Stills and Nash.

The troubadours, singers and soothsayers in the UK were also adapting the culture which preceded them, building on the work of the earlier collectors, archivists and traditional singers such as Ewan McColl, Bert Lloyd, Cyril Tawney and Hamish Henderson, and they rediscovered the older generation of singers and songwriters, to transform the meaning and convey the essence of 'folk music'. Ex-skiffle man Martin Carthy and his fiddling sidekick Dave Swarbrick, Jeannie Robertson, Shirley Collins, Roy Bailey and Norma Waterston were some of those in the UK who represented the bridging of the musical form, from its unaccompanied ballad singing days to its more adventurous, singer/songwriters, s u c h   as   John Renbourn, the incomparable Davy Graham, Bert Jansch, John Martyn, Nic Jones and the almost unclassifiable psychedelic magic of the Incredible String Band. Out of this whirlpool of creativity emerged the UK's equivalent to the US electric folk groups, including Pentangle, Steeleye Span, Fairport Convention and the Albion Band. So the influence of the 1960s folk revival was a profound one, stimulating an entirely new form of popular music, which is as flourishing and influential today as it was in the heady days of its formation.

There was a frenetic cross-fertilisation of styles, ideas and influences between the music of the two countries, from Carthy's tutelage of Dylan and a young Paul Simon to the encapsulation of the blues in the guitar playing of Roy Harper and Davy Graham. There was also an awareness of their musical origins in most of the revival exponents who, alongside their self-penned songs and instrumentals, included in their repertoires adaptations of the old ballads, work-songs, prison blues and shanties from which this new folk music originated. The folk revival assumed many forms, rejigged older musical lyrics and styles, and, despite its more experimental orientation, paid constant and loving homage to the folk music of the past, the music which inspired them in the first place.

The period between the early 1960s until the early 1970s, then, was the new music's most productive and febrile decade. Today's Nu-folk scene, includes such influential musicians as Mumford & Sons, Eliza Carthy, the Unthanks, Kate Rusby, Laura Marling and many other bands and singers. These younger performers have stood on the shoulders of the 1960s revivalists to maintain and constantly re-define the enduring traditions of folk music.

...and a Nu-Folkie Writes
By Bryony Hegarty, Autumn 2011 (49)

Today's new wave of acoustic balladeers may have grown up listening to their parent's '60s folk records but they have also had the opportunity to digest Rock, Punk, Punk-rock, Eighties Synth, Funk, House and Rave culture, and bland, bland, bland flat-lining of over produced releases that are more about the look of an artist than their sound. A return to acoustics is a logical response to a highly digital era – I've so often heard the reaction to glossy, produced music that the live show doesn't live up to the recording. In the Folk Tradition the live performance is the essence of the sound.

The Nu-Folk revival is enjoying a certain glamour, typified by P J Harvey's Mercury music award win. Putting the prize winners and high profile recording artists aside, Nu-Folk is also expressed in responses to the digital era of free music downloads and end of major record deals. 'Singing for your supper' through live shows, be they gigs or busking, and making direct sales of CDs to build your following 'from the ground up' is the only way forward. Or, in the case of the widely acclaimed Lisa Knapp, a tour by barge along the Grand Union Canal from Birmingham to London.

The prominence of folk from around the world, through high profile festivals such as Womad and radio champions such as Andy Kershaw, has broadened out the genre for young musicians, but the roots of both the '60s revival and of Nu-Folk lie in English, Celtic, Bluegrass and Skiffle sounds, and remain constant. In essence, acoustic live sounds are the people's music. At the heart of the music are rousing tunes such as The Chieftains 'Boil the Breakfast Early' (an '80s defining change for the band) and lyrics drawn from real-life stories.

Recently I listened to a group of Stoke Newington-raised, twenty-something musicians gathered around a table in a packed local venue. They played jigs and reels, Mary Hopkin and Joan Baez songs and original compositions. Included in their set was 'Deportees', Woodie Guthrie's protest poem (set to music by Pete Seeger) about plane crash victims who were being deported back to Mexico from California in 1948. I asked the band what drew them back to folk – the answer came as if the question were a little too obvious – 'the harmonies and the message in the lyrics', and I completely identify with the comment.

Whether it's Nu-folk, Old folk, Celtic folk, World Folk, we've moved on, but that doesn't disqualify new artists and audiences from enjoying an old form and drawing on its influences for their own self-expression. You can't move around the streets of Stoke Newington without passing young bearded men in checked shirts carrying acoustic guitars.

N16

FREE | Summer 2004 | Issue Twenty Two

On The Fringe
Mr Pitt Visits
Vortex Story
Mediaeval Baebe
Xword

the magazine at the heart of Stoke Newington

PART 2

Round and About

In this second part of the book, I have selected a variety of articles, letters, news reports, cartoons, memories and disputes which, between them, illustrate well the diversity of Stoke Newington life over the last twelve years or so. The content ranges from the communal enjoyment of the various festivals, the pointless hilarity of the 73 bus wars, the vagaries of the local Council and our artistic and dramatic endeavours, to the reflections of our local adventurers in foreign lands, the desperation of living on the streets, the views of the national press and the general grumpiness and perversity for which our little town appears to act as a magnet. There are enough fascinating articles and comments to provide several more collections such as this one but, for reasons of available space, I have selected those reflections which I hope will demonstrate as much as any other the humanity, humour and complexity of Stoke Newington life.

Death of the Festival?

By Rab MacWilliam, Autumn 2002 (15)

The Stoke Newington Festival is no more. An open letter from the Chair of the Stoke Newington Midsummer Festival Association, stated 'It is with great sadness that the Stoke Newington Festival will cease trading from today. Hackney Council ... made it very clear that there is no funding available to the Festival in the foreseeable future.'

Although the expansion of the Festival over the years meant an increasing number of installations, performances and artistic happenings across N16, the core of the Festival has always been the Sunday closure of Church Street.

Revellers came from all over London to join in the music, drinking and partying along the street and, although the crowd numbers recently necessitated a spill over to Clissold Park, the Church Street Sunday remained the highlight of Stoke Newington's year.

The Midsummer Festival Association, which has always run the event, believed it had no other legal option than to close. It had a number of debts, including money owed to the Council, and there was no way to gain the all-important matched funding from other arts funding bodies. To many, the Festival represented an opportunity to bring to a multi-ethnic, inner-city area a blend of all that was best in the contemporary arts. To others, it was the lofty, self-appointed guardian of a peculiarly middle-class definition of what constituted the essence of Stoke Newington: an unwelcome cultural imperialism which ignored the reality of most people's lives.

But there is little doubt that over the last ten years the Festival has made a significant impact on the social and artistic life of the area, and it has acquired a reputation well beyond N16. Only last year the Independent highlighted the event as one of the best festivals in the country and even the Hackney-bashing Evening Standard recently acknowledged its merits. Overall, a local consensus emerged that the Festival was an important and prestigious event for Stoke Newington and worth supporting and attending, due in no small part to the unpaid efforts of the volunteers and the hard work of the committee and director.

However, hidden away in a Festival press release earlier this year was the statement that the 2002 street festival would not be taking place, a decision which surprised and angered many local people and businesses. Would it not have been possible to have allocated some of the resources available away from what was a busy but essentially minority interest schedule of events in order to ensure the continuance of the street festival? Why was there no local consultation on this perverse and damaging decision? How did the Festival get into this situation?

We asked Kay Trainor, who resigned as director in 2001, to reply to a few questions which have been raised generally by our readers about the Festival.

You were with the Festival almost since the beginning. What event/performance (other than the street festival) are you proudest of? How do you feel about its termination?

There's so much I feel proud of: Parklight (which saw the Festival move into Clissold Park, and people stay overnight, Ed) of course; the cemetery event in 2001; all of the opera cabarets; storytelling at the campsite;

the DJ stages; the film about skateboarding; the tight rope walker across from the Tup to Helsinki; or just a memory of a woman so relaxed in the sun, dancing and dancing.

LBH pulled the plug and effectively killed the Festival. They are also the largest single creditor. Is this not an irony? In the light of this, should LBH write off the money they are owed by the Festival?

Of course they should but even if they did it wouldn't solve this year's deficit entirely. I also don't think it's beyond the possible to imagine that the council will fund the festival in the future. It was a direct and significant asset to local businesses on many levels.

The Festival was criticised by some local residents as elitist and unrepresentative of the local community. What importance did the Festival place on consultation with local people, businesses and communities?

As an organisation, we placed what seemed to other arts and community organisations, an insanely high level of importance on consultation. I think what the festival was trying to pull off was a very tough thing to do – to try to bring together so many different communities, and to do it in the middle of a busy inner city working community, closing its streets and filling its parks. Every year we visited every business on the street and we were constantly looking for ways of widening the consultation process. Public meetings were another way of consulting. Take Parklight, for example. There was so much fear about everything from noise pollution to a May Day riot, to concerns about the animals. In the end it was magical. One particularly vocal opponent stopped me in the street and said he was only sorry no one had turned up. It had been so peaceful he hadn't realised that 20,000 people had turned up over the weekend. And he lived right next to the park. It doesn't surprise me if some people use words like elitist, though – we were trying to bring really quite cutting edge and difficult stuff into the heart of a community.

Do you feel that the announcement of the cancellation of this year's street festival may have been a factor in LBH's decision to pull out? Was it a misjudgement to cancel the street festival?

I can only say yes. It was critical in terms of levering in the money from the council. Fifty thousand people can't be ignored very easily, especially when 65% of them are local voters.

Speak Out!
By Al Hanagan, Autumn 2002 (15)

What's happened to our Festival and what should the punter on the 73 omnibus do about it? Risking the charge of xenophobia towards Australians and residents of West London (*the new Festival Director*

was Australian, Ed), I have to wonder at the wisdom of appointing as lead organiser someone with no previous in either the Stoke Newington Midsummer Festival or north London. After all you would need to be exceptionally disconnected from the neighbourhood to decide to axe in its entirety its very centrepiece, the daylong Street Festival.

But that is exactly what the new paid leader and the volunteer Trustees decided to do. I am sure I would not have been alone in pointing out to them that the 'horse' is the Street Festival, the 'cart' the rest of the programme, and not the other way round. It appears that consultation was another casualty of the new regime. The organisers kept the news of their decision so low key that I suspect many of your readers are still wondering whether they got stoned and missed the Street Festival.

Having shredded their own best advert for sponsorship and funding, the organisers then find that a Festival-less Festival wins no brownie points with cash-strapped Hackney. How do our champions of a community festival respond? Well, they wimpishly throw in the towel. Not so, says the Chair of the Festival in a belated attempt to explain their decision to close down: 'Councillors and high profile figures have been strenuously but unsuccessfully lobbied.' Well, I don't recall anyone inviting me to have a pop at Hackney Council over Festival funding, I have seen no petition, no 'swamp the Council with emails or faxes' campaign, no 'get the bastards' posters, no 'Save our Festival' Gazette headlines, no mass demo. For God's sake, this is supposed to be a bunch of people that specialise in events, stunts, promotion and art installations.

Sadly, what seems to have happened is that the Festival leadership has lost touch with the diverse Stoke Newington publics, from parents, performers, punters, to providers. Without effective local relationships, the Trustees will have no more 'trust' in the support of the community than the community will have trust in them. So what is to be done? If the Festival has had its day, then let's leave it on the rocks to which is has been recently and resolutely heading. But beyond the cabal of the Director and her Trustees no one would seem to have been invited to set or participate in a new course.

For a Festival to be reborn there needs to be a mandate, and there need to be people to put the show back on the road. What the N16 Fringe did with inspiring and co-ordinating several days of pub gigs was great, but it's not a Festival, or at least not what I think of as a Festival. It doesn't have to be the same format as before, it will be whatever those driving, inspiring, and paying for it, make of it. But it does need a new generation of activists and volunteers and it must be an expression of the spirit of Stoke Newington.

Al was Street Festival Chief Steward from 1994 to 1999 inclusive.

Stokefest

Determined to fill the festival vacuum in Stoke Newington left by the demise of the official Festival, both the N16 Fringe and Stokefest decided to attempt to bring back some summer fun to the area. Read below about Stokefest, and over the page about the Fringe.

Starting Over
By Al Hanagan, Spring 2003 (17)

As the expensive wreck of the one time flagship Stoke Newington Festival sinks in the mire, the new look 'Stokefest' emerges. The date to keep your summer holidays away from is Sunday 15 June, 2003. The venue will be Clissold Park, and the weekend will also see N16 Fringe events and gigs at many of the usual Stokey haunts.

The one-day Stokefest event is themed as the 'Street in the Park'. So why the virtual street and not the street festival back by popular demand? Dominic Mandrell, from the core team of volunteers driving the Stokefest, is refreshingly frank. 'This is a new beginning. We are back to the basic ingredient of the spirit of wanting to express a festival and tapping in to all the talent and enthusiasm here in Stoke Newington and which was the old festival at its best. We just don't have the money, the infrastructure, or the in-kind services from Hackney Council to deliver a street festival this year. But next year? Let's see how this year pans out.' So, on the principle of mountains and Mohammed, the Stokefest team are targeting businesses, traders, schools and groups to take the street to the park. The idea is to produce branded stalls, performance art, installations, and the proverbial 'much more', to present all the participants in ways which will be entertaining and different.

No doubt the artistically challenging and provoking will also be present! Focusing on the children's interest appears to be a strong theme in the forward planning, with proposals for a circus tent, kids Ibiza, giant monopoly and a lost parents DJ zone. What materialises on the final programme will depend very much on sponsorship. Other ideas that are looking for funders include a theatre tent, community music stage, and wideworld tea dance.

Stokefest
Summer 2003 (18)

We asked the organisers of Stokefest what they thought about their Sunday event in Clissold Park in June.

The new Stokefest was, in the opinion of everyone, just about the greatest day out ever staged in Clissold Park. The temperature topped 26 degrees, and crowd estimates came in at between 15-20,000 people throughout the day. The volunteer organisers set out to create an inclusive, community event that combined a traditional fete with cutting edge arts, something everyone could participate in, and succeeded beyond their wildest dreams! Biscuit tin garden competitions, bouncy castles and circus workshops mixed with fire-breathing mechanical horses, a boxed art trail and a visually rich music and performance programme including Lost Vagueness, Continental Drifts, and The Lost Parents DJ zone amongst others. Radio One darlings Sweettoof, rubbed shoulders with the reggae zone pumping out a booty-shaking selection of eras and styles from Glady Wax and Solution Sound.

And it worked. Every nation, creed and culture that makes Stokey the buzzing heart of the borough were there. 'The day passed superbly', said Eric Stuart from Stoke Newington police, commending the organisers on a day entirely free of incident or arrest. All this was achieved in just six months by volunteers without the benefit of a single direct grant and with zero funding from the council. Indeed it was the disappointment local people felt when Hackney Council stopped funding the festival that fuelled this amazing show of determination and local solidarity!

A core volunteer team formed into a company: Open Source Productions. They were reinforced by local heroes who sprang out of the woodwork to perform superhuman deeds. Like Tony, who turned up out of the blue and volunteered to distribute publicity through the doors of local houses and got through 6,000 in one evening. He ended up becoming a one-man roadie crew doing everything from loading perimeter fencing in the small hours, driving equipment from north to south London and barely sleeping for three days. He loved it so much he said 'it has been like a holiday!' The amazing Emma and incredible Emmie took on many tasks including sourcing food donations from Stokey to Notting Hill to ensure the volunteers were fed. Even more remarkable, was Joolz, the builder of The Lost Parents DJ zone, who dragged himself out of a hospital bed after a heart attack because he simply had to be involved. He was moved to tears by the sheer amazing spirit of the day.

Financial support came from business sponsorship, charitable donations and advertising. All money was locally sourced. Everyone who worked on the festival this year whether as a performer or organiser worked for love – no one received a penny of payment. The festival was about friendship and community, and that is a priceless commodity. For our part, we were overwhelmed by the support we received. We were honoured to have so many different parties involved, and to see them all come together on the day to make something really special happen in our community. It demonstrates how much people in our area value the annual festival, and how much it really does make a difference to their lives and to the community spirit of Stoke Newington.

Stokefest Blues

We received the following Open Letter from Stokefest and printed it in our Summer 2008 (38) issue.

A huge thanks to all our hard-working volunteers, fantastic audience and the almighty sun for helping make Stokefest 08 another free party to remember! A special thanks to all who donated funds – you've kept us out of the red for another year. We know the entry gates were a surprise to some, but they were required conditions of the licence due to increased attendance. Hackney Council's premises licence confines events in Clissold Park to the Green Lanes/ Church Street corner, which is one of the reasons we had to fence off the dividing line. The police and security were monitoring numbers in the park and when the numbers came close to the licensable figure

at any one time (15,000), we were told to close the gates for just over an hour until enough people left. The police also implemented a dog ban in response to the heat and numbers of people they felt would attend. We know this made life difficult for many of you (and many of our volunteers) as no advance warning was given. In a few weeks we'll be making a presentation to both police and the council with our suggestions in the future. We'd truly like to expand the event in 2009 so it's not just a one-day park-based event but we can't do it alone. Some of us have given over 40 volunteer days (weekends, weeknights, sneaky lunch meetings) to help organise the festival but we can't produce a higher level of activity without more folks getting involved.

In Brief
Spring 2009 (41)

Stokefest no more, it appears. Due to the licensing requirements of Hackney Council and the local boys in blue, all outdoor events comprising more than 3000 people must be completely fenced in, in case people start enjoying themselves. All those thousands who attended the event last summer will recall the long wait to get into Clissold Park, with the police forcing long queues and pissing everyone off. Then, when you did get in, you could hardly move, as Hackney had allocated only a small area of the park for the festivities. In the face of such official intransigence and puritanical disapproval, you can hardly blame the organisers of Stokefest for calling it a day. What a shame. Still, the N16 Fringe (now the only fringe festival in the UK without an accompanying official festival) will be back in August this year with a quite amazing line-up of talent.

And that, I'm afraid, was that. Everyone involved in Stokefest gave it their best shot but they were ultimately defeated by the local police and council bureaucracy, who became increasingly alarmed by the realisation that people may be enjoying themselves.

Fringe Frolics:

Rab MacWilliam writes:

In early 2002, it suddenly struck me that a Festival should have an accompanying Fringe. If it's good enough for Edinburgh, it's good enough for Stoke Newington, went my thinking. My original idea was to hold the Fringe in a few venues and bars on the High Street as a sort of radical complement to the Church Street Festival closure day, and to promote local, alternative music, comedy and arts generally, under the promotional banner of *N16* Magazine.

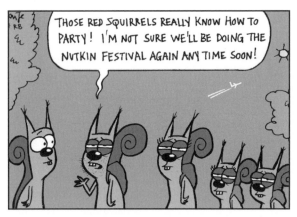

THOSE RED SQUIRRELS REALLY KNOW HOW TO PARTY! I'M NOT SURE WE'LL BE DOING THE NUTKIN FESTIVAL AGAIN ANY TIME SOON!

The project quickly gathered momentum when it was suddenly announced that the street closure would not be taking place that summer. Well, why not extend the Fringe to include venues on Church Street to provide entertainment for all those people who were looking forward to the annual Sunday jamboree?

Let's not disappoint them. We decided to promote and stage local performers, in particular musicians and bands of all sorts, in a number of bars and clubs over a summer weekend, ensure free entry to the gigs and demonstrate to the world the wealth of talent in our little parish. We'd print and distribute a programme, featuring the performers and venues, which would be sponsored by local businesses. We'd also develop a website for minute-to-minute updates, and include the programme online. Then we'd promote the whole shebang through leaflets, local advertising and *N16* Magazine, and bring a smile to people's faces and a tap to their toes.

And that's exactly what happened. The first N16 Fringe was a huge success, much more so than was expected by our little organising committee, which comprised Debs Butler, David Knight, Trevor Jones, Mathew Priest and me. The whole thing took several weeks of organisation (and a week or so to come down from), but it was worth it to see all the bars and venues crammed to capacity, and cheery groups of people lurching from gig to gig, knowing it was all live music and free. The N16 Fringe had arrived in a big way.

Thanks to the efforts of local advertisers and venues, numerous volunteers and, over the years innovative, enthusiastic music directors such as Mathew Priest, Warren Neill and Pete Bennett, the N16 Fringe continued its annual summer weekend incarnations until we decided to call a halt after the eighth Fringe in 2009. We had the option to remain as we were – a relatively small but massively popular local event – or to find major sponsorship and develop the Fringe into a much larger weekend or week of music and arts, with big companies inevitably becoming involved and beginning to call the shots. This is not something we had considered back in 2002, nor was it something we particularly wanted.

PUBS
PUBLIC HOUSES
TAVERNS
INNS

PLACES OF REFRESHMENT, CONVERSATION, BANTER AND BADINAGE – MINI-ROUNDABOUTS AT THE INTERSECTION OF CULTURE AND THE COMATOSE

So, in the end we agreed to take a deserved rest, and see what happened. The Fringe had taken up so many people's time for little or no reward, other than the pleasure and satisfaction of being part of such an increasingly prestigious, home-grown festival, lauded by local and national media alike. But we all had to make a living, and the pressures and time involved in developing and staging the annual weekend festivities militated against this sad but necessary fact of life.

However, the success and popularity of the Fringe over the years cannot be underestimated. Although our main focus was always on performers and

artistes from the Stoke Newington area, most of whom gave their services for free or minimal charge, we also cast our net wider for more nationally known musicians and artists. In this latter category were the likes of Hank Wangford, Mediaeval Baebes, Sam Brown, Tony Wrafter, Penny Rimbaud, Senser, The Popes, Billy Childish, folk singer and guitar genius Martin Simpson, and one of folk music's greats, Martin Carthy (who played three Fringes, the last one in 2009 accompanied by his daughter Eliza and who performed in front of a capacity, enraptured audience at the new St Mary's Church. 'How did you manage to get them, Rab?' asked the delighted Rector, Jonathan Clark. 'Contacts, Jonathan', I replied as mysteriously as I could manage, although it was mainly through luck and perseverance, the hallmarks of the Fringe).

It is invidious to select particular local bands and performers, as so many joined in, nevertheless any selection must include Luddy Samms, John Power, Miles Hunt, Monkey Island, City Farmers, Nazarites, Skull Disco, Corn Rocket Club, Plakka, Washington Rays, Morning Bride, Cesarians, Luxury Condo, Big Fibbers, Tad's ska disco, Michael Rosen, Jan Noble, Nigel Burch, Walking Wounded, Tim Wells, Drones Club, John Paul Holt, Dublo ... and so the list continues. We presented rock, blues, soul, folk, jazz, Turkish and African music, as well as poetry, drama, comedy, art and film, and conjured up weekends which few who were there will forget.

The venues ranged across Stoke Newington, from the Lion and the Others to Z Bar, Abney Public Hall via the old Barracuda to the Vortex, and from Yum Yum Orchid Lounge to the atmospheric, Old St Mary's Church, a sought-after venue for all our performers. Regular events stood out, such as sunny Sunday afternoon jam and ska sessions at the Auld Shillelagh, heavy rock evenings at the White Hart and energetic punk from Cornrocket Club at the ever-reliable Ryan's Bar.

Over the eight years of the Fringe's existence, we received enormous support from everyone, the events were hassle-free, and everyone involved had a thoroughly enjoyable time. In many ways, it's a pity it had to stop. The potential still exists should anyone wish to pick up the gauntlet and run with it. We wish you all the best if you do.

Thank you, and good evening, Stoke Newington. It was a big adventure.

In Brief

News In Brief was a regular feature in N16 *for our first ten years. It included small stories, snippets, comments, humorous asides and wry observations. It came to an end when we decided to concentrate less on news (we are quarterly, after all, and news quickly dates) and print more in the way of longer features of local and wider interest.*

Top rock band Dodgy, whose drummer Mathew Priest lives on Church Street, made national headlines earlier this month when they landed on the BBC Castaway island of Taransay in the Western Isles of Scotland in the middle of their 'Dingwall to Dingwalls' tour. Mathew says that they only wanted to entertain the castaways, but the inhabitants held a meeting and asked the band to leave, stating that rock music was one of the reasons they became castaways in the first place. Nothing daunted, the lads left the island, full of praise for the friendliness of the castaways.

Strange but true. N16 is a free magazine. It says so on the front cover. So why was a lady seen selling copies outside St Mary's Church a few Sundays ago? What was she charging? We don't know but we're sure it went to a good cause. From the sublime to the ridiculous: a local newsagent tells us that kids nip into his shop and nick copies of the free mag. Do they sell them as well? Perhaps they supply the lady. And it's nice to know we're so much in demand that at least one local school plans to send copies of N16 to prospective job applicants, and that a major property developer in the area has been using copies in its information packs for potential buyers.

A war of words has broken out between a local critic of the gentrification of Stoke Newington and Ballymore Properties, the developers of The Red Square apartments. Local critic (LC) objected to the use of twee, estate agent's language: 'All London's a Hollywood. All London's a location. North London's Bohemian Quarter' etc. LC launched a guided missile at the company's website accusing it of 'a property scam' that priced local people out of the housing market. The response was a B52 bombing raid of massive proportions.

After referring to cheaper locations, the company said that they were sure 'you would get an excellent deal in more exotic places such as India or Afghanistan. If you choose the latter you may need to invest in substantial military hardware, a fake beard, tanning cream and an updated version of the Koran!!!'Undeterred by this tasteful and sensitive comment, LC replied that he was opposed to the division of the area into 'wealthy property owners on the one side and poor tenants on the other'. Perhaps one reason why the company reacted in the way it did was because they are already sizing up the possibility of marketing trendy apartment in downtown Kabul or renovating some interesting caves in the surrounding hill: after all, Osama bin Laden is a well-known Arsenal supporter.

After many years of neglect, and strong campaigning by local residents, the Stoke Newington Assembly Rooms are to be saved and restored. The Council is now looking for a partner to undertake the renovation work and to bring the building back into use for both commercial and community use. In the past, the Assembly Rooms have been used for concerts, weddings, large family parties and local schools event. As for music, who can forget Dodgy's brilliant gig a couple of years ago or, at the other end of the spectrum, the annual Opera Cabaret. In the 1940s and 1950s, the phrase 'Going up Stokey?' meant the Assembly Rooms Saturday night dance (which, incidentally counters the criticism that the term 'Stokey' has been coined by recent incomers to the area).

Bring me the head of Daniel Defoe. The Clissold Residents Association have written to Hackney Council to complain about the removal of the plinth, headstone and bust of Daniel Defoe from the entrance to Stoke Newington Library. This follows on from the removal of the Chalmers Bequest – a collection of 17th-19th century oil paintings, carvings, water colours, porcelain and bronzes – in 1993. The letter complains that 'these items have resided here quite happily for many, many years as a feature of our local history and a number of our members are upset that more of our local "family silver" is being pillaged… we "dissenters" in Stoke Newington are most aggrieved that the items were removed without a by-your leave or word of explanation.' The great man now holds court in Hackney Museum, and Museum staff say that urgent repairs and renovation were required to the bust. But will they send it back once Defoe has been restored to a pristine state? And, while we're about it, can we have Marc Bolan's leather top hat back from the V&A?

Howard Devoto, Stoke Newington resident and former front man with legendary bands Buzzcocks and Magazine, came out of rock n' roll retirement to perform a short set at the Vortex last month. The occasion was to celebrate the fiftieth birthday of his old friend, local librarian and ex-Buzzcocks manager, Richard Boon. Howard performed with the Bikini Beach Band and received a storming reception from the partygoers. Halfway through their performance of the punk classic 'Boredom', Howard inexplicably became preoccupied with reading the *Hackney Gazette*. *N16* has strictly no comment...

THE NEW YORK POST in a recent article entitled 'True Brit – the very best of swinging London', sent in by a reader, contains the following:
COOLEST STREET
'The East End nabe of Stoke Newington has a rep for being self-consciously "alternative." While the sight of women in waist-length earrings shepherding children in rainbow knitwear along Church Street, the area's spiritual center, might be a bit granola, it's fun. Jam at Vortex Jazz Bar or flick through rare blues LPs at Totem Records. At Rasa, you'll find excellent South Asian fare.' The Yanks are coming...

A Stoke Newington library user reports that, when trying to find local band Bikini Beach's website (to blag a free invite to a gig) on the computer system there, he received the answer 'access denied'. Hackney Council clearly see themselves as our moral guardians and wish to shield us from such obscene words as 'bikini'. But what if you're trying to find out more about the 1954 H-Bomb test on Bikini Atoll in the South Pacific? Or making an academic study of the lyrics of Brian Hyland's lovelorn ballad 'Itsy bitsy teeny weeny yellow polka dot bikini' from the same era? Just do it from home.

The Sea Cadets, long resident on Church Street, have been forced to close. The unit was set up nearly 85 years ago, but they could not find a new venue. The centre was forced to close because the council wanted to be paid a full market rent instead of the peppercorn price that the Cadets had been paying for many years. The council suggested that they could move to the new reservoir complex but again they would have to pay the full market value. It makes you think.

Hackney Council has been heavily backing the Hackney Young Parliament. And a group of them came to talk to the June meeting of the Stoke Newington Forum and stated that they wanted more activities for teenagers. And yet at the same time the council was asking the Sea Cadets for a rent rise from £200 per year to £11,000. The Sea Cadet movement provides a wide range of activities based around sailing, and provides a healthy life style. At a time when the youth of Hackney are crying out for more support, it seems a strange decision to pull the rug from one of the few activities open to the youth of Stoke Newington.

So Hackney schools aren't good enough for Diane Abbott, who is sending her son to a private secondary school outside her constituency. The more educated, middle-class parents who send their children to local schools, the better it will be for the future of education in the borough. Surely Ms Abbott knows this, particularly as she is well known for her left-wing view on the world.

We seem to remember her critical comments on Harriet Harman and Tony Blair when they did something similar with their children. Certainly, young black males are the lowest achieving group in Hackney schools, but this should be addressed by engagement from within and not by shrugging off the Borough and going elsewhere. Particularly when you are MP for Stoke Newington and Hackney North.

Danny from the Fishery recently had an unusual request. A woman whom he guesses is from Russia asked him for a large salmon – guts and all. Danny was surprised because most customers ask for the innards to be removed. But the young lady insisted that the fish was fully intact.

She explained that the fish was an essential part of her erotic act at a Shoreditch club. Her act climaxes in intimate contact with the Scottish fish's innards as she rips it open. Danny politely declined the offer of a front row VIP seat.

The Written Word

The first Stoke Newington Literary Festival took place in June 2010, to great acclaim from locals and visitors: so much so, that founder and Festival Director, Liz Vater, decided in the light of the overwhelmingly positive feedback, to make the Festival an annual event. What with the Festival, Stokefest and the Fringe now all history, it's good to see that the spirit of local cultural enterprise continues in the area. Liz and her army of volunteer workers deserve our thanks and support for maintaining and enhancing the creative image and reputation of Stoke Newington.

Stokey Lit Fest Returns
By Liz Vater, Spring 2011 (47)

Tony Benn had a picnic in Abney Park cemetery where a local dog nicked half his cheese sandwich, Edwyn Collins raised the roof of the Town Hall with two rapturous encores, and Shappi Khorsandi prompted 200 people, en masse, to point towards Clissold Park and shout 'We've got deer!' You kind of had to be there ... A large proportion of the audience was from Stoke Newington but we attracted people from as far afield as Crouch End, Cambridge, Reading (no pun intended) and even – gasp – South of the River.

We're looking at extending the programme to include more venues and more events to accommodate what we anticipate will be a slightly larger number of visitors. We're working on some great collaborations this year, too, to provide an even more diverse programme. The Society for Curious Thought will be launching an installation at Lemon Monkey in the run up to the Festival, the well regarded Fire Station Bookswap will be popping by and there are lots of other goodies in the pipeline.

One of the strands that will run throughout the weekend focuses on Edgar Allan Poe, famous resident of the academy that once stood on the site of The Fox Reformed on Church Street. Robbie, the Fox's proprietor, has been instrumental in pulling together what promises to be a fascinating series of events. It's

too early to announce the line-up, but we'll be looking at Poe's extraordinary influence on literature, music, art, film and more. We're working with the wonderful pop-up cinema outfit The Flicker Club (www.flickerclub.com) who will be screening a Poe-inspired film and pulling together some other gothic delights.

We'll also be taking on some of the most pressing issues of today: the media, the importance of protest, the economy and chocolate. We'll be debuting some of the UK's most exciting new authors and unearthing some local gems from the world of poetry, music and comedy. We have some high profile comic names, some literary stars and much, much more.

Importantly, this year there's a full and very exciting children's programme featuring some big name kids' authors, as well as plenty of interactive workshops, storytelling and stuff with crayons. We're also looking at the influence that Stoke Newington and Hackney had on the emergence and development of the ska scene in the UK. The Phebes Club on the corner of Amhurst Road and the High Street has long gone, but together with The Four Aces in Hackney, the influential R&B records in Stamford Hill and local musician and record shop proprietor Roy Shirley, Stoke Newington was home to much of the burgeoning reggae and ska scene happening in the capital.

Our Own Lit Fest
By Bryony Hegarty, Summer 2011 (48)

Literary festivals aplenty seem to be sprinkled liberally around the country – Hay on Wye naturally springs to mind, as do Cheltenham and London's South Bank to name a few. Last year the Stoke Newington Literary Festival emerged in our increasingly acknowledged bohemian village.

What, you might ask, makes this festival different to any other? As one of this year's participants

remarked 'I'm in N1 aren't I?' The significance of his misapprehension jumped out – as we know Stoke Newington, N16, is a part of Hackney; the borough with the lowest literacy levels in the country. If actions speak louder than words, then the decision by Liz Vater, Director of Stoke Newington Festival, to donate profits to literacy initiatives in the borough of Hackney not only validates the Stoke Newington Literary festival as an outstanding initiative, it also activates the theoretical link from words to deeds.

Stoke Newington has been home to many artists, writers and musicians. Edgar Allan Poe, around whom much of this year's festival was programmed, lived in Stoke Newington for six years. There were big names from the lecture circuit, running alongside a focus on local issues and writers. Hackney MP Diane Abbott opened events in the town hall before swiftly moving off to chair African Diaspora Writers in the High Street bookshop. This was the pace of weekend with so much on offer one couldn't attend everything of interest. Speakers and audiences passed one another on the street, moving from one event to the next. The festival featured a strong children's programme – authors entertaining to packed houses with one of the highest concentrations of children per capita in the UK. This included John Hegley, David Walliams, Knife and Packer and Oliver Jeffers – literally animating his characters with a felt pen in hand and A3 paper to the wonderment of his readership.

Gavin Knight, author of *Hood Rat*, and Sean Attwood who blogged *Jon's Jail Journal* behind the bars of one of America's most notorious prisons, were in conversation. An hour of chilling truths on gang culture and penal reform was only too pertinent to the Borough. In many ways this discussion encapsulated one of the ambitions of the festival. As challenging as the issues raised, the authors and their audience made the links from literacy to positive outcomes and education versus punishment, to integrate and not ostracise members of society. A mesmerising

screening (hosted by the Flicker club) of Stephen Berkoff performing Poe's classic *Tell Tale Heart* was followed by conversation with former resident Berkoff. Alexei Sayle entertained with autobiographical tales, and bravely ran the gauntlet of local opinion about a line he used to use: ' What's on in Stoke Newington? Fuck all'.

Sunday had a strong bias towards examining music as an inspiration to read, write and listen. Chaired by Stoke Newington librarian and music industry figure (*N16*'s very own) Richard Boon, ex-manager of Buzzcocks, the Juke Box Fury Panel, revealed the tracks that inspired them to become writers. Paul Morley tapped into localism, a key part of his journey through music to journalism. He emphasised not the analytical process of 'describing what you hear', but the inspiration to write through evoked mood and idea. Charles Shaar Murray spoke as he writes with imagery-laden imagination about tracks that 'busted the fourth wall' and have 'musical verité'. Richard consigned his notes to the 'dustbin of history' and announced the 'evaporation of the debate' as the panel had sadly run out of time in a discussion that could have gone on at length. Winding up the festival, and chaired by former *NME* editor Danny Kelly, The Ska Panel: writer Colin Grant, Slits guitarist Viv Albertine, Newton Dunbar founder of Dalston's legendary 1960s Four Aces club, and the youthful but encyclopaedically knowledgeable Tim Burrows, debated the beginnings of ska, and the huge influence of Jamaican music.

This led to the post-show party with a live set from Viv Albertine. Tuning and chatting in between songs, about Sid Vicious, John Lydon, and the long scorching summer of 1976, she commented to her sound engineer 'the vocals should be louder than the guitar' capturing a seminal point about the ' post punk' mood. Spiky, funny, feisty she gave us 'Don't believe in Love': every man in the room was enslaved, every woman in awe. Howard Marks stood at the bar (Viv devoted a song to him) as writers, poets and speakers gathered for a brilliant climax to a festival that was creatively programmed, well attended and lofty in ambition.

Battle of the Buses

A few years ago, an outcry arose across the land. The subject which provoked this hoo-hah was a bus. The 73 Routemaster, the double decker, heroic symbol of our little parish, was to be replaced by a bendy bus. Agreed, the bendy bus was designed for the traffic-choked, wide boulevards of Paris and Frankfurt, and was not ideal for the neo-medieval tight corners of Stoke Newington, but there were several arguments in its favour. However, after fevered discussions, declarations of treason and passionate outpourings of loyalty (this is still only a bus, remember), the bendy was eventually taken out of service, and a newly designed 73 Routemaster was re-established, to local celebration, burning of bendy bus graven images and the public sacrifice of virgins (where did they find them?). So everything is back to where it was. What follows is a (very) brief selection of the correspondence we received about the 73 bus.

> **73 facts you didn't know (Spring 1999, issue 1)**
> - The 73 bus route was established at the end of the First World War and ran from Stoke Newington to Richmond
> - In 1968 the first 73 Routemaster appeared on the streets, replacing the older RT type buses
> - The 73 Routemaster fleet has travelled mileage equivalent to the moon and back (someone actually worked this out)
> - In the year ended 1997, the 73 bus carried nearly 12.5 million passengers

Regarding the 73 bus route, I can remember in the 1930s as a schoolboy the pirate and private buses, as they were called. There was the Westminster (chocolate colour), Claremont (red), Thomas Tilling (red), Public and Havelock (blue). The Westminster and Claremont were garaged opposite Penton Street in Pentonville Road. My father was a conductor on the Westminster bus. They paid for their own uniforms and caps which they wore with pride, winter and summer. As boys, my brother and I would go to the Angel Arcade opposite Liverpool Road and wait for the 73 bus which my father was on and give him his sandwiches for his lunch. In return, we would get on his bus and go to Richmond and return to the Angel.

I traded in a small place in Islington for a bigger place in N16 knowing I would evermore be reliant on the 73 bus. Nine times out of ten I get a seat and a comfortable, if lengthy, journey to work on an old Routemaster or new double-decker. By October, all these buses on route 73 will be replaced by (fewer) bendy buses. TfL issued a press release in January informing us how much 'more comfortable' it would make our journeys. Bendies can take up to 135 people (including 85 standing). Double-deckers 77 (5 standing). Am I missing something here? If there are fewer buses and only 45 seats, no one after the first two stops will get a seat during rush hour. And if you pack 85 people in self-same bus, make them stand for up to an hour, whilst hanging onto straps and poles, and send them down one of the bendiest routes in London, aren't they going to get a little tossed about?

The TFL stats sound impressive, but they are rubbish: bendy buses increase congestion by sheer length, they cause roadblocks as drivers pile up behind them afraid to overtake, they are more dangerous to cyclists and motorbikes, they are packed with non-paying passengers abusing the open-doored system, they cause motion sickness, elderly passengers are getting knocked around, and you don't want to stand anyway. A common question has been 'How do you get two past each other in Church Street?' Answer: all parking in Church Street will henceforth be banned. While passengers will relish a faster journey to work, many shop-owners are concerned that business will be affected by car users avoiding shopping/eating in Church Street altogether.

I was sad to wave farewell to the Routemaster. On what is quite possibly the most depressing journey ever now, all aisles are blocked with people, so access and exit at bus stops has become an issue with people being trapped in doors and what may actually infuriate me most, no card readers on the exits apart from the front door working! I wonder, does anyone in City Hall or LT have to use the bendy bus or are they deliberately keeping it away from their own routes!

I love the bendy bus. My enjoyment of these marvels of innovative engineering grows each journey. My most significant new experience was seeing a person in a wheelchair decline the offers of confused, surprised, flapping passengers, concerned she was attempting to board a back door. She informed them the driver did know she was there and that having pressed a button, she'd board perfectly well without them. She promptly

rolled in over an effective ramp mechanism. The sight of people with mobility problems on London streets is incredibly rare compared to Sydney and other cities in my experience. London's notoriously inadequate transport provision for the disabled seems to be finally under effective consideration.

I've always loved bendy buses. Bendy buses are a piece of social engineering that brings the best out of us. Passengers move aside to let mothers park their buggies, people offer their seats to those 'less able to stand', and they have disabled access. I still remember my first gas-powered Mercedes bendy cruising down Church Street. Three doors opened and we were all aboard. There might not be many seats – less likely now with the extra buses – but we were on the move as the bendy turned into Albion Road with surgical precision. At last, after 30-plus years' service, Arriva has consigned the bone-rattling, suspension-less, diesel-belching Routemaster to where it belongs – the scrap heap of history.

There are three kinds of vociferous opposition to the bendy bus. First, there are those with a yearning for the past that never existed. Bring back the Routemaster! Hey, let's go the whole hog and revert to the Victorian, horse-pulled omnibus. Second, some cyclists claim that bendy buses are dangerous. Stokey cyclists come in three types – the bad, the ugly and the unspeakable. Although a tiny minority, the unspeakable are unaffected by the bendy. They are usually aggressive young men travelling at high speed on the pavements, making pedestrians paranoid about getting a bicycle tyre up their orifice. The ugly are cerebrally challenged

teenagers who veer across Church Street, usually on one wheel, cutting up traffic. They are an accident waiting to happen. The majority of Stokey cyclists fall into the 'bad' category, as in a bad or fleeting acquaintance with the Highway Code. They are easily identifiable by their ugly protective headgear, earnest expression and hideous attire. Would you try and overtake (on the inside!) an articulated lorry? No? Then why would you want to overtake a bendy bus that has in clear huge letters on the back 'THIS VEHICLE IS 18 METRES LONG'? Third, there are motorists who hate the bendy. Usually builders-arse van drivers or the school-run brigade who pooter along in their people mobiles, destroying the ozone layer while delivering their darling kid(s) to the school gate. Why can't these anti-social, selfish individuals use public transport like the rest of us?

I was alarmed to read the piece (*above*) on bendy buses in your last issue. Firstly, when the Bendy Buses came into circulation there were no warnings displayed on the back of the buses. The subsequent number of accidents and injuries that resulted. and consistent lobbying from cyclists and other road users, forced TFL to introduce the current stickers. Secondly, the decision by Ken Livingston to put these buses on our streets was taken I believe from an economic standpoint and not as a result of their suitability to London's streets and traffic. The fact that the buses have had overheating problems and some have even caught on fire is well known and documented. Whilst this problem now seems to have been rectified, it still does not solve the problems the buses have negotiating the largely medieval street plan of London. The buses in many cases contribute massively to the general slowdown of traffic owing to their relative inability to take sharp corners and negotiate obstacles when compared to standard double decker buses. Lastly, and perhaps most alarmingly, it seems clear to me that any saving in carbon emissions that the bendy buses may give is all but lost as a result of the traffic congestion problems they contribute to, and the fact that buses with driver-operated doors and without a conductor mean more time has to be spent at bus stops, which in turn means more time spent holding up other traffic.

It is an absolute travesty that Route 73 has lost its Routemaster buses. Not only were they the most appropriate bus design on their inception in 1956, but the design has yet to be surpassed in terms of its practicality and ergonomics, so much so that they remain to this day the symbol of the capital itself. The reason Routemasters are being taken out of service are firstly economic and secondly due to emissions. Whilst I agree with the need to give value for money and reduce emissions in public transport, it should be noted that no real effort has been made to re-design the Routemaster or design a bus like the Routemaster which incorporates so many of the features that made it such a practical bus. For only some of the reasons I have listed above, it seems to me obvious why large numbers of people are choosing to cycle in London.

Your Letters

The letters printed in these and other pages are just a small selection of the correspondence we have received over the years. In most cases, I have omitted the writers' names. The point they express is the important thing.

I wonder what you make of this load of pretentious codswallop which appeared recently in the *Sunday Telegraph*. All too ironically entitled 'Changing Values', the piece sought to justify the £500,000 price increase (since 1991) of a house in Stoke Newington Church Street by quoting the (ex-Islington) occupant and, thank goodness, would-be vendor: 'the area has changed. It used to be very working class, but now it is fashionable, with restaurants and a jazz club. My sons say they realised the area was changing when, suddenly, attractive girls started appearing on the street.' Ah, that's the secret of Church Street and no doubt why, as the article points out, the 'barristers and bankers are rediscovering the area!'

Diane Abbott's comments about the police in the July issue of *N16* didn't do her credit. I'd have thought that as a black woman she would be wary of blanket condemnations of whole groups of people. But by stating that 'police officers in Stoke Newington in the past had a well-deserved reputation for corruption and brutality', that is what she did. The simple addition of the word 'some' would have made all the difference.

I had need to phone Hackney Council's Bulk Collection service to dispose of two armchairs. They were willing to collect for a fee of £10 to be given to the driver on collection. This service as far as I know used to be free. Instead of helping to keep our streets clean, people will be dumping more beds, mattresses, furniture etc, because they cannot afford or are not prepared to pay this charge. I wonder sometimes what we are paying our Council Tax for. It's all very well saying 'Old Stokey' is coming up in the world when already our streets are in a disgusting state.

Our first visit to Stoke Newington or 'Stokey' as it is often called, took place late October 1998. We were advised by two well travelled visitors to Stokey that we had to first board the infamous No 73 bus to see Stoke Newington in all its glory. Pub names escape us, as the alcohol took hold, but we are assured we visited most of the splendid public houses and eateries along the way. Judging by the size of our hangovers the following morning, I think it is fair to say we wholeheartedly imbibed the 'Stokey' atmosphere. An apology must be made to our new friend for the 'liberation' (ahem) of a certain bottle of

brandy and a further apology to our colleagues for dropping said bottle in Russell Square. Hope to be back this year - we may even descend for the 'Stokey' Festival: watch this space and lock up your brandy! Ciao!

I wonder if a reader can give any information about a local Stamford Hill character? I first saw him when I was a young child in 1937. My mother and I were on Stamford Hill when we saw this man with shoulder-length hair, unheard-of for a man at that time. My mother told me he was a hermit who was quite old (she said 'about 80' although he looked to be 35-40.) She told me he lived alone and was very healthy because he never ate meat, walked everywhere and lived a healthy life. He always seemed to move between Stamford Hill and Clapton Common. I kept seeing him over the years, but last saw him in Safeways about 6-7 years ago and I fear he must have passed on. I very much wished to talk to him, but never did, as I respected his privacy. Even if he was 'only' 40-50 years old back in 1937, that would make him a very old man when he died and he did not look it. I'd love to know more about him.

Regarding the 'Stamford Hill hermit' - during the 1970s and early part of the 1980s, I used to see someone similar around the Clapton/Stamford Hill/Stoke Newington area. He was known locally

Speech bubble: OLD PEOPLE'S CLUBS, NURSERIES, BOWLING GREENS, ANIMALS IN CLISSOLD PARK ZOO AND DUCKS FOR SALE!!

as 'Father Christmas' but we called him 'Mr Natural' because of his resemblance to the Robert Crumb cartoon character. Dressed in the most fantastic combinations of Indian print sari lengths and dayglo furnishing fabrics, he was hard to miss. Lots of jewellery too, anything shiny – I once saw him with a chrome Mercedes hub cap on a string around his neck. He was old, but ageless really, maybe 70, maybe 80 and always very purposeful, very focused on whatever his personal hermetic mission was. I tried some conversation once, but he turned his eyes away and would not speak. Same person, or someone else?

As a native of Stoke Newington I must say I cringe every time I see or hear the word 'Stokey'. This area, in all its long history, has never been termed so until recent years when, its existence discovered, it appeared in the Press with this 'jokey' name. Now it proliferates throughout your otherwise excellent magazine.

Through research and discussion with long-term residents of the parish, it seems that 'Stokey' was in common usage as far back as the 1950s. Does it really matter?

You could rename N16 'Colonial Times' because that's the truth of it. Your rag makes me puke! It's a pat on the back for how successfully the middle classes have swarmed in. And your obsession with the 73 bus! Sure, it's big and red and maybe a little fantasy gets projected, but for chrissakes it's just a bus! You walk around Hackney like it's an old curiosity shop. The letter in your last issue said it all – 'an interesting cultural mix of people who appear to live alongside one another harmoniously'. A woman said to me in the park once that she wouldn't let her kids watch Postman Pat because there weren't any black people in it, and I looked around the playground and all I could see was 'wellys' (people from Tunbridge Wells). You're either squatting and calling yourselves anarchists, or just plain buying up the place. You talk as if it's a community without acknowledging the fact that you destroyed an ailing community to get what you want. You strut around like you're street hip. You even get Ali G's jokes, but it takes a bit more than sticking little Milo in an Arsenal shirt to be a fan.

I agree with what what your correspondent wrote in the last edition of N16 – your magazine should be renamed 'Colonial Times'. It is a magazine for people who spend holidays 'up the Dordogne in a camper van' or like Sally Watson, who you quote as saying that she is having such a problem finding a private nursery for Georgia and Tabatha that she 'may have to move to Highgate just to find one'. The problem is that the Watsons will be replaced by more rich young people who will move in and continue to take over what pubs and cafes we have left, and show off to us about it in the pages of N16. As the middle class takes over more and more of the Borough, the IWCA will continue to seek to involve and represent what is still Hackney's working-class majority.

Hackney Independent Working Class Association

The area has done nothing but continue to boom over the last few years and it's now more popular than ever. The cuisines in the restaurants resemble a round the world trip in food. You could certainly never die of thirst as there are enough pubs and bars to suit everyone's taste. But when we start to think about entertainment and activity in this community – especially for younger people – not a lot is going on. There are many cultures in the area but we hear hardly anything about their activities. No, we don't necessarily want a massive rave scene in the locality, it's far too small for that. One of the problems of living around here is that everyone knows each other and what they get up to. It can certainly slow you down! There should be a wide range of well-publicised activities for children and older people. What about a proper Community Centre? But it's really down to us to make our voices heard to ensure that these things are provided. So why aren't we doing more about it?

Our House Wino

Peter Grogan began writing for N16 Magazine *on wine and assorted bevvy in Spring 2000, and he's been a regular and prized contributor ever since. Now one of the UK's top wine writers, Pete has reviewed virtually every establishment selling wine in Stoke Newington and beyond, and his regular musings and 'tastings' are one of the funniest and, almost as an aside, most informative columns in the mag. As examples, here are two of his articles, concentrating on alcohol appreciation from very different ends of the social spectrum.*

A 'Frilling Night
Spring 2002 (13)

When a pith-helmeted Robbie Richards hacked his way through the impenetrable jungles to the north of Newington Green in 1981 in search of the fabled land of Stokiana his friends thought he'd got a touch of the sun. Whether it was heatstroke or a stroke of genius that drove him on we may never know but he made it to that happy land and set up shop at The Fox in Church Street. Approaching its twenty-first birthday, The Fox, now Reformed, has achieved 'local institution' status and provides everything necessary to sustain life for its devoted habitues.

Among many other things, Frills – The Fox Reformed Imbibing and Low Life Society – features fortnightly wine-tastings. I went to one focussing on Australian Shiraz, which was probably a mistake, as it's a subject I only marginally prefer to straight algebra. Nonetheless, it was intelligently tutored, there were proper tasting glasses and so on, and a good enough selection of wines to point up the range of styles and quality that can emerge from a single varietal in different hands.

One stand out, however, was the only blended wine, Element Shiraz-Cabernet Sauvignon, which The Fox stocks by the glass. From Western Australia, it's a wine with a lovely, deeply saturated colour, fabulous glycerol-laden body and an intense nose of super-fresh blackcurrants. The explosive (and long) black-fruit flavours of the Cabernet are given a greenly herby, dill or fennel, edge by the Syrah. This blend is not used, to my knowledge, in 'Old World' France, maybe because in the days when they were working these things out, the Rhone seemed a very long way from Bordeaux and people stuck with local varietals. No such problems in the 'New World' of the Pays d'Oc, however, whence comes La Fourcade Cabernet-Syrah. Somewhat closed and much less extracted than the Aussie, but with a good, smooth body and herby flavours this is certainly nothing to offend, but Element was a show-stopping act to follow.

Bergerac Sec Belingard is a product of another match made in heaven, Sauvignon Blanc and Semillon. The Sauvignon is always in your face first – in this case in a high-strung, very slightly smoky, gooseberryish sort of a way – then the Semillon comes from behind to fatten it up and give it some roundness in the back of the mouth. Maybe it's something to do with age, but a lot of straight Sauvignons seem quite harsh compared with this classic and, mercifully un-vogueish blend. I'm not sure what goes into the leggy, blonde Cotes de Gascogne La Fourcade, but the refreshing, crisply grapefruity flavours suggest some much under-rated Ugni Blanc and I could drink a lot of it. Fat and oaky, Gallo Sycamore Canyon is text book, mid-range California Chardonnay with solid body, zesty fruit and a slightly tarry finish. The Frills house claret, M de Montesquieu 2000, is a nice example of what is known, in one of my favourite bits of wine-speak, as a 'light luncheon claret'. It is soft and candyish, light in colour and body, with redcurrant flavours and just a touch of oak. The makers have eschewed any troublesome tannins – this is, after all, a mere baby to be drunk at 18 months of age.

The Bum's Rush
Winter 2005 (28)

These are happy days indeed for our park bench pissheads. They're getting drunker, faster, cheaper than ever before and you know what? Some of the stuff doesn't even taste too bad.

In terms of bangs for your buck there's no more competitive sector of the market than the alcohol-dependent, so I've worked out a handy 'pence-per-unit' ratio which you might like to keep by you in case of tough times ahead. As this is a scientific survey, I have used the prices in my local corner shop. They may be somewhat inflated but I reckon that this is where I would be most likely to stagger for my first 10am belter, rather than arrange regular white-van trips to a cash-and-carry near Luton.

It's not so long ago that such horrors as Thunderbird, Cyprus sherry and VP 'British wine' were the staples of the 'wino list' and, to put things into context, I sprang 27p per unit for a bottle of the latter – the 'Medium', as it styles itself. (Medium what, exactly, is what I'd like to know?). In a spirit of scientific rigour I tried it at park-bench temperature, on the assumption that the outdoor life doesn't usually allow for much in the way of refrigeration – except at night, I suppose. It has quite a strong 'nose' of lime pickle, and that can't be right, can it?

There's also something there that whisked me back 35 years to some murky liquid that came out of my first chemistry set. I'm glad I didn't drink whatever it was all those years ago because it might well have tasted something like this – thin, sour and metallic. There's not much booze that goes down the plug-hole chez Grogans but you wouldn't make a mud pie with this.

Why would anybody, except me, pay 40p per unit for a bottle of Thunderbird at 13% alcohol. What is Thunderbird, anyway? Why does it smell of melons and taste so horribly chemical and sort of bleachy? I bought the last bottle on the shelf – maybe it's the last bottle on the planet. Let's hope so. Carlsberg Special Brew (27p per unit) has spawned a hundred imitators in the stupor-strength lager category, and I've always rather liked the slight whiff of honey and the malty, creamy taste.

The sheer weight of alcohol – at 9% it's the same strength as many a German wine – means it tends to stick in the craw somewhat after the first few tinnies, probably just as well really, isn't it? Tennent's Super (25p per unit) has not just the same alcoholic content but something of the floral characteristics of many better German wines as well. It's cleaner and drier than Spesh but with the same maltiness. Rather lovely, really.

It's almost colourless, almost odourless, almost tasteless, but White Star Cider (19p per unit) will leave you completely legless. It has the alcohol content of a small town and notes of saccharine dissolved in vinegar, but this is it, folks – the cheapest hit out there. As for Diamond White Cider (24p per unit), ditto the above – the only difference is the price. Nobody ever drank these because they liked the taste. In fact, did you ever see anybody other than a wino drinking one?

At 30p per unit, Argini Soave 2004 is the cheapest plonk in the place. It's thin and a bit tart, but it's really quite refreshing if chilled to near zero. Clearly, it can't compete for your last three quid. And when that's gone, don't even think about Methylated Spirit (2p) – liver damage, blindness and death await you. And it doesn't taste very nice either.

You can read all Peter's articles on our website or his own website petergrogan.com.

Indian Memory Man Joke
By Rab MacWilliam, Autumn 2004 (23)

Looking through some back issues of N16 the other day, it suddenly occurred to me that we have never published any jokes. How sad is that, over six years? To redress the balance slightly, here is a much abbreviated version of one of my favourites.

Twenty-five years ago, Alec and Morag were about to get married in Glasgow. 'Where'll we go on honeymoon, hen? Rothesay?' says Alec. 'Nah, that's boring', says Morag. 'I was reading the other day about Florida. Let's go there'. So off they flew across the Atlantic, landed at Miami, hired a car and headed down to the Keys. Driving down the Interstate, Alec noticed a gleaming, newly painted wooden sign with the words 'Indian Memory Man, Next Right' inscribed on it. 'This looks interesting', thought Alec and pulled the car into the turning.

The couple walked down a freshly mown, well-tended path until they reached a brand-new canvas tepee. Alec pulled back the entrance flap and there, in the centre of the tent, sat a cross-legged young Indian, his jet-black hair crowned with a single eagle's feather, who stared at them with a deep intensity. 'I am the Indian Memory Man. Ask me any question and I will answer it', he said. 'OK', said Alec, 'who won the 1923 Scottish Cup Final and what was the score?' The Indian replied immediately. 'Celtic. 1-0'. 'Amazing' said Alec, something of an expert on Scottish football. 'How did he know that?' The couple congratulated the Indian, left the tepee and began their holiday, soon forgetting about the encounter.

Glasgow: the present day and a Silver Anniversary. Alec and Morag decide to celebrate by returning to Florida and retracing their honeymoon all those years ago. Back they go on the plane, hire a car at Miami and drive off down to the Keys. On the way there, Alec spots a faded, wooden sign, hanging from a post by one hinge, containing the barely legible words 'Indian Memory Man, Next Right'. 'I wonder if he's still there', thinks Alec and pulls into the turning. The pair push their way through an overgrown path, through the dangling palm fronds and reach a dilapidated old tepee.

They open the flap and go in. In front of them is the same Indian, although now sporting a mane of flowing white hair and a full chief's headdress. The intensity of the stare is undiminished. Morag takes Alec to one side. 'He's obviously now an important man', she says, 'treat him with respect'. Alec says 'I know how to do it. I've seen it on the telly', walks up to the Indian, raises his arm with outstretched palm and solemnly intones 'How'. The Indian looks up at him and replies 'Penalty. 35th minute'.

Back To Schooldays

Education has always been a contentious issue in Stoke Newington. The arrival of academies has stirred things up still further. This is a brief, edited selection of what readers have had to say about local education.

Straight To The Point
By Sue Heal, Winter 2002 (16)

At the start of this term there were over 80 11-year-olds languishing at home in N16 because no secondary place could be found for them in the locality. And the situation is on course to get considerably worse. Stokey Comp, or Stoke Newington Tap Dancing Fame Academy as I believe it likes to be called, is monstrously oversubscribed with a sizeable pocket of Islington kids having fled the truly dire sink secondaries in their home borough. Personally I think the comp is just Flavour Of The Month and from what I hear has some serious problems which are being swept aside in the frantic race! for a place – any place – which isn't in the wilds of E5 with flick-knives optional. But I digress.

The fact is if you don't live in a campervan parked outside the gates you can forget Stokey Comp. And, as 80-odd parents have recently discovered, can be reduced to gazing balefully at a depressed Archie or Amy across the kitchen table, struggling with logarithms for the first time in 30 years while work goes hang.

I bumped into the parent of a 10-year-old this week, recently moved from N16, who used to vigorously sing the praises of Stokey's most fashionable primary. She and hubby were called to see said son's new head in Westminster (bog standard state) and told bright Little Jimmy was roughly 18 months behind the national average for his year group and would be playing serious catch up for some time to come. 'Apparently, Sue, he can paint wonderfully expressive pictures but has no idea where to put a comma.' Scales had not merely fallen but been ripped from her eyes. I suppose if you shovel them straight into the Comp you're none the wiser.

Letter in response, Issue 17, from the headteacher...

I have had the article written about our school shown to me by a concerned local trader. He was rather surprised and alarmed by the characterisation and blanket generalisations made in your article which do not reflect his impression of the school.

The truth is whether you like to accept it or not that this is a good school, in fact a very good school which serves a balanced mix of children: 33% band 1; 33% band 2 ; and 33% band 3. The numbers from outside Hackney are small, and we have just had an OFSTED document which places our results in the top 10% of

schools in the country (not London) that have similar challenging intakes. We are not satisfied or complacent about our achievements and are still rapidly improving and constantly changing to respond to the issues we are presented with.

I am not afraid of criticism based on evidence; what I do object to is the publishing of what amounts to little more than gossip about the school, the community we serve and more importantly the very many good young people who come to this school, behave well, work hard and achieve excellent results. I also object to the snide and patronising tone of your piece, which cannot hide the lack of any real research or evidence for your assertions. Some research might have helped in the article: you ask for contributions, but have never approached me to 'grace' *N16*.

I am therefore offering you an invitation to see the real school, warts and all, without any cosmetic doctoring by me. You can talk to students, they can show you around.

Back to Schooldays
By Sue Heal, Spring 2003 (17)

Sue accepted Mark Emmerson's invitation to tour the school and to find out how the school, now called Stoke Newington Media Arts College, is meeting its challenges.

Stoke Newington School Media Arts College is a big place, housing 1200 students from wildly differing backgrounds. For almost three years 41-year-old Geordie Mark Emmerson has been guiding the tiller. 'I'm not going to sit here and say this school has no problems. In many ways the school reflects the wider community in Stoke Newington. It's a complex mix with those expected to achieve highly and many disadvantaged kids,' he says, 'but it's a vibrant, succeeding environment. The kind of school I wish I'd gone to and want for my own kids. We're improving delivery all the time. We currently have 570 applications for 240 places.'

Emmerson strikes me immediately as a steely realist. He's had a fairly rapid rise up the education career ladder and I suspect won't collect his carriage clock in Stoke Newington. Sandy haired, short, although not as short as he thinks he is, suit, tie, a mite prone to management speak, there's lots of 'delivery outcomes' and 'managing down'. Yet Emmerson knows full well he straddles that old line between Stokey's dafter middle-class parents, who see authoritarianism behind every rule, and kids with home lives so wild and chaotic they'd reduce the place to rubble if they weren't reined in. 'I'd known the school for some time before I came here and in my opinion it was too liberal. And I do call myself a liberal, although some of the parents might disagree with that,' he says with the hint of wry smile. 'I'm a firm believer that children need boundaries. I immediately saw my major priority as sorting out behaviour, and that's still true.'

The kids obviously know where they stand with him. The place is knee deep in contracts, sanctions and codes of conduct all based on mutual respect. An anti-bullying policy has just been introduced. GCSE grades are undoubtedly on the up and half-a-dozen of the leavers will eventually end up at Cambridge. There is absolutely no doubt that this is a vastly improved school. Art exhibitions, touring theatre companies, dance evenings, field trips, acres of after-school clubs, young writers' workshops, cabaret nights – the place is a dizzying round of events, most with a heavy media slant. The school has video-editing suites, a sound-recording suite, a theatre/TV studio seating 220, a drama studio and digital cameras galore, although all looked a little careworn. There is a rather gloomy, dark

air about much of the place. I told Emmerson that, out of his £5 million budget, a few pots of paint wouldn't go amiss. 'Well 80 per cent of that budget goes on staff salaries. And we've been re-equipping, for example the science labs. This school is a work in progress.'

One of the big debating points at present is the comprehensive admissions quota system. The children must be evenly split between the three main ability bands, which in effect means large numbers of bright local kids cannot get in while others come from as far away as Clapton. 'It's under discussion', says Emmerson warily. 'Do we want a local school firmly rooted in the community? Our catchment area locally is now only 600 yards. Children who attend William Patton cannot get in. My own children wouldn't stand a chance of getting in. And they (the schoolchildren) have so many opportunities which I wish I'd had at my school. It's easy to knock being in Hackney, but I love it. It's challenging, vibrant and interesting.'

I believe him. We know. But people have got to be prepared to talk about what's wrong, otherwise what hope is there. Some of his parents have given me a rough ride over recent weeks. Once they've calmed down a bit and loosened their grip on my throat, many Stokey parents have expressed two major concerns. One is persistent anti-social behaviour by a hard-core pocket both in and outside the school, which Emmerson is resolutely determined to stamp out. And the other is the thorny issue of homework, which many claim is either not set, inadequately marked or often simply not challenging enough.

What do I personally think now after my visit ? What would I want for my own daughter? Something which I've long suspected doesn't exist. A school with Stokey's vibrant energy, cultural and social diversity, challenging ethos and a head who understands and respects the complexities of how children learn. Plus top notch exam results, solid traditional teaching, a bright tidy building full of wellbehaved, highly motivated kids who don't smoke dope with Mum and Dad. Forget it, huh?

It's Academic
By Bryony Hegarty, Spring 2011 (47)

A few years ago, the *Observer* magazine identified Stoke Newington as 'The Best Place in Britain To Be A Parent', with the UK's largest number of babies per capita. These statistics make education a key concern for the neighbourhood. We're all bracing ourselves for the ever deepening cuts that the media forecasts and the politicians promise. So how are things looking at our local schools?

The Learning Trust will make cuts to the tune of £8 million by December 2011. The initial fear of a mass cull is not as bad as it could have been. It is thought that the offer of voluntary redundancy will make up a significant tranche of this.

Academy status is now an option for primary schools as well as secondaries. In secondaries the cost of conversion itself is £25,000 in the form of a government grant (i.e. from the taxpayer) which would be surely far better spent on education itself. A number of Academies (nationwide) are finding themselves in financial trouble as costs have exceeded budget forecasts. The building of academies in Hackney was a means to secure funding for new schools when there was a dire shortage of school places. A choice of different types of school is now a reality in the borough.

At Stoke Newington Secondary, a successful Community school, a feasibility study into taking academy status suggests that there are no real advantages and some potential significant drawbacks. No actual financial gain when the figures are analysed and a number of extra responsibilities and liabilities for governors of academies who, in law, become company directors. At the school the prospect of compulsory redundancy has been kept at bay for this year, and one-to-one tuition for students with additional need in core subjects has been maintained. Students and staff have benefited from recent building improvements.

A number of our local schools are rich in cultural diversity with a strong parent voice. There has never been a more important time for parents to get involved to preserve standards and to find out what the cuts will mean, especially in vulnerable areas such as learning support and affordable after-school provision.

School Wars
By Bryony Hegarty, Winter 2011 (50)

A short walk away from Clapton Girls School (one of Hackney's most recent converts to academy status) author, journalist and campaigner Melissa Benn spoke at Pages of Hackney bookshop on Lower Clapton Road, about the current changes in education and her book *School Wars*.

Education is an issue central to all our lives, be it our own experiences, or how we plan to educate the next generation. Nothing seems to challenge our principles quite so effectively as the choices (or lack thereof) to be made over our children's education. In modern times, the issue of state education has been a hugely divisive issue. Some parents have had an easier choice than others, depending on if you happened to be in an area of the country with poor local schools or within walking distance of several high-achieving secondaries (reflected in the prices of property around schools).

In certain areas of the country, supposedly rational, educated adults, have found themselves lying on admission forms, using false addresses, moving out of their large houses in down-at-heel areas to squash into tiny flats in 'better postcodes' near higher-ranking schools, during the application process. Others have turned to the Church to secure places for their children in 'Faith Education', thus further draining a representational balance in local schools. These actions have seen one adult judging another for setting a poor example to their children through deceit or hypocrisy, with the frequent riposte that for the sake of one's children's education it was justifiable; with the return accusations made to the parent perceived to be 'braving the local school', as caring less about their child.

biggest changes in our school system since the post war creation of the Grammar /Secondary modern model, in one year in power, with the move towards the 'charter' model and franchising at the same time as we've witnessed the failures of the City.

In conversation with Gareth Evans, Melissa Benn tracked the history of post-war education, and discussed the Academy and Free Schools programme, opening the debate to the floor. Issues around the ethos of the new models were discussed in terms of educational environment, access and exclusivity. Naturally, the changes in Hackney were central to the conversation. The creation of new schools and conversion of existing ones now means that N16 is the only corner of the borough to have a community school, Stoke Newington School. While Mossbourne Academy is hailed as a national success story, interestingly the two schools have similar academic results, and as was acknowledged during the discussion, a lot of 'good practice' that has been implemented, such as individual tracking of students, is not intrinsically linked to Academy status.

While we are worrying about the arrival of another Sainsbury's in the neighbourhood, 'chain store education' is becoming a reality, with sponsors such as Co-op and the Christian ULT (with a number of its academies having been judged inadequate), ARK and Harris Federation. One issue that this debate flags up is that, while so many politicians and policy makers continue to educate their children privately, they simply don't have the vested interest in creating the best system possible.

From this situation one can see how the first of the Academy schools introduced by New Labour sold well as a concept to parents who wanted a decent education for their children and could not or, on principle, chose not, to pay for education. New buildings and promises of enhanced funding appeared to hail the dawning of a new era – although, to many, the 'incentives' to convert seemed a little too good to be true, and in practice money pledged was not always handed over. Hackney is at the heart of the education debate, having transformed from a borough with failing schools and too few places in secondary education to accommodate its children (notably school places for boys), to a thriving centre of education. The new model has been pushed through here at great speed.

In *School Wars*, Melissa Benn digs beneath the veneer of the story and gives an overview of how we have come to this point and where we may be going. The book charts education from the post-War era to today, and examines how we now find ourselves in the clutches of a new model which has been put into practice before widespread awareness and understanding of its implications have filtered through the general public. Academies and Free Schools are now, in law, the model for state education. As Benn points out, the current government, with no mandate, made the

In Brief

Regular users of Stoke Newington Library will be missing a familiar face behind the counter from this month, as Odoligie Ogiemwonyi (better known – by his choice – as Fred) returns to his native Nigeria, to assume his hereditary title of Enogie (Chief) of Oben. After working for the Hackney Library Service for 14 years, Fred had a duty to return to his people after the death of his father, to oversee (with a Council of Elders) an area the size of Hackney. His priority on arrival is water. Makes a change from stamping books. His colleagues and the piles of books awaiting his usual careful attention will also miss him. He would have liked to have taken the Benin bronzes in the British Museum back home too, but that's another story. His coronation is in July. Hail to the Chief.

The paradox that is Stoke Newington was vividly illustrated on Saturday 17 July. At the western end of Church Street the Stoke Newington Village Fete was taking place. An enterprising, entertaining and community-oriented day out in Clissold Park – featuring chess and backgammon tournaments, stalls selling local produce and proclaiming the virtues of local organisations and businesses, a kids' Tai Chi competition and a hot air balloon (no doubt fuelled by the energy emanating from local public houses) – were some of the many attractions on offer. Forget the postal code and you could have been in rural Berkshire. At the other end of the street, meanwhile, a very different scene was unfolding. The police had sealed off the High Street after a serious stabbing only a few hours before the Fete began. So which is the real Stoke Newington?

N16 believes that Stoke Newington is generally a pleasant place to live, where the various communities appreciate and tolerate each other's culture, behaviour and lifestyle, and where people make an effort to get along together. There are exceptions to this, but exceptions prove the rule. However, it is salutary – even if it has to take a senseless and brutal attack with a knife – to be reminded that we live in the inner city, with all its attendant problems (to underline this, last month police armed response cars screeched into Church Street when two kids were seen to be carrying guns, which turned out to be fakes). There is a tendency to self-congratulation in Stoke Newington, and *N16* is not blameless in promoting this. But we should remember that we are not exactly under the editorial scrutiny of *Country Life*. Be careful out there.

It's been a bad few months in Stoke Newington. Mohammed Iqbal, one of the brothers who run the Shaheen Superstore on the High Street, lost his life in a car crash and the front of the store was immediately covered in tributes. Sunny Crackmell was savagely attacked in Upper Street and died from his injuries. Balloons were released in his memory in Clissold Park. And earlier this month Brendan Kirby, ex-landlord of Steptoe's, died unexpectedly in Phnom Penh, Cambodia.

Stoke Newington resident Tjinder Singh and his band Cornershop had a massive hit back in 1997 with 'Brimful of Asha'. It looks like he's going to repeat the success with Cornershop's latest single, 'Topknot', selected by the *Observer Music Monthly* as Song of the Month. The mag labelled them 'one of England's greatest bands' and described the single as 'a genuinely beautiful take on Punjabi folk, backdropped by a loping funk beat and breathtakingly lovely guitar ... the perfect sonic antidote to a summer dominated by the fat meatheads waving the flag of St George and the sad jingoistic success of Ukip.'

So according to the *Observer Magazine*, 21 November, Stoke Newington is the Best Place in Britain To Be A Parent, and has the UK's largest number of babies per capita. This was attributed to our 'strong, child-friendly Mediterranean atmosphere' and an influx of 'young Bohemian types'. No mention was made of the 25,000 strong Hasidic community who are not known for their unwillingness to raise large families and must help to skew the statistics. A local resident was also quoted in the article as saying (and this does appear to be irony-free): 'A visit down Church Street on a Saturday is a must, just to see all the three-wheeler buggies.' *N16* was so moved by this revelation that we have decided to launch a Three-Wheeler Buggy Appreciation Society. We will also investigate the cultural habits of their owners, such as the need to walk side by side up one of the narrowest pavements in North London, forcing pedestrians onto the road to overtake them and risk being squashed by a psychotic bendybus. And also why they beam at little Milo and Chloe when the little darlings scream at a thousand decibels in local restaurants and cafes, while strapped into the iconic machines.

Listeners to BBC Radio 4's 'Open Book' last month will have been amused to hear Stoke

Newington Library staff discuss items found in returned books. Apart from the obvious – bookmarks – other items cited included travel cards, bacon rind, a razor blade, £150 rent money (safely returned) and a snapshot of a naked man in an obvious state of excitement. Not returned, as the borrower could not be identified – his head was cropped out of the picture.

More on the *Observer's* article last November about Stoke Newington being 'the best place in Britain to be a parent'. 'Urban Fox', the *Times* Online Correspondent wrote the following: 'My own obsessive property disorder makes me think, wrongly, that this is the kind of write-up that will have all residents gloating and calling the estate agents at dawn to see how fast local property prices have shot up overnight. Not to mention Hackney Council opening the champagne to congratulate itself on so successfully drawing in a relatively wealthy demographic in a poor part of town and keeping them so happy.' Fair enough, but the downside is 'There are no secondary schools here', the disgruntled residents chorus. 'Or none where your children might pass exams.' When the first child in a family turns 11, 'the whole family moves away.' What's wrong with the fast improving Stoke Newington School?

An alarming beer mat has appeared in the Rochester Castle, courtesy of the Metropolitan Police. All in black, it bears the legend 'Relax, enjoy your drink. No one in this pub can tell you're a wife beater'. On the flip side it threatens 'we will arrest you immediately' and 'we will track you down'. While *N16* certainly does not condone violence against women (or, with certain exceptions, men, for that matter), the offensive assumption is that all male drinkers are also potential wife beaters. Is this beer mat to be found in some of the hipper West End wine bars? Or in police staff canteens?

Stories have been appearing in the Press recently about the possibility of the Orthodox Jewish community in Stamford Hill moving elsewhere. *N16* asked Rabbi Herschey Gluck, from the Walford Road Synagogue, if there was any truth in this. He replied: 'Owing to the scarcity of affordable housing in the Borough and the many young families coming on stream, we have been looking into options further afield, including Milton Keynes and Thames Gateway. These options are at the drawing board stage. We are certainly not considering relocating the community, just facilitating and catering for the needs of a growing community.' So it appears that one of London's most interesting and distinctive communities will be remaining with us in Stoke Newington for some while yet.

Newcomers are increasingly the lifeblood of Stoke Newington, but it's encouraging to discover that some people have deeper ties to the area. Frances Rickford, who lives in Alkham Road and is editor of *Learning Support Magazine* aimed at support staff in primary schools, contacted us about her family's history in Stoke Newington. Her children are at least the fifth generation of her family to live here. Her great grandparents ran an ice-cream parlour in the 1890s where the chemist shop now stands at the junction of Green Lanes and Church Street, and her grandmother and her sisters used to churn the ice cream on the pavement to sell to people coming out of Clissold Park. Another set of great-grandparents lived in Albion Road at the turn of the century, making artificial flowers. Her grandparents were married at St Mary's in 1914, and her great uncle died in the First World War – his name is on the war memorial in the Library and Frances has a postcard he sent from the Front to his family, who then lived in Queen Elizabeth Walk. Frances's mother Betty was born here in 1920 and christened at St Mary's. She and her parents moved to Palmers Green when Betty was a child, and Frances knew nothing about the link with Stokey until after she moved here with her partner from Islington in 1986. Both her daughters have grown up here, attending Jubilee and Grazebrook Primary Schools and Stoke Newington School.

We spotted on TV at the end of October local librarian Richard Boon (he dropped the 'e' – his joke), aka N16 Fringe's very own MC Ricky B. Richard, a regular contributor to *N16*, was on the box by virtue of his career in the late 1970s as Buzzcocks manager, and he was a talking head (and hat) in a programme on the band The Fall, fronted by his old mate Mark E Smith, a colourful and somewhat outspoken character. As Richard reminisced (with some authority and perception), it was not hard to perceive a sense of nostalgia for those heady days of Manchester punk. Never mind, Richard, the Fringe will soon be back.

Local cryptic crossword solvers will have been amused by a clue in Wednesday, 15 February's 2006 puzzle in the *Guardian*. It is as follows: 'Speaking first to boy at college, being interrupted by footballer from a London suburb (5,9)'. This is not a difficult clue to solve. Can you work it out?

Arts and Drama

N16 *has always covered drama and the arts, in the form of both listings and reviews, from the Hackney Empire and Arcola to local productions and galleries. We have space here for only a very small number of contributions over the years. However, n16mag.com is constantly being updated with all the latest artistic happenings and events. Make sure that you visit the website and there will almost certainly be something for you.*

Hackney Shed
By Richard Boon, Summer 2004 (22)

They brought the house down. Twice. On two sold-out, standing-room (and ovation) only nights at the Boilerhouse Theatre, Stoke Newington School, 52 young members of Hackney Shed theatre group performed their version of the Broadway musical *Annie*. This landmark performance celebrated the third anniversary of the group and was its most ambitious project to date, involving children not only on stage, but in all aspects of production, from front of house to props and make-up, through to the technicalities of lights and sound. Having previously written and performed several musicals including *Thumbelina*, *The Silver Sword* and *The Grinch* and, in June 2002, contributed to performances in the Mall marking the Golden Jubilee, this was the group's first venture into Broadway theatre.

Formed in January 2001 as an outreach project of the Chicken Shed Theatre Company, the group's stated aim is 'to provide an exciting, relaxed and informal atmosphere for children and young people in the Hackney/ Stoke Newington area to come together and produce theatre'. Run on an entirely voluntary basis, Hackney Shed holds term-time workshops for young people from the ages of 7 to 16 – at which later age, while still able to attend, members are encouraged to become 'practitioners', assuming more responsibility and taking a leadership and guidance role for younger members.

The founding principle of the Chicken Shed Theatre Company is that theatre should be an experience available to all, regardless of ability, in a culture that equally embraces young people with special needs and the able bodied. All are seen as being capable of making a contribution. One of the Hackney Shed's coordinators, Nic Harris, explains the group's central 'inclusive environment': 'We aim to provide a safe and stimulating space for children and young people to work creatively using drama, music and dance. Chicken Shed's ethos is our backbone and Hackney Shed sets out to be non-exclusive, enabling children from all social, economic and educational backgrounds to achieve their full potential, helping each other to produce great results.'

While children's theatre has lately become a growth area for aggressive commercialism, the Shed's approach demands commitment from all. Nic continues, '*Annie* was a great testament to the massive effort of everyone involved to really put Hackney Shed on the map. We will begin again with a new project in September and are always receptive to new members – adults and children. Anyone with an interest in helping with the sessions – choreographers, musicians, drama practitioners, or behind- the-scenes with sewing, set- design or administration – is very welcome.' And as for the brought-down house, given that the capacity crowd consisted mainly of proud parents, siblings and friends of the cast and crew, at *Annie's* conclusion there was not a dry eye in it.

Saturday Night Empire
By Helen Griffiths, Spring 2005 (25)

Five stand-up acts and a compere at the beautifully refurbished Hackney Empire for a tenner on a Saturday night. Just brilliant. Russell Brand hosted the evening admirably. A loud, gangly and very physical presence, with a delivery bizarrely redolent of Michael Crawford in his incarnation as Frank Spencer, Brand nevertheless managed to be oddly endearing. His guilt regarding his onanistic indulgences in front of his cat struck a chord with much of the audience.

Ed Byrne was by far the funniest act of the evening. His act included some fairly typical, albeit very funny, spleen venting on the subjects of George W Bush, the voting American public and the smoking ban in Northern Ireland. However, his true genius lay in proving exactly why it's a terrible idea to have a relationship with a comedian. The vitriol he directed at his apparently shallow and vacant ex-girlfriend was evil and twisted, bitter and brilliant.

I found the quiet and deliberate delivery of Arthur Brown a little too stark, a juxtaposition to the exuberance of the first three acts. The audience were fairly raucous by then and it was difficult to get them to appreciate this shift. I think, given his fame and standing, he would have opened the evening well, and Kerry Godliman could have been spared the slightly shaky start she had when the audience weren't quite so responsive. Both she and Rhod Gilbert shone, however, and it seems likely that they may well be two more very famous graduates of the Hackney Empire School of Comedy before too long. Alastair McGowan, the headline act, is committed to raising the profile of the Empire and ensuring its success in its newly refurbished incarnation. His seamless transition through the familiar repertoire of scathing impersonations of the rich and famous is truly remarkable on a bare stage devoid of the make-up and props of the TV version. And his impression of Eddie Izzard was inspired.

Bryony Hegarty became N16 *Magazine's Arts Editor in early 2011, and her reviews of local drama, music and art have quickly become a regular feature of the magazine. Here are some edited examples of her reviews.*

Anna Karenina
By Bryony Hegarty, Spring 2011 (47)

Nabokov described Leo Tolstoy as 'a robust man with a restless soul, who all his life was torn between his sensual temperament and his supersensitive conscience'. In Helen Edmundson's stage adaptation of his classic novel *Anna Karenina*, Anna describes her affair with the Count Vronsky as 'shameful, rapturous and frightening'. The production captures the essence of Tolstoy's characters in an ambitious piece of physical theatre from a talented young troupe of performers. Director Max Webster gives a contemporary reflection on the human propensity to succumb to powerful desires that, when pursued, will become our downfall.

Webster's conceptions are funny, dark, moving and do not shy from exploring fear and the power of desire. Staged with little set, the main props are chairs, which are used to evoke train journeys, love-making and dance, in skilled and impressive choreography, inevitably reminiscent of Theatre de Complicité, given

Webster's association with the company and his training with Jacques Lecoq. There is an imagined dialogue throughout the piece between the characters Levin (believed to be a self-portrait of Tolstoy) and Anna (whose lives are connected but not intertwined) as, following separate paths, they seek happiness, love, and the meaning of life. A microphone is used to signal these communications, which I didn't find an entirely successful device. The first act is a fast-paced portrayal leading up to the heady heights of Anna's love affair; comic interlude comes in the dramatisation of a scene at the races, where Elizabeth Twells moves from being Anna to become Vronsky's horse 'Frou Frou', and later in the 'cardboard cutout' evocation of Vronsky, as Ann tries in vain to get him out of her mind. Andy Rush is a convincing Vronsky. The Company sustains the momentum of this highly energetic performance through her descent into desperation.

The stream of sound includes original compositions, electronica, Peter Sarstedt, Bob Dylan, and features live music from the performers. This shrouds the piece in a timeless framework, and gives the reeling sensation of Anna's transition from dutiful wife and mother to the woman who must live, love and ultimately die. The presence of a hooded figure in Anna's mind the 'dark omen' who visits her, entwined with her deep and passionate longing for fulfillment is disturbing and dramatically powerful.

Expanding on straight choices for women of duty and unhappiness, versus scandal and sacrifice, Edumdson emphasises three strands of female experience in Dolly (Sophie Waller) the betrayed, lonely wife, Anna who gives in to desire and its consequences, and Kitty (Maryann O'Brien,) both heartbroken and heartbreaker for whom love with Levin is ultimately fulfilled.
Anna Karenina was presented at the Arcola Theatre

Nae Wimmin, Nae Cry
By Bryony Hegarty, Spring 2011 (47)

'That man to man, the world o'er shall brithers be for a' that', wrote Robert Burns in his poem 'A Man's A Man for A' That, considered to be Burn's supreme expression of egalitarianism and a forerunner of 18th-century liberalism. Two centuries later, Bob Marley went on to write: 'One Love, One Heart, Let's get together and feel all right'.

'Two Bob One Love' is an annual event, inspired by a great Scot and a great Jamaican, with the aim of breaking down cultural barriers and celebrating two of the world's most prolific poets, whose birthdays fall within weeks of one another: Burns 25th January, Marley 6 February. The event is the brainchild of Stoke Newington-based Scottish DJ Steve Clark. Last year's inaugural event won the support of Benjamin Zephaniah, Denis Bovell and JC Carroll. For 2011, the line-up featured poets, musicians, a music biographer, soap opera stars, Jerk Haggis and rum and whisky shots.

Clark exudes a warm Celtic welcome as he greets us at the door with a wee dram to get the night off to a good start. He is resplendent in tartan and bearded for a final few hours before loosing his whiskers, all in the name of swelling the coffers. As the bar filled, and those attending seated themselves, proceedings commenced in traditional fashion with the Selkirk Grace from Clark; Gary Fairfull the Shoreditch poet and bon-viveur, of Found legend, addressed the Haggis. Following on after the 'Toast to the Lassies' from Colin Levy, the 'Toast to the Laddies' came from Nicola Duffet and Claire Perkins on flamboyant form, Duffet giving a cockney element to the proceedings to great comic effect. Jerk Haggis was not just a novel concept but decent fusion cuisine and disappeared off plates. It was followed by an equally popular Jamaican Rum Cake.

Journalist and writer Chris Salewicz read from his book *Bob Marley: The Untold Story*, regaling a tale of time he spent with Marley in Jamaica, and Marley's support of young political activist Michael Bernard. Numbered among the musicians the Jambila Music Band, set things in motion with mellow rhythms. Bringing an air of Gallic sophistication to the evening was Barbara Alcindor (of French Affair and Groove Armada). There cannot have been an uninspired soul in the house by the end of the Two Bob One Love night.

A Doll's House
By Bryony Hegarty, Summer 2011 (48)

Nora is the 'doll' her bank manager husband talks down to, the coquette who panders to his indulgences. But, internally, she holds a secret with steely pride: she borrowed money when her husband was ill and now repays the debt out of what she can spare from the housekeeping. As she is threatened with exposure, and then faces her husband's threat to remove their children from her care in the wake of such scandalous revelation, Nora's self awareness becomes heightened and she draws radical conclusions.

With a surrealist set, Greek chorus and piercing sound design, Alex Crampton's production of Ibsen's A Doll's House focuses intently on externalising expression of Nora's inner turmoil. The evocation of her children in the drama through puppetry both concentrates the child-parent communications and adds a quirky extra dimension to the piece, again accentuating the focus on her mental anguish. The choreographed dance element to this very physical production is largely played out through the chorus. The set design by Irina Borisova has the symbolism of domestic bliss literally suspended just out of reach. This is a beautifully performed production which teases out all the nuances of Nora's 'confined' existence, from her husband's view of her as woman child, to her concealment of responsibility through play and manipulation. Yet, ultimately while a highly enjoyable evening, Nora's final departure lacked the sense of enormity it entails. The banging of her front door as she heads into the unknown was said to send reverberations across Europe in 1879. The exit made

here seems a little light-handed.
Ibsen's A Doll's House was presented at the Arcola

Local Artist
By Bryony Hegarty, Summer 2011 (48)

The L-13 gallery is an independent, contemporary art space that 'seeks to reinvigorate and subvert pre- conceived ways in which art is considered and produced, blurring the distinctions between art production and exhibition. 'The combination of Stoke Newington artist, musician and writer (as well as N16 contributor) Pete Bennett, with New York-based painter, Jeanine Guidi, curated by Billy Childish at L-13, was an engaging concoction.

With a watercolour effect (so often the domain of soft, washy landscape), Pete Bennett paints suggestively, projecting big urban evocations and representation of idea and feeling over literalism. Grand scale
graphic markings, and line drawings in colour pencil that abstract but evoke form. Guidi's moody-blue, smudged, feminine and carnal explorations co-exist in harmony. A number of her works are untitled bold/naïve images that speak for themselves. The artists' catalogues offer a link between the characters and their creations. Bennett is introduced by Peter Doig, commenting on the intense and 'painterly' quality of his work and his early inspirations from 'Pac Man to Braque man'. Somehow Bennett's biography, (produced on original pink, recycled paper, printed on a vintage Gestetner 360 duplicator) with his acrobatic ancestry and precarious arrival in the world, is all evoked in his 'Man Falling' series of 4 (acrylic) paintings; with the sensation captured of the void beneath one's feet, that we've all sensed in dream. Guidi's catalogue opens with a description by Billy Childish of days spent in their shared Zurich studio, as he painted happily whilst a few feet across the studio, she set fire to her canvas and chucked it out of the window into the snow. This seems a far away proposition from the work produced here.

It is refreshing to find a show that narrates ideas, art for its own sake in the fulfilment of self-expression. Tastefully, and in the spirit of anti-commercialism, there are no price tags in sight although the artists wholeheartedly deserve to sell the works, if that is their intention.

Core Arts
By Bryony Hegarty, Summer 2011(48)

In 1992 artist Paul Monks set up studio in an empty space in Hackney Hospital. With the arrival of the Homerton Hospital, and most of the old unit closed, only the psychiatric wards remained. Patients soon began visiting Monks as he worked, escaping their controlled, clinical confines and responding to the artist's environment and tools. This led to the development of initiatives to provide creative opportunities for patients at the hospital. In 1994, with Monks as director, CORE ARTS became a registered charity with a mission statement to 'use the arts to break down many of the prejudices associated with people with mental health problems and promote access and participation'.

Nineteen years on, the project has a diverse and multi-faceted brief, encompassing art, music, writing, horticulture, and creative business enterprise. Members come to CORE via a referral from mental health services. Within a spacious former school building, they have access to facilities such as a painting studio, pottery kiln, recording studio, and a large venue/gallery space. A number of professional artists, musicians and writers work at CORE as tutors and co-ordinators. Together with the members, they devise individually tailored creative work plans. Members, who have often initially accessed the service at a time of acute need, can go on to become volunteers helping to run the service. 80% of the trustees are currently or previously have been members. The creation of two agencies, Core Design and Core Landscapes, both of which donate their profits to CORE ARTS, has generated further funding, and has led to the employment of members of the horticulture project. There is a satisfying symmetry to the relationship where, for one particular contract, former patients are now landscaping the grounds of the Homerton Hospital.

A combination of creative innovation, good organisation and high demand seems to lie behind the success of this initiative. CORE ARTS is an organisation working at the cutting edge of community services, arts and mental health and can be regarded as a benchmark for mental rehabilitation. Current thinking in public health strategies is very much in favour of empowerment from within and individual self-motivation – rather than the imposition of a regime from the top down. CORE by its very nature and evolution and, in its unique essence, has grown organically out of an interest and demand from the mentally ill who have found self-expression and a recovery strategy, and active participation in managing the organisation. The success of the project has been achieved through integrity, not plain good intention.
Core Arts 1 St Barnabas Terrace London E9 6DJ
www.corearts.co.uk

Letters

Having lived in Stoke Newington for most of my life and worked here through my adult years, I come into daily contact with many of the locals... however it never fails to surprise and confuse me to hear the term 'village feel' used in the same sentence as the word 'stokey', though I do not wear sandals out nor do I suffer from any trendy eating disorders, such as vegetarianism. I can't help but think the lack of these character traits hinder my vision when out and about in Stoke Newington. I often ask myself if the people who live in Stoke Newington have ever been to or seen a village. I know most of them disagree with televisions but have they avoided the beautiful sights of *Postman Pat*'s village through their childhood, or never managed to catch glimpse of *Last Of The Summer Wine*'s scenery to use as a comparison? Maybe if they had, they would notice the signific ant absence of dry stone walling and sheep throughout N16, as well as realising that sofas on the corners of streets, yellow signs that say 'commercial robbery', care in the community candidates who walk about and shout at themselves, and parking restrictions don't really fit into the backdrop of a Yorkshire village, nor would a cemetery be classed as parkland. Please help me to understand and fit in!

I stumbled upon your mag and must say 'well done'. I read the Luddy Samms article (*see page 49, ed*) with a broad smile on my face and can recall the James Brown concert at the Knokke blues festival he mentioned. I too played at the Three Crowns for many years and the story of how the then tenant was treated by the police and subsequently framed but found not guilty at Crown Court was typical of a political move to shut down live music venues at that time.

There's a new beggar sitting at the Halifax cash point. Last night I tried to withdraw cash to be met with the usual chant of 'can you spare some change?' – nothing surprising so far but when I replied with 'no, I'm sorry' I was threatened with 'well I'm gonna rob the money from you instead, then'. Feeling rattled, but not standing for that kind of nonsense, I gave the chap a piece of my mind. To my astonishment, a few ill-informed and unhelpful do-gooders in the queue told me I was wrong to chastise him! What on earth is wrong with these people! Surely we should not stand for aggressive begging and threats?

I read your magazine with a mixture of awe and disbelief. Why? I left N16 in 1969 and moved to Australia in 1973. I worked in Church Street for too many years at Victory Engineers after a regulation working class upbringing in Winston Road and Albion Road Central. Note the 'Central', it was important at the time – putting it a notch or two above Frankenstein's Castle [Wordsworth Road]. Okay, getting to the major question. Where do all these customers for this plethora of culinary delights come from? If they are not within walking distance, where do they park? As I remember Church Street, there were about two 'raffs' in the whole street. The one nearest to our works was run by two or three large ladies of an older dynasty. They produced doorstep toast with lashings of butter and bacon sarnies. It was beautiful toast, I have to say. They had a fire going and pushed the toast onto the grill at the front, giving it a lovely smokey flavour. I am dead serious when I say, how can these raconteurs spout on about their glorified fish and chips costing only £47.20 per meal. If it is any tastier than the F&C on Albion Parade in the old days, I'll eat someone's hat. And for variety, how about Pie and Mash from Cook's in the High Street. Not forgetting the liquor mixed with a generous helping of vinegar. I admit the pies were a little dodgy. It was rumoured that some of the meat was horse. That never bothered me at at the time – I thought most of the gee gees I wagered on were better off in a pie. Before I go – don't let them do anything to the 73. Some of my fondest memories as a kid, were sitting on the wall opposite the bank at Newington Green and counting the caravan of buses emerging through the snot green fog. Maybe the record might be broken! I have a suggestion for London Transport. Forget the bloody bendy buses. If they must have a change, bring back the good

old solid tram. Good for the tourists and the raffs. When the pole comes off the wire, everybody can get off for an aperitif or something. Unfortunately, it is too late for the ladies with the toast to make a come back – they have been serving tea and ambrosia toast in the Elysian Fields Olde Cafe for a long time now.
Bert F. Errington, Queensland, Australia

It was with regret that I read about the closure of Totem Records in Issue 24. It was the first shop I entered on Church Street when I moved to the area in 1998. Much of my record collection originated in those crowded racks. Much time was spent searching for items to spend my wages on and I was never disappointed. And if Tony or anyone else is wondering, I still haven't managed to shift that collection of early 1960s Electronica. Totem will be sorely missed, even from the other side of the world.
Toby Roberts, Sydney, New South Wales, Australia

I also read the piece on the closing of Totem Records. Unfortunately, those behind Totem Records were, I believe, responsible for their own demise. The owner and his staff were usually quite rude and uncooperative, and the records over-priced (and he wouldn't allow you to listen to them!). What does he expect if he lives up to the stereotype 'grumpy-record shop owner- who-can't-be-bothered'? He also made the mistake of not stocking at least a handful of the latest releases, something which another new record shop in the area should do. I'm a completely devoted vinyl addict and of course it's sad to see

a record shop close, but I used to go into Totem regularly and I'm not surprised it shut. Don't moan about rents going up – think about your own attitude to your customers!

I first moved into London (N5) in '97 and then N16 in '99. I am going to SW5 during this summer to be nearer my young family. The fucking up of the Coach & Horses, the presence of things like Fresh & Wild, the odd Hoxton twat, and the absence of Totem Records and a decent den of iniquity I could handle. Now there are joggers... JOGGERS, people. I saw a bottle blonde who looked as though she had bathed in Cambell's cream of tomato soup the other day. The transient nature of the population has always provided me with entertainment of all kinds and sated my appetites. I do believe that now is the time to go, because the efforts to change the area into Crouch End will backfire and you will end up with a second-hand Wood Green.

I should like to make a comment about your article about Chomsky (*issue 25*). You quote without comment: '...international terrorist network... it was Taiwan, Israel... that's a kind of international terror network...' This is a strange comment to make at a time when your own life is being threatened by enemies of Israel. It sounds more like the kind of antisemitism used by Hitler, Ford etc when they wrote about the menace of the International Jew. I am sorry that you do not like Israel, but how does mindless hatred help anybody?
Charles Heller, Toronto, Canada

What I would like to know, but suspect it will be consigned to the 'one of life's little mysteries' category, is how long it takes to put up (or move) a bus shelter. I am referring firstly to the one that was once at the bus stop near Stoke Newington station, but that one day, suddenly, wasn't. It disappeared overnight (at least a year ago now) and, I fear, will never be seen again. I have written to Transport for London several times, who informed me that they were moving the site of the stop (to accommodate bendy buses) and that, as soon as that was done - it involved Hackney Council doing some prior road works - the shelter would be re-erected. Well, it took HC months to get round to the work (quelle surprise!) but now it has been done and we await the shelter. And have been awaiting the shelter for months. Actually, even the temporary bus stop has now disappeared and passengers stand vaguely around where a bus stop once was and shelter might one day be. As I write this, the sun is pouring down, but all-too-soon it will be the rain and wind and winter. Are we to be abandoned to the elements for ever?

'The Lottery Project From Hell'

The Clissold Leisure Centre debacle stands as an example of crass incompetence and mismanagement by all involved in the saga, a shambles on a scale never again likely to be matched in Hackney. From the initial estimate of around £12 million in 1998, the final cost, when the building finally opened for good in late 2007, was £45 million. Local author, journalist and lecturer Ken Worpole (www.worpole.net) presided over the whole sorry affair for N16 Magazine in these four articles.

J'Acuzzi
Spring 2000 (5)

As the scaffolding and security fences slowly come down on the site of the gleaming new Clissold Leisure Centre, the gasps are not so much of admiration, but of 'Why so long?' and 'How much?'

The saga of the new Clissold Leisure Centre – whose opening date, now a year and a half overdue, is still uncertain – has been surrounded by a wall of silence equal to that of the Kremlin in its worst years. Hackney Council claims that an ongoing dispute with the contractors prevents it from making any public statement on either costs or timetable. Sport England, declining to comment on these matters, simply asserted that Sport England's contractual agreements with the Council are 'not in the public domain'. And in an article in the Architects Journal on 9 March 2000, the architects responsible bluntly refused to discuss the financial problems of Clissold Leisure Centre, saying, 'We do not want to fuel further rumour about this issue'. Strange, therefore, to remember that Hackney Council insisted at the outset that 'the success of the Clissold Leisure Centre depends upon the active participation of local people in the project.' Go figure.

Meanwhile the District Auditor has sharply criticised Hackney Council in his annual report for allowing Clissold Leisure Centre to overspend by an astonishing £10.6m, which, given that originally the centre was only going to cost £10m (£13m by the time the contract was signed), seems to indicate serious mismanagement somewhere. Rumour has it that the total bill is now approaching £21 million, half of which will have to be found from Hackney council tax payers, by cutting other services, and selling off more of the family silver. Things, then, couldn't be worse, or could they? Another rumour has it that despite being intended to be self-financing in revenue terms – because of all the state of the art fitness equipment, squash courts, sauna and jacuzzi rooms for hire at commercial rates, as well as the two swimming pools – in fact it will need further subsidy, if it is to fulfil its community obligations. It is worth remembering that the Council's own leisure strategy stated that it operated in a socioeconomic climate characterised by:

'high levels of unemployment... high levels of social exclusion among young people... high levels of poverty restricting opportunities to purchase leisure services'. But where is this money to come from? Clissold Leisure Centre has become a financial albatross around Hackney Council's neck, into which it has to keep pouring money in order to get the wretched thing finished. Several Hackney councillors have told me that it is like a great gaping hole into which council money is poured by the lorry load, but which never seems to fill up.

As a result, massive cuts are being made across the board across all services, causing collateral damage on an unprecedented scale. Hackney Council, it seems, is having to decimate Hackney's many long-standing arts and leisure services in order to save a prestige new lottery project which will almost certainly be handed over to a commercial operator to run. The irony of this scenario is not lost on an increasing number of local people. One unhappy effect of the Council's continuing political in-fighting and corporate mis-management has been to set different parts of the borough against each other. The Haggerston Pool Community Action

more able to handle outside contracts any better than it can manage its own services: 'Like many other authorities, Hackney is increasingly outsourcing its services as well as entering partnership arrangements with outside agencies. Whilst such methods can lead to improvements in service delivery it is vital that those commissioning services have the required expertise to specify properly and then manage the contract with the outside providers; this is often not the case at Hackney.' There is no doubt that, once finally opened, Clissold Leisure Centre will be a landmark building and a wonderful facility. Yet over £20 million of public money has now been spent bringing it to fruition, only with the likelihood that it will be handed over to a commercial operator before it has even opened. The time has come, surely, for the Ombudsman to join the District Auditor for a bracing dip.

Not Waving but Drowning
Spring 2001 (9)

The public has now been told that the cost of the new Clissold Leisure Centre is currently running at £26.7 million – and still incomplete – even though the original estimate was in the region of £11 million. More than that, the building is now two years late, and people are still impatiently waiting to breathe that elusive smell of chlorine, damp swimming costumes and wet paint. They are advised not to hold their breath, as the opening date is being deferred yet again at the time of going to press.

'Never apologise, never explain', is the watchword of political life today. Those with long memories may recall that when the project was announced, Hackney Council proclaimed that 'The success of the Clissold Leisure Centre depends upon the active participation of local people in the project.' However, although jointly funded by Hackney Council and the Sport England Lottery Unit (both public bodies), the long history of mis-management and financial incompetence surrounding the building of the Leisure Centre has been conducted in total secrecy. The latest report on this sorry saga was presented to the Council's Policy and Finance Executive Committee on 26 February, but was declared to be an 'exempt item', to be discussed only when the public were excluded. So much for open government.

Group claims that the need to bale out Clissold Leisure Centre was responsible for the abrupt closure of the well-known and well-loved Haggerston Baths (now to be re-opened again after packed protest meetings and day and night campaigning). The fact is that today the destinies of all of Hackney's leisure centres are linked. On 1 July the Council is likely to contract out the management of all of the Council's leisure facilities to a commercial operator, chosen as a result of competition. It is assumed that the operator will have to find the capital investment needed to bring Haggerston and the others up to scratch, although of course it will have the showcase Clissold Leisure Centre, presumably handed to it on a plate.

It is unlikely that Hackney's present Leisure Centre budget is very much more than that needed to cover the returns on the capital investment which might be needed to be made by the new operator. Which leaves the crucial question as yet unanswered: where is the money to come from to underwrite the non-commercial uses of these crucial local health and sports facilities? As the District Auditor's most recent report on the Council's abysmal finances notes, the Council is no

More than that, the building is now two years late. The question as to who will manage it, according to what kinds of pricing and concessionary policies, remains completely in the dark. The chances are that this new Centre, wholly financed by public money, will be handed over to the private sector to run once it has been completed. A Council which once prided itself upon its social vision has become just another economic basket-case, selling off as many public assets as it can, wholly – and rightly in Hackney's case – one has to concede convinced of its inability to finance, manage or run any kind of service efficiently or successfully. Not waving, but drowning.

A Flume with a View
Winter 2001 (12)

Well over two years behind schedule, and possibly £16 million over budget, it looks as though Stoke Newington swimmers will be getting their feet wet soon. Hackney Council staff are now adamant that the pools will be open in February 2002, even though the rest of the centre will not come onstream for a few months after.

The private contractor franchised to run all of Hackney's leisure centres, Leisure Connections, are now doing the final fitting out. Has it been worth the wait? The natural light in the main pool is wonderful, and so are many of the sightlines and vistas as you move around the building. The Centre includes two pools, a dance studio, several gym areas, squash courts, sauna, catering areas, and probably much else, though on my visit an air of suspicion towards all 'strangers' in the building, made me keep my questions to a minimum. What is perhaps the most astonishing thing about this new building is that it seems three times as big on the inside as it does on the outside, so much so that you wonder if you will ever actually visit all its spaces and facilities in a single day.

Only the most mean-spirited critic would fail to praise the skill involved in designing these expansive flows of space and volume on such a relatively small site. First impressions count, and there is no doubt that the architects, Hodder Associates, have designed to impress the world (if not the local residents who have had to foot the bill). Clissold Leisure Centre is already being talked up as representing a new era in swimming pool design, and expect to see a trail of visiting dignitaries from the architectural and sports press beating their way to the door to praise this beautiful building. Nobody on first entering the large, airy spaces of the reception area, cafe and main pool can fail to be uplifted by the sheer spaciousness of the whole complex. The centre is, if nothing else, a triumphant exercise in steel, glass, natural light and cool precision. Serious swimmers and keep-fit fanatics will love it; others, particularly families with young children, may find it slightly intimidating.

But it does not feel child-friendly. One suspects that the, blue plastic flume (children's water slide) was resisted by the architect, and only put in under duress. It seems totally out of keeping with the austere, clinical architecture of the rest of the spaces and fittings: rather like finding a bouncy castle in the entrance of the Tate Modern. The flume itself is almost vertical and ends in a small pool no larger than a cattle trough, and there is no baby pool or paddling pool, unless I am mistaken. You can see some problems arising as young children (and their carers) begin to realise that this centre is not really for them. The training pool, which functions equally

as the women's pool on occasions when there is a need for segregated bathing for the Orthodox Jewish and Muslim communities, has been surrounded with opaque glass to allow total privacy. This gives it an austere, almost chilling, atmosphere, lightened only by the elegant Swiss railway clock (often favoured by minimalist architects). One wonders how long staff will be able to resist the temptation to add a few indoor plants and playpens to offset this attitude of architectural high seriousness, which borders on clinical depression?

This is probably very good architecture indeed, but that is not quite the point. Is it appropriate to the needs of the particular community in which it has been built? Remember that Stoke Newington is in the midst of an extraordinary baby boom, as the teeming crowds in the children's playground in Clissold Park confirm. Yet this is not a 'community facility' so much as a high-level sports facility, which Sport England – in its typical colonialist mentality – may feel that this part of London needs. Certainly they have never replied to any of my phone calls asking about the degree of community consultation which went into the project.

Some Hackney residents I have spoken to feel that four cheaper pools spread around the borough and focused more on school and family use would have been a more equitable way of spending the very large sum of money spent on this flagship building. The other architectural oddity appears to be that the designers have chosen to make a feature of the glass lift, which is immediately visible as you enter the Centre. Glass lifts are part of the design vocabulary of shopping malls and corporate headquarters, but in a low-rise community facility they are principally there to allow older or disabled people to access all areas. Yet the use of glass makes the users of the lifts a public spectacle; some, indeed many, may prefer otherwise.

All new buildings have teething problems, but it will be interesting to see how the public responds to this bold but severe design. This is given most other leisure facilities and amenities in Hackney have developed a 'leisure aesthetic' of blu-tack, amateur posters, balloons, equal opportunities statements, and lots of babyfriendly and family-friendly programmes. This, however, could be like walking into a hi-tech corporate HQ, monitored by the style police and staffed by laboratory staff dressed in white.

Broken windows, shattered dreams
April 2004 (21)

Walk down Clissold Road past the recently opened – and even more recently closed – Clissold Leisure Centre, and you will notice that already three of the large glazed panels at the front of the building have been smashed and now covered over with corrugated iron.

An official communication from the Mayor posted in the doorway suggests that the Centre may be closed for a long time, while disputes about whose fault this failed building ultimately rests with are resolved, and money is found to have the centre refurbished and made safe for use again. However, as any street-smart citizen will tell you, leave a few windows broken in a building like this for more than a week or two, and vandalism begins to spin out of control. This is the 'broken window syndrome', beloved of criminologists, who tell you that failing to fix the most minor of acts of vandalism means that, pretty soon, 'there goes the neighbourhood'. Clissold Leisure Centre, once described by its architect as 'a catalyst for regeneration', opened in February 2002, two years' late and massively over budget. It was subsequently forced to close its doors in November 2003 owing to multiple faults and building design problems which made it unsafe to manage as a public facility. If the total cost is now agreed to be £31 million – as the notice on the door now admits – and the Sports Lottery Fund gave £10 million, then it means that Hackney residents paid a cool £21 million for a pool that was only open for 21 months and may possibly never open again.

Given that in the original budget, Hackney Council (that is to say Hackney residents) were only required to contribute around £1.5 million, and ended up having to find £21 million, then many might concur that 'we was robbed'. The scandal is now of such proportions that stories about Clissold Leisure Centre fill the national press and airwaves, as well as causing a serious amount of heart-searching in the planning and architectural magazines. Ominously, Mayor Pipe admits that the costs of making the building useable again may run into additional millions, money which the Council simply does not have. Note, too, that Sport England announced in January this year that 'Lessons have been learnt. I doubt if we will be putting more money into Clissold.' The whole sorry saga could fill volumes, but the issue that has caused most bitterness amongst local people and swimming groups is that the project has been shrouded in secrecy from start to finish. As local swimming coach Peter Cottle said in a recent local radio interview, 'We're just ignored. No-one takes any notice of us at all and no-one's been in touch with us from the council by phone or letter.' Another swimming coach, Greg McNeill, told the Guardian, that once the centre opened and faults were noticed, 'When we said all this we were called whingers.' On the same radio programme as Peter Cottle, local Tory councillor, Eric Ollerenshaw, claimed that: 'The majority of councillors have not got a clue what is going on because we are told this is in the hands of the lawyers and it is all confidential.'

Mayor Pipe was wrong when he said that many people would be disappointed by the closure. People are not disappointed so much as angry and bitter about the whole scheme – and have been from the very beginning, when it was obvious that the scale of the project was beyond the capacity of the Council, its management capabilities and budgets. Not only that, the Council's ability to deal with external contractors seems seriously at issue, and there are now rumours of a major falling out with Leisure Connection over customer refunds and other operational liabilities. A dark cloud of hopelessness about the Council's ability to deliver the kind of leisure facilities that people want, seems to have settled over the Borough, and beyond. Finding out what went wrong, attributing blame and apportioning costs, could take years, and in itself cost hundreds of thousands of pounds in legal fees. Meanwhile local needs for exercise, recreation, sport and fitness now remain unmet.

Eventually, and after much nervous anticipation, the Clissold Leisure Centre finally opened towards the end of 2007, to the relief of those who had been waiting so long that their beards were scraping along the ground. The consensus was favourable, there was little doubt that it was architecturally spectacular, and the facilities were of a high standard. Under the management of Greenwich Leisure, it appeared professionally and efficiently operated. And it's still with us, and seemingly doing good business. But it certainly was a struggle.

Did It Really Happen?

Nick Webb wrote several articles for N16 featuring imaginary memories and letters written by historical figures associated with Stoke Newington, all written in the vernacular of the times. Here is one of them. It concerns Daniel Defoe caught in a time warp on Church Street and finding himself in a 73 bus.

A miraculous tour through the District of Stoke Newington by Daniel Defoe of this Parish, Spring 2002 (13)

It was passing strange. Ensconced in The Knackered Horse Inn, scarce two hours ride by spavined nag from London, I was enjoying some Argument with MacWilliam, a fellow pamphleteer, on the vexatious Scottish question, when I found myself with a mere half pint of porter inside me falling into a gentle and then, by degrees, a profound swoon. Recovering swiftly – for since my days in Newgate, now long past following the success of my many writings, I have a gift for tolerating beer and spirits that none may equal – I found myself in a state that, even recollected in the safety of my home, my wits can barely apprehend without dread. In truth, I appeared to be on some sort of huge carriage drawn along a road of astonishing smoothness without any sign of horses. Prodigal in its use of glass, this nightmare vessel offered me the sight of the very Inn in which I had been speaking with such a masterful marshalling of Logic a moment earlier. It passed before me at a speed that doubtless would have made it hard to breathe had I been outside. Even now I recall it with terror.

Now I have always been a seeker after forbidden knowledge, but imagine my bewilderment when I beheld all around me people of many colours who at first I took to be demons so strange was their attire and so grim and woeful the expressions on their ravaged faces. So affrighted was I by this vision that I turned instead to the window; but where I expected green fields and market gardens there burst upon my sight endless rows of terraced housing, and everywhere vessels without horses roaring along at a velocity that I could scarcely credit. And behind the windows of those fell contrivances were people – people, like those in my own carriage, whose faces bore the marks of weariness and defeat as if they had been ingested alive by the devices that transported them at such unnatural speed.

Sensible to the horror of my situation but nonetheless determined that my duty as a Man of Letters was to observe all around me, the thought that pierced me to the quick was this: I must be in hell. Had the Almighty taken revenge upon me for a lifetime of Dissent? Yet somehow still the bones of the Earth seemed familiar. Was not that the rise where so many victims of the great distemper had been interred – and who was

Mr Costcutter that he should so recklessly construct a hostelry atop a plague pit? But bit by bit as my horror receded and I looked upon the shape of the land, I came to understand that I was still in Stoke Newington, but by some astonishing intervention of providence I had been carried from 1728 unto the far future.

To what a melancholy pass had society fallen! I recollected when as a boy I was introduced to the great thinker, Mr Hobbes, who impressed upon me most cogently the notion that without the fiercest imposition of Order – perhaps at the hands of an absolute monarch – mankind, left to its own devices, would degenerate to the estate of the animals. From the signs of those around me, clearly such a catastrophe had come to pass. What else could explain the variety of human life stock such as I had never witnessed before, or the maddening Babel of languages of which only the insinuating tongue spoken by the perfidious French was familiar to my ear? Had our island been invaded since the days of George the Second? In truth I have always distrusted the intentions of the Dutch and, if this essay should be found among my papers in centuries to come, I have no doubt that my suspicions will be revealed to have been well founded.

My musings on this point were interrupted, however. 'Where did you get that cool wig?' My wig had been purchased from the finest perruquier in Bond Street, but it was – like all its kind – damnably hot. 'Pardon me, Madam, are you addressing me?' The young woman on the bench in front of me had swivelled around. She was an extraordinary sight, with no wig and the short hair of a boy. In her left nostril she had inserted a jewel, possibly a small diamond. This I recognised from my investigations into the life of Andrew Selkirk, whose misfortunes became the inspiration for my most famous book, as the mark of the concubine of a chief of the Anthropopagi from the islands of the Great Southern Ocean. Despite this blemish, she was a comely wench with a saucy look of challenge in her eyes and a most immodestly tight bodice of some unknown material clinging to her body like a voluptuary friend.

'Oh,' said she, 'you're in character. Fancy dress party, is it? Who are you doing?' At this point the other woman on the bench also turned around and revealed herself to be, if anything, even more handsome. It is a truth seldom acknowledged that a man in mortal peril for his soul will often feel the urging of certain appetites, as if he could compensate for the immediate danger of extinction by an act of generation. To my surprise I found myself answering with a roguish smile: 'Why, madam, I do for any party that will pay me for my scribblings. But now I am lost and, like Vergil, I need a Beatrice to guide my spirit through this foreign land.'

The other woman, to what end I have never been able to discern, opened her cherry lips and said: 'Fruitcake.' By chance it was the random utterance of a disordered mind. God save us, I thought, perhaps we were hurtling towards some new Bedlam. 'Stylishly sustained fruitcake though', said the first woman even more mysteriously. 'Madam', said I, 'I know not about this confection to which you and your beauteous friend make reference, but I do know from my humble efforts at verisimilitude for my work, Moll Flanders, something about pleasure. Is it possible,' I lowered my voice to a discreet whisper, 'that you are gay ladies?' 'None of your business', said the nasally bejewelled woman, 'but as it happens we're proud to be gay. Do you have some problem with that?' 'No, madame, indeed not', I said. 'In fact I have a guinea in my pocket, and would be happy to get off this frantic carriage and discuss our further commerce in some private room if you could recommend one. I fear my acquaintanceship with the area may not be current.'

Readers will struggle to give credence to what happened next, but I swear to it by all that's holy. Instead of haggling with that delightful mix of concupiscence and flinty-heartedness that characterises the many charming working women of Drury Lane, this creature drew her fist and smote me with incredible force upon the chin.

Instantly I fell into an endless pool of darkness. When I awoke it was to the familiar smells of ale and pheasant pie, a pleasing speciality of The Knackered Horse, and also to the sound of my friend MacWilliam discoursing yet again on those flaws that undermine the Act of Union to the detriment of his fellow Scots. Yet every word I have set down here is the truth, and I leave it to posterity to decide if I had for a moment lost my mind or if, as I suspect, some weird mechanism had carried me through time itself.

Nick Webb: An Appreciation
By Rab MacWilliam, Summer 2012 (52)

Nick Webb's erudite, historically well researched and elaborately sustained spoofs were a feature of the magazine from 2002 till 2004. They featured such local characters as Edgar Allan Poe, Charles Dickens visiting his publisher on Church Street, Mary Shelley, a visit by William Pitt to Newington Green, King James I's stay at the Three Crowns and several others. Their apparent veracity fooled not only a few of our readers but also the Islington Gazette.

Nick Webb, who has died at the age of 63, was a regular contributor to *N16* Magazine between 2002 and 2004. He specialised in witty spoof articles, supposedly composed by historical figures linked to Stoke Newington, such as Daniel Defoe, King James I, Edgar Allan Poe and Mary Shelley, and written in the style of their times.

I first knew Nick in the mid-1970s when we worked together in book publishing, and we kept in touch. He was an extremely clever, very funny and widely read man, and it was little surprise to me that he enjoyed a successful career in the publishing world. He was also Douglas Adams' official biographer, and the first publisher of *Hitchhiker's Guide to the Galaxy*. In recent years we used to meet at the Rose & Crown – he was a long-term resident of Albion Road – and his company was infectiously hilarious. I was shocked and saddened by his sudden death, as were all his many friends in the literary and publishing world.

Stokey Press Watch

Between Issues 28 and 37 Victor Ardern kept us informed on press coverage of our parish. Below, we reproduce some of the insights he discovered into how the national (and international) media perceive Stoke Newington.

Winter 2005 (28)

For the last three months, much of the national and international press in which the words Stoke and Newington juxtapose has included the names of former resident Ibraham Muktar Said, whom I believe recently moved to Belmarsh, South London, and Diane Abbott, who apparently is still very much in our midst.

In fact, the right honourable member for Hackney North & Stoke Newington seems to be ploughing two fertile furrows at present. One week she's one of the 49ers who, according to the *Scotsman* have caused our Tony's '3115 day reign to unravel', the next, she's telling the *Independent* that if she had three wishes she'd plump for being a 'best-selling author', being 'able to play the piano beautifully' and having 'the height and physique of a willowy Somalian beauty'. She has also opined on Mrs T's legacy at 80, and 40 years of civil rights and social inclusion. All very commendable stuff, but what about the roadworks?

The good people of N16 do seem to make excellent pulp for the weekend supplements. Apart from the usual travel pieces in which 30-something N16ers discuss the need for 'a well-run kids' club for Maisie' (*Sunday Times*), there was:
- The 'youthful British editor of *National Enquirer*' in the *Observer* who 'has traded his 3-storey period house in ST NE for a spacious loft apartment in New York's SO HO'.
-The chief executive of a major publishing empire in the *Independent* who 'prefers to take public transport from his home in Stoke Newington'. It can only be hoped that he takes the 'seventy free' as the tabloid hacks have dubbed it and not the No 393 on which, according to the *Daily Mirror*, a woman 'was taken captive by the angry driver after she asked him to stop using his mobile at the wheel'. It's all a far cry from the 1950s when, according to government papers made public last month, a chap called Joe Coral was 'for a bookmaker in Stoke Newington ... not a bad sort of fellow' (*Sunday Times*).

Church Street was accorded its usual press inches. At one end of the main artery, William Patten School saw lengthy articles from both the *Times* and the *Daily Telegraph* concerning the laudable scheme of 'sending restaurant chefs into school kitchens in a bid to improve meals and educate young palates'. This should ensure every under-10 in the area demands all the family provisions are sourced from Fresh & Wild.

Everyone's favourite supermarket came in for a light joshing from Liz Jones in the *Evening Standard* who was unimpressed by 'a woman who decided to survive a week shopping only at Tesco ... That's what most people do for the entirety of their lives'. Her challenge was to shop at F&W: proudly she announced 'her bill came to £167.83... and I have two meals'. At the other end of the street near Clissold Park the press had a mini-frenzy over the plight of a 16-year-old who was dropped in a dustbin by a local bobby for allegedly being cheeky. 'You've Bin Nicked' screamed the *Daily Star*, whereas the rest of the Fleet Street's finest seemed undecided on the rights and mainly wrongs of the incident.

N16 crime stories were rather thin on the ground. In point of fact, we're very white collar round here these days. Excluding the 17-year-old reported in the *Daily Mail* whose family came from Stoke Newington and who admitted to 15 burglaries and asked for 1,396 other offences to be taken into consideration. It was a 'Forged Bus Ticket Racket' (*Evening Standard*) and a FSA warning about an unauthorised investment firm 'that is believed to have promised returns of 10% a month but spent the money on spread-betting' (*Guardian*) that were picked up on.

Spring 2006 (29)

And the winner is ... Stoke Newington Church Street, which, weighing in at a whopping 26 letters, was in January awarded 'London's Longest Street Name' by *Time Out*. It should sit well on the mantlepiece next to the Largest Bus Down Smallest Street award won last year. The good old 73 'Happy Bus ... The best thing is it's free' (*Evening Standard*) again featured in several stories regarding fare dodging and the proposed £40 fines. Most people questioned felt it was excessive, but one rounded view came from a Stoke Newington resident who told his inquisitor 'provided the money goes back into improving public transport I would be fine with it'.

Enfant terrible of the pop world 'Potty Pete' (*Daily Star*) Doherty wins the award for most column inches in an N16 context since Issue 28. The poor chap had plenty of unwanted press, in which almost every story had the phrase 'due to return to' or 'held at' Stoke Newington Police Station' within it. The *Montreal Gazette* stated that he was 'arrested in the town of Stoke Newington'; everything's always bigger in Canada isn't it! The *Irish Examiner* reported that 'his behaviour on Dunlance Road caught officers' attention'. Hang around any street in N16 for a few minutes and you'd probably have a Black Maria full, if that's the prerequisite for being arrested these days. Whilst Mr Babyshambles is reinventing himself as Oscar Wilde, N16 pop fans might want to get acquainted with Doloroso. *Time Out*'s Future Sound of London Special enthused that 'this Stoke Newington-based bunch are turning heads with their impressive brand of dark, Bowie-tinged art pop'.

If a good book is more your thing, *Time Out* had a look at 'excellent independent bookshops'. Stoke Newington Bookshops on the High Street was included, although the testimony 'one fan says I always seem to see a book I want to read when I'm browsing' was about as bland as a plate of Fresh & Wild brown rice. If you happen to be in there supporting a local bookstore why not support a local writer?

A final nod to London's weekly listing. Last month saw their semi-annual pointless North v South of the river issue, in which Walworth Road was described as 'like Upper Street without the panzer-sized pushchairs, Stoke Newington Church Street without the hipsters and smugness'. Surely we're the buggies and N1 are the smuggies.

Our esteemed MP was as ubiquitous as ever in the nationals and her regular *Evening Standard* column. However, it was in the Cornish press, of all places, where she grabbed most print. 'MP asks ministers to stop Darkie Day' headlined the *Western Morning News*. Apparently our 'prominent black activist' has tabled a Commons motion to 'stop the controversial festival in Padstow' where 'blacked-up townsfolk parade through the streets to commemorate the end of the slave trade'. Locals seemed to feel it was none of her business.

Summer 2006 (30)

According to the *Evening Standard* 'some in Stoke Newington now claim to live in Hackney because it sounds edgier and cooler'. To be fair, who can blame them when as local resident George Alagiah pointed out in the *New Statesman* 'an area which has been a refuge for London dissenters since the 18th century, is now home to thirty-something couples who drink wheatgrass shots and obsess about school catchment areas'.

'Danny Williams a solicitor at a City firm specialising in corporate takeovers ... with a flat in Stoke Newington'

(*The Times*) would be a fine recipient, only Danny isn't real, he's the main character in another novel, the recently-to-paperback *Utterly Monkey* by Nick Laird. As if fictitious corporate lawyers within our midst wasn't bad enough, the *Daily Star* has even managed to unearth 'an office worker from Stoke Newington' – he was commenting on bird flu, of all things, in a piece tastefully headlined 'Cluck that'.

These days, there's obviously plenty of money floating around the area for a fortunate few, including Dr Sanjiv Gupta the '£270,000 a year GP' with the 'Mercedes with personalised number plate' (*Daily Express*) and 'shabby London surgery' (*Evening Standard*). Wherever you stand on the recent GP pay debate, you have to feel a bit sorry for the Stoke Newington doctor who became the human face of this national story. No matter how many times he tried to explain that 'it is nobody's business but mine what I earn ... my pay is only £130,000 with the remaining £140,000 spent on staff costs' (*Daily Express*) no one seemed hear him. The *Independent* put his alleged salary as on a par with The Duke of York, Jade Goody and Cherie Booth: put that way I'm sure most in N16 would agree that, being responsible for the health of 9,000 of our ranks, Dr Gupta probably deserves his £130K.

Locals with disposable incomes large or small should think about dispensing with as much of it as they can locally. 'The village that thrived until the traffic wardens appeared' headlined the *Evening Standard* in a piece that focused on Stoke Newington as part of the paper's 'campaign to save London's small shops'. Mark Prisk, shadow minister for small business, came visiting, they reported, and 'was immensely impressed by the range and quality of shops'. Several local shopkeepers were quoted, including Georgie Cook from Hub, saying 'rent hikes, parking restrictions and ruthless traffic wardens have put off customers. I've seen many of the nicer shops in Church Street forced out of business. If, as we fear, Tesco and Starbucks move in, it will be the beginning of a downhill slope – even the end of the street'.

Autumn 2006 (31)

Recent headlines all saw members of our community involved in some way or other: 'Monster returned to Britain and had 3 killed' (*Sun*), 'Robber killed man for his Louis Vuitton briefcase' (*Standard*), 'Karate chop killer faces life' (*Times*), 'Head of Ferrari cocaine gang jailed for 21 years' (*Standard*) and, most depressingly, 'Killers left baby lying in blood of dead mother' (*Standard*).

Factor in a Brazilian rain forest of print concerning alleged terrorists from our midst, and much of the summer news emanating from our Republic has been as depressing as the August weather. The odd ray of sunshine has peeped through the clouds, however. A fine piece by local resident Michael Goldfarb in *The New York Times* entitled 'Where London comes together' gave a modicum of hope. He noted that 'in a world slowly splitting at the seams, Clissold Park is like a dream'. There, 'some of the most intractable conflicts in the world seem to have been resolved or at least temporarily ignored. Kurds and Turks, Jews and Muslims, working class and middle class all coexist'. One reason he puts forward is 'the bedrock British custom of queuing. There are only four swings, far too few for the number of kids who use them ... but parents take care to wait their turn. The Hasidic Jew nods to the woman in hijab and the exchange of swings takes place, with none of the coiled resentment seen in American playgrounds.'

Swing shortages in the park are never a problem come the summer holidays. The *Observer* seems to know why. Apparently we're all swimming in the mud at festivals. A piece on The Big Chill stated that 'it looked like someone had organised a mass outing from Stoke Newington, I lost count of the number of thirty-something couples pushing state of the art buggies'.

I'm sure autumn will see normal service resumed, as the future of N16 and their creators go about doing what they do best. In an article titled 'How can a whole area be allergic to gluten', Christina Patterson of the *Independent* noted that in Stoke Newington cafes 'you can't read a paragraph of your paper without a perfectly enunciated little voice demanding a 'babycino' (hot frothed milk, apparently) or an organic flapjack. Or an adult voice telling little Emily or Sam or Tallulah that if they eat up their lentil lasagne they'll get a lovely mango lassi. A soya one, of course. For these are the fussiest children on the planet, born to the fussiest parents.'

Another reason why, according to the *Observer Food Monthly* 'London's yummy eco mummy central Stoke Newington' has the first all-organic farmers market in the UK. Whisper it very quietly, but many of these parents may well be voting Conservative next May. Looking for answers to the question 'So could you vote for Cameron?" the *Guardian* came to 'comfortably pinkish Stoke Newington' looking for the answers.

With so much depressing news around I'll leave you on a note of optimism. The *Evening Standard* interviewed a selection of London 18-year-olds who had just passed their A Levels. One of them from Stoke Newington wants 'to be the first female United Nations secretary general'. I'm sure we all wish her well in her quest.

Autumn 2007 (35)

The *Guardian Diary* claimed to have overheard the following – 'Young mother in Clissold Park to toddler in push chair ... 'No darling, you can't have cous cous with pasta – they just don't go', and *Time Out*'s Overheard Underground eavesdropped that 'It's

pretty much impossible to get to Stoke Newington'. The 'emotive subject' of baby feeding in the *Sunday Times* reported that 'admittedly, an organic café in Stoke Newington is not the wisest place to be seen with Cow & Gate, but did the mother who opened a jar of baby food in Fresh & Wild really deserve the sharp intake of breath and disapproving stares?' An *Evening Standard* journalist and local resident even touched on what is surely N16's biggest cliché when he claimed that he had 'started to treat my local neighbourhood as a village' before going on to ponder on the joys of Clissold Park and Abney Cemetery.

If it's the summer and you're an editor with a paper or the *Evening Standard* to fill, you can always fall back on that staple we British just love – property prices.

According to the capital's finest, 'Londoners have 3 times less living space and the £200,000 national average (for a house) buys you a meagre 549 sq ft in a poky one-bedroom flat in Stoke Newington'. A few days before, the paper had headlined with 'Cycle all the way to the bank and save £125,000', stating the not unobvious, namely that living near a tube costs you more. According to their extensive research 'the greatest savings were to be found between the districts of Highbury and Stoke Newington. Stokey is without a tube station and about a mile further from the West End but otherwise it would be quite difficult for a Martian to tell the two Victorian neighbourhoods apart'.

Believe it or not, there was some serious news from the area to keep dinner party conversation flowing when house prices and baby feeding have been exhausted. The 21/7 terror trial in which 'ringleader Muktar Ibrahim, 29, of Stoke Newington' was one of four men to get 40 years for their failed suicide bid was discussed at great length – although the *Daily Mirror*'s headline describing him as 'Chemical Wally' for his 'bungled bomb mix' probably won't go down as one of the more sensitive stories of the year.

The ongoing saga of 'Bin Boy' also came to a conclusion. The *Daily Telegraph* screamed out '£4,000 for teenager dumped in a litter bin by police officer' after he allegedly 'pelted people with conkers on Stoke Newington High Street'. His out-off-court settlement was meat and drink to those in the press with less liberal leanings. The *Sunday Times* felt 'maybe we need yet another set of bins for our front gardens – a red one for lippy troublesome teenagers and guaranteed weekly collection by the council for melting down and recycling'.

Spring 2008 (37)

So far, 2008 has seen press comment about our Republic dominated mainly by a couple of political knockabouts. Home secretary Mrs Smith's comments

about the borough certainly got our Ms Abbott hot under the proverbial; she claimed in the *Independent* that 'Jacqui is quite wrong to suggest Hackney is a no-go area for women after dark ... she needs to get to know inner-city London. She will find it is not the nightmare scene from a Hogarth engraving that she seems to imagine.'

The *Evening Standard* reported that 'to prove her point she brought MPs and journalists for an evening stroll through Stoke Newington' where 'Committee Chairman Keith Vaz was shown the pubs and restaurants of Church Street with other MPs'. Now, obviously our main drag is awash with many dangers. In point of fact, according to the *Evening Standard*, it's one of London's 'accident black spots for mobile phone users who crash into lampposts'.

However, the paper chose to go for a gentler ridiculing of the area's perils, claiming 'Stoke Newington where intellectuals and artists driven from their traditional haunts by high house prices buy and gentrify. The only clear and present danger in Stokey is that a minor poet with a collection of haikus on the ghastliness of George W Bush will stop you in the street and bore you to death.'

Our other political limelight came in the shape of what the *Daily Mail* called 'Labour's Golden Couple' and the *Daily Express* 'Mr & Mrs Greedy' one day and 'Mr & Mrs Insufferable' the next. Yes, you've guessed it, esteemed politicians Ed Balls and Yvette Cooper. The Press Pack were united in their indignation of their 'neat footwork to get the public to pay £44,000 a year towards the cost of their mortgage on a second home in fashionable Stoke Newington' (*Evening Standard*) 'even though they are based in London during the week and their children go to school there' (*Daily Express*).

Wherever you stand on this story, surely the most shocking thing to come from the coverage is the fact that property prices are patently plummeting in the area. One day, the *Daily Express* had the Ministers' Stokey house 'valued at £700,000', then, two days later, in the same paper, it was 'worth £650,000'.

The word 'insufferable' came up again, this time to describe Arsenal supporters in an amusing column in the *Evening Standard*. It took our two main arteries as analogies for the Gunners and Spurs. 'The High Street leads to Tottenham, Church Street points to Arsenal... and it seems to exemplify the difference between the clubs in recent years: Tottenham the slightly grotty, dangerous but somehow more honest; Arsenal the trendy, appealing but, dare we say, a touch overrated ... where they sit smugly watching their matches in gastropubs, bray- ing and grunting'. Aah, you really must try the Smoked Lamb Quesadilla with Goats Cheese and Caramelised Onion at The Auld Shillelagh; it's to die for.

Letters

You write in your article 'Monkey Business' (*issue 12: see Jan interview on page 62 of this book*): 'In fact, she's not the only member of Jan's family who contributed to his "calling". My dad was in a band called The Joystrings. They got to number 45 in the charts in 1964 with a song called *It's An Open Secret*. And if anybody reading this has a copy, then let us know and we'll get Jan senior to sign it for you. Y'see, that's community in action again!' My question is. Who is your dad who was in The Joystrings? I do not know a Jan. Maybe you can help me on the way, and besides I have the record *It's An Open Secret* .
Cor Quint, Holland

More Monkey Business. Herr Quint's Curious Conundrum and the Perplexing Puzzle of The Joystrings: A Humble Response With reference to Mr Cor Quint's remarks regarding The Joystrings song 'It's An Open Secret' (and his comment 'I do not know of a Jan (Senior)'. May I endeavour to enlighten him?

Although, as aficionados of one of the '60s top beat combos will know, beater of the mighty skins in The Joystrings and owner of the finest pair of cheekbones this side of Ginger Baker's Air Force was a certain Mr Wycliffe Noble, it would not be an inaccurate, albeit a highly metaphoric description, to use the words Jan Senior to describe the father of the young gentleman featured in the interview you refer to. I have known Mr Jan Noble, (aka Wycliffe Junior – hereafter referred to as simply 'Junior'), one of our most highly regarded, if not always upstanding, members of the literary community, for several years and have had the always entertaining and rarely dubious pleasure of collaborating with him in various musical projects, most recent of which I gather formed the core of Mr Priest's interview. May I say that he has inherited many of the very excellent qualities that his father possesses: an almost metronomic sense of time (if not, in his case, punctuality), a strong sense of idealism, libertarianism and those afore-mentioned good looks – as many of the ladies of the borough will testify.

Returning swiftly to the matter in hand, however, I must offer the opinion that, although the song *It's An Open Secret* is a great single, The Joystrings were primarily an album group: show me a better Christmas collection than 'Well Seasoned': it contains none of the tedious commercial trappings that have become associated with the winter season, has some highly individual re-workings of blues standards and more importantly contains, what I regard to be, their finest track, *Keep Me In Your Love*. Nestled away in between the carols and candles is such a glittering bauble of beat-pop psychedelia that, if one were not aware of the strict Temperance of the band, one might fancifully suppose their influences came from some of the more exotic sources that fragranced the creative juices of pop-groups of that era.

As for acquiring an autograph for your copy, Mr Noble would, I'm sure, be flattered at such a request. He is a now a fit and healthy octogenarian residing in a beautiful self-restored house overlooking the River Thames, has his classic Sonor drum-kit set up in a study at his home and, when not conducting his daily business and attending anti-war demonstrations, can be sometimes seen coaxing the equally rakishly handsome visage of his vintage MG around the byways of Surrey. Thankfully, he did not, like many of his contemporaries of our most colourful decade, succumb to any Green Manalashis, decide to re-dedicate his life and logic to yogic flying or feel the necessity to make a pilgrimage to Africa to 'discover' 'rhythm'. Henceforth, examples of his excellent and humanistic architecture can be seen around the capital, gently chastising the excesses of modernists who did not feel the necessity to enable those less fortunate amongst us to access their creations: a most notable example being the graceful curve of the disabled ramp that softens the rather brutish and

fairly bland post-war constructivism of the Royal Festival Hall complex.

Finally, I hope this has helped clarify your thoughts on the subject, and in conclusion may I perhaps venture that we all give a resounding hallelujah for Mr Wycliffe Noble (aka Jan Senior), The Joystrings, his eldest offspring (aka Junior) and of course their fine music. Surely you must agree with me that a contemporary re-working of 'Keep Me In Your Love' is long overdue by one of the groups of young pretenders who have the audacity to call themselves modern beatcombos?
Yours faithfully, Sambuchus Nero, RFS Cert Arb, Ma (Chelsea), (Part Ret)

I was amused to read about the Rio cinema. I confess that I haven't been to a movie in Stoke Newington for more than 40 years. I guess prices have gone up somewhat since the days when I paid two shillings. The article informs us that if anyone objects to the prices, they can go on an expedition to 'the outpost known as Edmonton'. Now, it just so happens that I live in an outpost known as Edmonton. But if anyone wishes come here to see a cheap movie, they will need to plan on a nine-hour flight across the Atlantic, and over Greenland and Baffin Island all the way to western Canada.
Norman Temple, Edmonton, Canada

Congratulations to recent letters concerning of the near-lunatic introduction of bendy buses into London. But there is another point that seems to have escaped people's notice. That was that TFL want to 'give value for money and reduce emissions' for the London public. Why doesn't this apply to the thousands of jet aircraft that fly straight over us every week? In Highbury and Stoke Newington, we are now directly underneath the flight paths of thousands of jet aircraft going into Heathrow. They come in from both the north-east and north-west Heathrow stacks, turn over Crouch End and Finsbury Park (or somewhere thereabouts), and scream over Highbury, Islington and Stoke Newington on their way down to the landing path to Heathrow. I've spoken to BAA about it, spoken to the CAA, and all that they say is that 'nothing has changed in the way that air traffic is conducted over London.' I beg to differ. When the wind is from the west, I (and thousands of other people in Highbury, Stoke Newington and Hackney, I imagine) am woken at 6 am, and have to endure the racket of thousands of jet engines

going overhead till 11 pm. Why has it suddenly become convenient for Heathrow Air Traffic Control to do this? Why do we have to take the brunt of noise and pollution from two streams of aircraft from the east and west turning into their final approach to Heathrow? Why are they flying so low, so continuously on one path, and why over N5, N10, N16, E1, and N1? (We're at least 15 miles east of the airport!). I've read on the HACAN (a lobbying group against aircraft noise, first started in west London) website that BAA has finally admitted that 50% of all traffic into Heathrow is now routed over Highbury, Islington, Stoke Newington and Hackney: 'BAA has confirmed that half of all flights landing at Heathrow Airport are routed over densely-populated areas of North London. Planes land over London when the prevailing west wind is blowing.' God knows what would happen if one of these planes came down.

Long may you live. What a joy to have gone to Clapton Library and picked up your mag. I've never written to a mag in my life. But now I've some time on my hands (I've just become a member of the Arse Scratching Club – 50 and unemployed) and I thought I'd write to you to let you know that *N16* is a mag I would recommend to my pals. I've lived in Hackney all my life and was born in Stokey (Lordship Road). All you hear is Murder Mile, crack houses and shootings. What a breath of fresh air *N16* has brought to our house. Keep it up and good luck for the future.

Hello from Canada. I, too, came from Stamford Hill and went to school in Stoke Newington. I also live in the wilds, in Ontario, Canada. If I need to go to the cinema or theatre I have to travel 2 hours or more. It is better to wait until the DVD or VHS comes out. We were lucky in the '50s and '60s to get to appreciate good theatre and good movies (films) now we have to travel to see them. You are so lucky to be in London and able to see whatever you want to. We just left to make a better life for our kids.

On the Streets

It's not all café lattes, £1 million houses, expensive shops, four-wheel drive motors and comfortable 'bohemian' lifestyles in Stoke Newington. The experience of some people is rather different, and not one you may envy.

Smack and Crack: Getting Clean in N16
Anonymous, Winter 2009 (43)

You don't know me, chances are you don't know anyone like me, in which case this piece may be nothing more than a quick dip into someone else's misery as you sip your lattes in The Spence or grab a few minutes 'me' time at home before the kids come back from Clissold Park with the nanny. No, you don't know me but you do see me. You see others like me too. Outside the Abbey National on the High Street? Begging by the Nat West at the bottom of Church Street? Selling 'stuff' by Abney Park gates?

The estate agents hate us. The PCOs move us on. Some people give us money. Some people give us food. Some people give us a piece of their mind. Some people spit or urinate on us. 'I fucking hate you junkie scumbags'. Not as much as I hate myself, mate. Some people are less able than others to hide the fact they can't even look at us, pretending we don't exist. We do, though. But that's about all you do when things have come to this. We exist. That's it. Same shit different day always waiting just like Lou Reed said, except most of the time we are not waiting for a man, but a 'boy' who works for a man, a teenager with too much jewellery and contempt. Jewellery paid for by 'us' in conjunction with the growing contempt as we call from various phone boxes in N16 asking where to meet, having somehow accumulated the ten or twenty quid required to bring relief from our existence.

It wasn't meant to be like this. I had dreams once. I wanted to be a footballer like Kenny Dalglish, until it became apparent that I wasn't good enough to emulate the 'king'. I changed the posters on my wall. Keith Richards replaced King Kenny and in some respects I eventually managed to do a pretty good impersonation of good old 'Keef'. I managed to form a few bands though but I got the equation wrong. Sex and drugs and rock'n'roll? For a while, maybe.

Until it was just the drugs. Thought I could stop anytime. Really believed I could. Until I tried to. Ten years ago I completed a rehab and after a couple of years living in a hostel was given a flat on Amhurst Road. I had never been to Stokey before and always found enough drugs elsewhere in the metropolis. Soon found them here, though, I asked a guy on the street one day, which was a mistake. Not the fact that I'd asked him, he knew plenty of teenagers with bad attitudes and expensive jewellery. My mistake was thinking I could have 'one'. My thinking had already

become clouded due to the fact that after 18 months 'clean time' I'd decided I could handle a drink. Just one of course. I had one. A can of Special Brew. Then I had some more. A few days later the 'Brew wasn't really cutting it so I had the first of what would become many 'conversations' with my new friend. And Stokey had another junkie in the Parish.

And so it came to be that I spent the best part of the first decade of the new millennium scuttling through the side streets of Stokey in search of teenagers who could assist me in my painfully elongated journey to the place 'we' go when you no longer see us outside The Abbey National, Nat West or Cemetery gates.

Which is where? Jail? Yep. Not for very long but it didn't work anyway Rehab? Yep. Plenty of times but for me they didn't work either. A cemetery or crematorium? Ah! Not me, obviously, but I can think of at least ten people I knew who will no longer trouble you as you amble up Church Street in search of the perfect cup of coffee. Ten people who I waited by 'phone boxes with, sat in stairwells and took drugs with, chatted about nothing of any consequence with, identified with, exchanged numbers of teenagers with ... existed with. I don't recall if we ever laughed, but I very much doubt it, maybe just after we'd met our teenager and done what we had to do. Mostly though, there was a lot of silence.

You don't know me but you see me. Where? These days you see me pushing a buggy along Church Street, playing with my 18-month-old daughter in Clissold Park; sometimes you see and hear me as I play my guitar at acoustic evenings in N16; sometimes I'm shopping. I am no longer hopeless. ! I have hope! I am never alone. Why? I haven't used a drug or had a drink for over three years. Nothing. That's right, nothing at all, no smack, crack, methadone, valium, coke, pills, weed, Special Brew ... nothing. And, fuck me, it feels good.

Do you have many drug- or alcohol-dependent visitors, I ask Mike? 'Yes, we do have some, but trouble is rare. We have visitors with no drug or alcohol problems, but several with mental health issues. We also have visitors who are lonely and come along for the social interaction. We find it can give them a focus on life.'

NLAH also provide other services to the homeless. Twice a year they run a mobile X-Ray unit, and every three weeks a Homerton Hospital nurse-led TB 'find and treat' team, as well as offering flu jabs, HIV screening, blood pressure and heart tests, and even haircuts. They also run East European Narcotics Anonymous meetings – 'there is a real need for this' – on Wednesday evenings from 8pm, and also provide English classes every Wednesday. They also operate an outreach venture on Saturday mornings, going out around the parish talking to and feeding the homeless. It must be said that, without these dedicated and caring workers and volunteers, the outlook for the homeless would be bleak indeed in this area.

How is all this funded, then? 'We spend a lot of time filling in application forms', observes Mike, wryly. The NLAH receives grants and money from a number of sources, including West Hackney Parochial Fund, Trust For London, Irish DION Fund, banks, various city guilds, benefit concerts and other fund-raising events and individual donations. In total, the NLAH needs approximately £60,000 per year to continue to operate, so could always find a useful way of spending more. They received a regular grant of £10,000 a year from Hackney Council, until this funding was withdrawn last year. 'This was something of an inconvenience at the time', comments Mike, 'but we now have an excellent volunteer to help compensate for this shortfall'. Aside from further corporate and individual financial assistance, what else would you appreciate in terms of donations? 'We need donations constantly. We are always looking for ideas for fundraising, volunteer drivers, volunteer legal advice, camping gear and warm clothing and blankets.'

So what happened? I found a way out. It might work for you if you need it too. It's not for everyone. But if like me you've tried and failed for too long by your own best thinking, then try a meeting of Narcotics Anonymous. If you think you have a problem with drugs, any drug it doesn't matter what or how much, we are not really that bothered in what you use, but we are certainly bothered about what you want to do about your problem and how we can help. We've been there.

Ain't got no home, anymore
By Rab MacWilliam, Winter 2011 (50)

I met up with Mike Tomes, Centre Manager of North London Action for the Homeless, a man who is doing his best to ensure the homeless are fed and looked after, particularly over this period of gross conspicuous consumption and indulgence. Mike works with three part-time staff (chef, outreach and liaison workers) and a pool of around 40 volunteers at St Paul's Church on Stoke Newington Road, across from the police station, where the NLAH moved nearly five years ago. The NLAH itself began seventeen years ago in a synagogue in Amhurst Park, and then moved around various locales before settling down at St Paul's.

The main services provided by Mike and his team are lunch between noon and 1.30pm on Mondays and dinner between 7 and 8.30pm on Wednesdays, both freshly cooked, 3-course vegetarian meals. The cook, Lucie Galand, raises funds by making chutney with the service users and sells it at the farmers' market, held every Saturday morning behind the church, and she has also raised money to open the NLHA's own vegetable garden. The meals are attended by up to 80 people per session. 'We attract the homeless and vulnerable', says Mike. 'We don't preach at all. They come in, eat and go. We serve them at the tables and respect their dignity'.

I asked him if he sees homelessness as being on the increase around here. 'Well, it's certainly not decreasing, it's an increasing problem. It's difficult to give the reason. It could be that our services are becoming better known, but our numbers are certainly increasing. There has been a massive increase in the number of East European homeless, and also a recent increase in middle-class people who seem to have fallen on unexpectedly hard times.'

It's easy to walk past homeless people on the way back to your warm flat, but it's a damn sight more righteous, selfless and human to help, financially if you can afford it or, rather than hanging around the pub, with your spare time. It doesn't take a huge mental leap to see that it could be you out there.

Mortimer Observes

Mortimer Ribbons, owner of Ribbons & Taylor, was a regular columnist for this magazine until his untimely death in 2009. His dry wit and often hilarious observations from his vantage point on Church Street – in particular his struggles with Hackney Council, the constant repairing of Church Street and the travails of life generally – always enlivened the mag, and supplied a personal and perceptive insight into each issue. This article was the first of many which he wrote for N16.

The Golden Eggs
By Mortimer Ribbons, Summer 2005 (26)

Summer's here and Murphy's hard at work on the street again – not. He spent half of last year resurfacing it – and it looked really good for a couple of weeks – before the holes appeared for the cable TV. Now we're replacing Victorian water mains. Didn't we do that in 2003? Or was that the Victorian telephone lines? We've all got used to it. The temporary lights have become a permanent fixture, slowly blinking out the seasons, and we live in an endless traffic jam. No need to smoke cigarettes anymore because the air round here's equivalent to twenty a day at least.

Scientists in California have apparently halved state

road-mending bills by inventing a shovel that leans on itself. We need the same thing on Church Street. And we need some towering giant at the Town Hall to decree that all the services should be mended at the same time. And then that the road should be filled in to allow people, cars, bikes, buggies, beggars, and bendy buses to move freely along it. And to be able to stop, too. If you're trying to run a business, then it is desirable that customers and suppliers should be able to park somewhere. If people can't stop – and at the moment they can't even get off the bus – then they won't buy anything. The Council takes the view that cars are illegal and immoral, and it is therefore their duty to make as much money as possible out of them. To this end, it has gradually choked off every side road off every shopping street with Controlled Parking Zones. The pattern is familiar: a questionnaire comes round asking if you'd like to pay eighty quid to park outside your house? Everyone says no, leave us alone. Then the Council counts all the postal votes they sent to Mongolia, adds

them to the number of dead people who would have voted yes, had they been asked, and declares a CPZ. Each time they do this it becomes a little easier: by now, they have managed to manufacture a very genuine parking problem for any streets that remain.

A parking warden recently was writing out a ticket for a man who had parked his van in a Residents' Bay outside his hardware shop. He pointed out that he had just paid three hundred and twenty pounds for a Business Permit and that the four business parking spaces within walking distance had all been parked on by people with Residents' Permits. The warden, annoyed at this waste of valuable ticketing time, finally asked what was so special about him just

because he had a shop there? Had I been there, I would have told this ignorant and officious clod what is so special about it. Church Street is the Goose that Lays the Golden Eggs. Property values round here are measured by their proximity to Church Street with its park, cafes and shops. And every move that the Council, the planners and the developers make seems to be designed to damage the shops. If the hardware shop becomes a restaurant because there are no parking restrictions after six o clock, and if the rest of the daytime shops follow suit, then the Goose won't lay any more. Local custom is our backbone. It's wonderful to see our friends and neighbours in the shop every day but we need visitors too. And we need to treat them right. How about opening the car park behind the Town Hall to visitors? It's jealously locked and guarded at the moment, but I'm sure the Council workers who drive in to work wouldn't mind taking the bendy bus instead if it were explained to them that it's all for the general good.

Controlled Parking

Ours is now a street of shame where every day you can see 'speeding, 'dumping' and even 'mainlining' (down to Liverpool Street). We desperately need a CPZ treatment. For a contribution of only £1.50 a week we can help dozens of drivaholics to find a decent parking place near their home and loved ones and keep their habit under control. Some of the real derelicts and unlicensed users might even give up altogether. Then once more we can walk freely and safely along our street.

Church Street businesses imagine their trade is car dependent. The actual research evidence is that 92% of Stoke Newington town centre visitors do not come by car, and just think of the traffic jams if any more did. Independent research also shows that car shoppers spend over a period no more than those who go by bus, and that those who walk to shop spend 50% more than both. One thing is certain – not one Church Street business will believe a word of it.

Only in Hackney could the powers that be come up with a parking scheme that leaves an island of uncontrolled streets surrounded by Controlled Parking Zones. People in local roads have not had regular rubbish collections because of cars parked on the corners making it impossible for the dustcart to turn into these roads. Wheelchair users can't get down the sloped bit of pavements for the same reason and children cannot see past the tightly parked cars to make sure it's safe to cross. Dare to park in the middle of the road to unload shopping rather than ferry it from hundreds of yards away, and one risks the wrath of impatient drivers. I have witnessed people I know to be reasonable human beings arguing over parking spaces. Tyres have been slashed and car bodywork damaged.

Before CPZs people could at least park somewhere in the area, if not in their own road. People without permits are well and truly stymied because they can't park in either a CPZ or in the non-controlled roads. I suppose they had to provide somewhere for commuters to park so local businesses didn't get seriously miffed by having to shell out £300 plus per employee for a business parking permit, or am I just being cynical? The current chaos is not helped by the fact that many people who are in CPZs have decided to take advantage of free parking rather than buy a permit that would enable them to park in their own roads.

Controlled parking – as a small business – is a bit of an issue. At a recent meeting of local businesses everyone in the room – around 40 – had been adversely affected by the recent CPZ extension. Since then, our sales – and I know many others – have noticeably dropped. Customers have come in fuming because it has taken half an hour to find somewhere to park, they can't park for long and we'll be lucky if they come back. It means they spend less time and money in the area as a whole.

And yet many residents go out to work during the day (which is why we rely on customers coming in from outside the area), so the side streets stand half empty because of the resident only bays. And don't forget all the service businesses that now have to pay thousands of pounds to park their vehicles around the borough when out on jobs. As a business we are supposed to pay £320 a year for a basic one-zone permit, which is insane considering there are too few business permit bays and often nowhere to park. This means that prices have to go up to cover the extra costs.

It is the ripple affect of something like CPZ that ends up devastating businesses. Added to that we've had to swallow a rise in business rates and a general economic slowdown. Does anyone really appreciate how hard it is to run a small business in Stoke Newington at the moment? The area needed CPZ – regardless of why – but the way it has been introduced has been poorly thought out and badly implemented. Residents and businesses have been pitted against one another – and it is something we must stop. Without the independent shops and restaurants the area would not have the 'villagey feel' that we all know and love. And without the residents who are attracted to that we have no businesses. The Stoke Newington Business Association is now in talks with Hackney Council to try and get changes made to the CPZ.

They are listening and have already made minor changes – like allowing customers to pay per minute in the Wilmer Place car park (behind Whole Foods) instead of only one, two or six hours! They are also looking to make more bays into shared use so businesses and their customers can park in the day. The Council will conduct an extensive review of the CPZ in March next year. I urge all residents and businesses to respond to any surveys and consultations and tell the Council what you think. Unless of course you are happy to see Stoke Newington turn into another cloned High Street.

In Brief

Italian football has recently been hitting the headlines. But how many of you knew that the man who created Italian football – the father of 'calcio' – came from Stoke Newington? Dr James Richardson Spensley was born in this parish in 1867. He arrived in Genoa in 1896 and set up the Genoa Cricket and Athletic (later 'Football') Club in order that expats could play against the crews of visiting British ships. He only played two games for the club (apparently, he was a useless goalie) but he was president of the club until 1907. Several sources claim that he also created the worldwide scouting movement. He died on the front line in Mainz, Germany in 1915.

Beware of rapacious terrapins, causing havoc among little Clissold Park ducklings. According to BBC's Radio 4 'Today' programme in mid-September, the little carnivores are lying in ambush, leaping out and attacking the fluffy duckies. Worse, apparently they are foraging along Church Street, their beady little eyes searching out their next dinner. This seems barely credible, given that the little beasties seem to move about one yard every two years, a view supported by local councillor, who dismissed the idea as a moral panic. Watch out, though. You never know.

There was a lot of police activity on Church Street on a Saturday morning, towards the end of May. We counted at least 30 squad cars from the Met and City of London Police, with heavily armed officers, and a helicopter circling overhead. They also shut down the street for a couple of hours between Booth's and the Daniel Defoe. The reason – an officer was stabbed in the thigh outside Safedale Chemist, and the hunt was on for the perpetrator, who was caught soon after the incident. The good news is that the officer concerned is apparently OK. However, given the size of the operation, you'd have been forgiven for assuming that Arsenal fan and international terrorist Osama Bin Laden and his trusted lieutenants were holed up in Abney Park. Would a civilian involved in a similar incident have received this amount of attention?

Stoke Newington surfers are falling off their boards in disbelief at the latest series of adverts from Debenham's. As part of a supposedly spoof series of ads – Dundee Dog and Duck Darts Club, Hastings Ladies Kickboxing Club (you get the picture) – the department store is attempting to sell its trendy and expensive clothing by attempting to be funny, in a somewhat arch way, and ending up by being patronizing. Indeed, the Stoke Newington Surf Club (based on the New River opposite Clissold House and currently awaiting a wave machine) – one of the societies which Debenham's think they have invented – are currently consulting their distinguished lawyers about this disgraceful and illegal appropriation of their name. Both Club members are deeply upset about this. Surf's up.

What bliss it is to be alive in our little parish. The new edition of *the Lonely Planet Guide to London* states that 'East London has emerged as the capital's rising star'. Also that 'Stoke Newington in Hackney is a wonderful blend of hippies, yuppies, gay and lesbian couples and pockets of Orthodox Jews and Turkish Muslims, all living in the most unlikely of harmonies.' And in Abney Park Cemetery 'the atmosphere of the whole place is nothing short of magical' (that'll be before it gets dark, then). Although it's a good thing to talk up N16, let's not forget the muggings, murders, sad junkies, non-stop police sirens, people living in decrepit council estates and all the other problems of inner-city life, including two fatal stabbings at the end of March. Reality should occasionally intrude.

Tesco Express is now open on the High Street and, despite the prophecies of some local soothsayers, the seven plagues have still not arrived in the parish. *N16* understands the continuing arguments concerning the allegedly negative impact of Tesco's dominance in the food retail industry. And we have read all about Tescopoly. There are undoubtedly some areas where a Tesco's would not be appropriate, but this is a high street and, so far as we remember, high streets have always been full of large shops selling lots of stuff. Specialist food retailers, such as the Fishery and local delis, should remain unaffected, and Tesco's arrival, although probably initially painful for the largely Turkish foodshops, should provide opportunities for diversity and greater efficiency, where necessary. It should also mean more people leaving the cosy confines of Church Street and visiting the no-man's land of the High Street, thereby bringing more trade into what has always been Stoke Newington's main thoroughfare.

Extract from the USA's own *Washington Post*, 13 June: 'First mentioned in the Domesday Book, a land survey completed for William I in 1086, and meaning 'new town in the woods', Stoke Newington today very much retains a village charm. Cheaper than Islington, it has long attracted struggling artists, including many British independent filmmakers. 'Stokey', as residents affectionately call it, is also multicultural, multiracial and multigenerational. The neighborhood is compact and friendly, with most of the action centered on charming Stoke Newington Church Street.

Best for: Indie shopping. The chain-store creep that has infected most of Britain's high streets has yet to hit Stoke Newington, so small independent shops dominate, including a good range of second-hand bookstores and coffee shops.

Most charming feature: A peaceful resting place for past and present North Londoners, Abney Park Cemetery (Stoke Newington High Street, with an entrance on Stoke Newington Church Street) is a delight to wander through on a pleasant day. Be sure to search for the massive abandoned chapel, which is crying out to be a shoot location for a rock video.'

Multigenerational? Eh? And Nando's, Halford's, Tesco, Oddbins, Fresh and Wild *et al* are not chain stores? Still, nice to get a mention from over 3000 miles away. Thanks, dude.

We mentioned this a couple of years ago, and it seems to be getting worse. We are referring to the environmental nuisance and irritation to the public of constant police sirens in the area, particularly in the High Street. When we asked the Met Press Office about this back then, we were told that there are no official criteria and that individual police drivers can turn on sirens when they see fit. Now, clearly, there are cases when our local police have to clear the traffic to prevent crime or catch up with the perpetrators, and sirens are necessary for this. However, they seem to be roaring up the High Street, sirens on, every ten minutes or so. Surely serious crime around here is not that bad? A recent case in South London involved a police car, siren on, in a bad accident. Reportedly, the officer was returning to his station with a Chinese takeaway. N16 is not implying that this occurs here, but why turn on the sirens when the nearest cars are hundreds of yards in front or in the middle of the night, when the roads are virtually empty? Our local police have a difficult job to do, but why alienate the public if it's not necessary? Anyway, patrolling the pavements, which they don't do, would probably be more effective in cutting back local crime than screeching around in their high-powered plodmobiles.

From Church Street to Wall Street. Local artist David Downes, whose drawings appeared on the front cover of the first two issues of N16 Magazine, has been carving out quite a career for himself over the last ten years or so. His distinctive paintings have been displayed in Fox's Wine Bar, the Library Gallery, and a variety of other locations, including recently the Riverside Gallery in Richmond, the Lion and John Jones in Finsbury Park. He has also been artist in residence at the BBC. After an exhibition at St Bride's Church in the City, he was commissioned by Goldman Sachs to execute sixteen paintings of New York scenes which will initially be exhibited at the Hudson Building in mid-October, then moving to Goldman Sachs on Wall Street before ending up at the World Trade Gallery in Manhattan. Visit www.daviddownes.co.uk for more information.

On 15 April 1989, 96 Liverpool fans lost their lives attending a football match against Nottingham Forest, the semi-final of the FA Cup played at Sheffield Wednesday's Hillsborough football stadium. The fans were crushed to death in the Leppings Lane end of the ground in a tragedy caused by organisational negligence. Stoke Newington is home to a vibrant Liverpool community, with both reds and blues represented. John Power, Stoke Newington resident, ex-La, Cast and currently recording as a solo artist, was asked by Liverpool Football Club and the City of Liverpool to supply lead vocal on the recording of 'The Fields of Anfield Road', in order to commemorate the 20th anniversary of that dreadful day. The idea is for the song, which was released on 26 March, to be as successful as possible in order to remember this tragedy, and allow all those affected to grieve. Justice has never been done.

Building work has now started on Clapton Library, which is to be refurbished and expanded thanks to a major restoration project that will return the Grade II listed building to its former glory and create more room for improved facilities. It will reopen in Spring 2010. When completed, the refurbished and expanded library will have enhanced facilities and dedicated areas for all ages. The new extension will include a wheelchair accessible entrance and a lift providing improved access for all. Hackney libraries continue to provide a home delivery service for those who find it difficult to visit a library because of limited mobility. The library's stock disposal has also unearthed some unexpected discoveries. A book by H G Wells, *The Bulpington of Blup*, which was checked out of the library on 1 September 1939 – the date of the invasion of Poland, marking the start of World War II in Europe – was not returned until the summer of 1999, some sixty years later. This may well be a record for the return of an overdue library book, claims Hackney Council.

It's six in the morning in Stoke Newington and, if you haven't got a hangover, you're lying in bed listening to the birds singing (or the foxes howling), Suddenly you hear a deep rumbling noise, getting louder by the minute, Yup, the first flight out of Stansted is heading your way to be followed by at least another twenty in the next half hour or so. They tend to take off an hour or so later from Luton. But the Stansted rumble is a bit like 'I've got you, babe' from the movie *Groundhog Day* – irritating as hell, but there's nothing you can do about it. Apparently, Stansted 'has a strict policy towards noise emissions' which will no doubt be aided by its expansion plans and the number of new airlines queueing up to acquire slots there.

Vote Local

I'm always surprised why people stand for election to anything, particularly when they have no chance of winning. However, there is something admirable about their indefatigable determination to make their opinions heard in the public arena. Both Suzanne and Knigel deserve much respect for having done just this.

Showy Breeders and Badly Behaved Sprogs
By Suzanne Moore, Autumn 2010 (45)

Strange as it may seem I do sometimes venture out occasionally into the wilds of Stoke Newington. I refuse to live in fear of gypsies, tramps and thieves. But there is one thing I am scared of. I am afraid it might have even lost me the election. It is more than likely that I lost not because Diane Abbot is ... well Diane Abbott ... and she had the entire Labour Party machinery behind her and all I had was a few snazzy leaflets. It was because I dared to speak out. I broke the final taboo. By accident obviously.

A nice young man with a camera came round to interview me for some dashing website. He had interviewed the other candidate's about their 'policies'. I did well on the Third runway and the Tobin tax I thought, although most punters I met seemed to be more concerned with the legalization and drugs and /or parking. Then of course there was the enthusiast for assisted suicide that I met in the Leisure Centre. He promised to vote for me as I nodded energetically and ensured him that I was totally for people killing themselves. That's politics for you.

Anyway, the David Frost of N16 also nonchalantly asked me about what I liked about Church Street. The stress of campaigning got to me. I admit it. The dam burst. 'I don't go there much. I really can't stand it. I hate the way people in Stoke Newington actually believe they are the first people in the history of the entire human race to have reproduced. I hate baby cinos and stupid bloody shops where children's T-shirts cost £50. And baby Pilates and infant yoga and toddler drumming. BUT what I really hate is those bloody ginormous buggies that hog the pavements.' And that I am fairly sure is why I am not your MP as we speak. It's not that I am the child-catcher in Chitty Chitty Bang Bang or anything. I like kids. It's the parents that are the problem and the equipment that I loathe.

What are these ludicrous pram/pushchair efforts that cost millions of pounds? What are they for? They are the SUVs, the 4-wheel drives of the selfish middle classes. And they should be stopped. They are taking over our streets. What is wrong with a little collapsible pushchairs that folds up like umbrella? Yes, I know a McClaren buggy ate a child's hand or something but they are tame enough. These massive

buggies are being pushed about by the Jeremy Clarksons of parenthood though somehow they imagine themselves to be hip and free. So it is all about fashion and status. It is not even child friendly. Certainly not citizen friendly. And, Christ, what is with the jogging with buggies deal? What fresh hell is this? In your face fitness and fertility. It must be stopped immediately.

So must this awful attitude that the workers – yes, the workers of Stoke Newington – who serve in pubs and restaurants for less than the minimum wage are basically there to provide free childcare for these often badly behaved sprogs. Sure we can celebrate being a place of showy breeders. I am one myself and have spent many an idyllic afternoon in Clissold Park picking up germs from the paddling pool and being sexually harassed by the swings. But my point is that we seemed to have managed without basically putting our kids in fake cars.

And what about encouraging them to... you know, walk around... I thought that was meant to be good. Babies are babies. Lovely if they are yours. Fairly boring if they are not and mostly you wouldn't notice them if they didn't get in your way. Which they don't if not strapped into some aisle-blocking monster cart. I don't know if it's a yummy mummy thing, an N16 thing, I just know that talking about banning these vast juggernauts that clog up Church Street is akin to kitten strangling outside Olive Loves Whoever.

Suzanne lives in Stoke Newington and has worked as a columnist for the Guardian, Independent and Mail on Sunday. She has three children and stood unsuccessfully as an independent candidate in the 2010 General Election for Hackney North and Stoke Newington.

Loony Election Memories
By Knigel Knapp, Autumn 2010 (45)

I wasn't going to stand in the election this time round. I'd done what I wanted last time. And I knew everyone was really pissed off with politicians of all parties – what with the expenses scandal and everything. But then two strange Scotsmen in The Rochester Castle persuaded me I should stand again. Here is what happened.

6 April: So they've finally called the General Election. Right! Let's get on with it!

12 April: The manifesto launch was a rip roaring success! I gave away loads of badges and posters and even a few copies of the manifesto! The Royal Sovereign was packed, The Fibbers (Knigel's band, Ed) were great, even my speech went ok. The raffle was rather marvellous and people asked questions and I managed to answer some of them. And Reuters was there to film it all! Coming to a TV near you soon, or more likely somewhere in the Far East (he's right: he featured on Singapore TV).

13 April: New Transport Policy Launch. On 18 April I demonstrated the new Loony-bike on the river Thames near the Houses of Parliament. The Loony-bike is a floating bicycle, capable of speeds up to 10mph. They're great, environmentally friendly and they will get the nation fit if everyone starts using them. And what with global warming everyone might have to use them when the sea levels rise. In the meantime we might have to build a few more canals and that can only be good for the unemployment figures.

20 April: I handed in my nomination papers and £500 at the Town Hall yesterday. I haven't heard anything from them so I'm presuming it's all alright. Which means I'm doing it! Vote for me, vote for me and the Raving Loonies!

22 April: So there are nine other people standing in North Hackney. The usual three, the greens, the Christian Party, three independents and a bloke from something called the Magna Carta Party – who they?

27 April: Spent the weekend campaigning in Mid-Wales with Lord Offa of the Dykes. Friday night we spoke to loads of people in every pub in Brecon. Lord Offa got promises of votes from pretty much everyone he met! Saturday night was Lord Offa's Victory Party. He's celebrating already! Sunday a slow drive back to London and now back campaigning in Hackney.

1 May: Out campaigning on the streets again and met Suzanne Moore. Then to the Rochester to draw a raffle. Lots of interesting conversations with the locals.

6 May: We couldn't organise a victory party in Stokey because of the Tottenham v Man City game last night, so The Big Fibbers went over to East Mosely. Got back about lunchtime for some last minute campaigning in Dalston. Then home and a lie down. Right – I'm off to vote now. And I think I'm going to vote for myself!

8 May: 182 votes! Thanks very much all you loonies out there. If everyone had been allowed in to vote, I might have got a few more. Thursday (election) night was a very strange affair. We arrived at the town hall at about 11.30pm to find some very angry people who hadn't been allowed to vote. I'd be angry too. After talking to them we wandered inside and began the long wait. The 15-hour wait! It was supposed to be all over by 4.00am but it took until almost 11.30am on the Friday morning just to finish verifying the three votes. It took just 2 1/2 hours to count the parliamentary vote and so by 2.30am – surprise, surprise – Diane Abbot was announced the winner. She actually spoke to me this time! It had been an interesting but knackering night, so home to bed. No photos of the announcements I'm afraid. My official photographer had wimped out hours before.

Knigel came in somewhat short of the number of votes required for his deposit to be returned. We're sure he'll be back.

The original editor of N16, Tim Webb, wrote a perceptive and often hilarious series of sketches based on attending Hackney Council Meetings down in Mare Street. They ran from Issues 6 to 19. Eventually Tim, tireless as he is, had enough. Here is the first sketch, featuring Mayor Joe Lobenstein, in the Summer of 2000. Like all the other articles in the magazine, these can be found in the back issues of our website.

The Coronation of Joe Lobenstein

Early evening trade was brisk in the Samuel Pepys pub in Mare Street. People were finishing their drinks before setting off for an evening's entertainment. They had an exciting choice within only a short walk. Just up the road at the Hackney Empire, the Rocky Horror Show ('fast, funny, sexy' – *Daily Mail*) was packing in the punters. Next door, at the Town Hall, the cast of the rocky finances show – the councillors at their monthly meeting – were also ready for curtain up. A new Mayor was about to be elected.

Inside the council chamber, the councillors and their guests scrambled to their feet as the mace bearer demanded that we 'be upstanding for the Mayor of Hackney, Councillor Joe Lobenstein, MBE !' Joe, long-time scourge of socialism and now Mayor for three successive years, entered stage right and plonked himself in the Chair. His chain of office gleamed across his plump mayoral chest and stomach. A military looking man, dressed like the governor-general of a small Caribbean island, sat at the end of the platform. A councillor told me he was the Mayor's driver. In fact, he was the Deputy Lord Lieutenant of London, paying a visit to see local democracy in action. A fire alarm started to ring in the corridor outside. Eric Ollerenshaw, Tory leader, leapt to his feet. Was he going to lead us to safety through the flames? No, he only wanted propose a 30-minute adjournment to consult his group. We were mystified. What was going on? Back to the Pepys for a quick half pint. The moment we had all been waiting for finally arrived. The nominations for the new Mayor. Which dynamic, creative figure would they choose? New Mayor, New Hackney. The Liberal Democrats nominated Councillor Howard Hyman. Who he? Then it was the turn of the Tories. Eric rose again. 'We nominate Councillor Joe Lobenstein.' Oh no. Did we hear right? Not again. Say it ain't so, Joe. Don't worry, here comes Jules Pipe, leader of Labour, the largest group. Like Tony Blair, he'll modernise us. The forces of conservatism will be blown away. We breathed again as he launched into a eulogy about Laz Oleforo, Deputy Mayor and all-round good guy, hard worker, dedicated and principled. Great, Laz is no loser. Cometh the hour, cometh the man. We waited for Jules to finish. But his last sentence began with 'however' and we blinked. Amazingly, he went on to say the nomination of Laz would not be pursued and Labour would be backing their ancient enemy Joe. Howard Hyman received 13 votes and Joe romped home with 37. A few Labour hands seemed to be raised rather reluctantly. A shout of 'Oh, Blimey, what a stitch-up!' rang from the public gallery. A group of about ten protesters were working themselves up into a state of noisy indignation. 'What about the people of Hackney?' No one in the chamber took much notice, so they started to shout back at themselves. 'Hang your heads in shame!' they cried. 'They know no shame!' came their reply. 'Rubbish!' they accused. 'Yes, that's what they are rubbish!' they echoed. Obviously renewed with fresh energy and confidence, Mayor Joe told them to be quiet or be thrown out. 'You're not allowed to touch us!' they shouted defiantly. So they threw themselves out.

Joe made a gracious speech of acceptance – his fourth in four years – and said that even though he had met the Queen, the Duke of Edinburgh and Prince Charles, his favourite people were 'Mr and Mrs Hackney'. He nominated 'my lovely wife Bella' as Lady Mayoress. Bella smiled radiantly as Joe praised her abilities in providing sandwiches for his guests. The Bella effect worked miracles. Harmony broke out all around the chamber. First names were used, political rivals were thanked and appointments shared out between the parties. Bouquets were presented to the staff. We then adjourned to a nearby room to drink wine and consume mountains of sandwiches. Hackney can relax. In the first year of the new millennium our civic figurehead will enshrine the eternal values of the past. Joe's our man. Again.

Tim also wrote, in the same issue, an article which neatly encapsulated the increasing pretentiousness of much of the Stoke Newington Festival, which was to close in 2002 .

Revealed: Festival Highlights

Responding to criticism that this year's Stoke Newington Festival reached new heights of pretentious twaddle and obscure happenings, recently appointed Festival Director Tracey Amen confirmed that she plans a fresh approach to next year's events. 'The others screwed up big time', she stated. 'All those failed actors, unknown performance artists, bogus attention-seekers and art students on the make, plus unreadable language in the programme, really pissed off ordinary people like me who live around here.' Pushing aside her bacon sandwich, she continued, 'we believe that our sort should have what they really, really want, not a load of poncy stuff imported by middle-class tossers who spend more time in the Dordogne than in Dalston.' She let *N16* have a quick peek at some of the main items next year.

SUNDAY. Grand opening and speech by the **Mayor of London, Ken Livingstone**, outside the newly privatised Stoke Newington Town Hall. Moving into Clissold Park, and accompanied by the **Queen Mum**, Ken will inspect the ponds for signs of newt life. In Church Street the stalls will be stocked with good British food, including fried Mars Bars, prawn cocktails, fish fingers, mushy peas, creamed rice and custard, bangers and mash. **The Stoke Newington Firefighters' Male Voice Choir** will perform a medley of Cockney songs and football

chants inside Booth's Bar. The main event of the day will be the **White Van Grand Prix** around the High Street one-way system. Drivers wearing England replica football shirts will force each other off the road. They steer the van with one hand, the other free for giving the finger, mobile, and cigarette. The surviving driver and his mate will win a Cross of St George banner, two tickets to England versus the Faroe Isles in Euro 2004 and a training course in plastic chair throwing.

MONDAY. Let's Go Cruising! A mysterious walk at dusk in Abney Park Cemetery. Shadowy figures flit behind the gravestones in the old boneyard. You may have a brief encounter of the closest kind.

TUESDAY. A Night in the Cells. Stokey's finest will perform an arrest and body search if you act in a suspicious manner near the police station. You will be cuffed and then booked by a real desk sergeant before being led to your own private cell. At 4 am you will be woken and given a mock kicking or 'restraint'. You will be released without charge at 7am after a good breakfast of hot tea and cold porridge. Too old at 80? Don't believe it. Sabrina's Sauna and Massage Parlour kindly provides **Helping Hands** for senior citizens. Feel the relief. Men only.

WEDNESDAY. A Tour of Local Pub Toilets. Have you ever felt confused when you are caught short in the pub after nine pints of lager and a Thai meal? Why is there no toilet seat? Where is the bog roll? Which is the hot tap and why doesn't it work? Does the door lock? All questions answered by your highly qualified tour guide an ex-pub landlord. Bring your own air freshener.

THURSDAY. The Dead Cat Show. Has your moggy recently passed through the great catflap in the sky? Turn your moment of grief into a window of opportunity. Enter the competition for the most alternatively beautiful deceased feline friend. Missing ears, teeth and claws score points.

FRIDAY. Kylie and her posse of gorgeous gals provide **Lap Dancing for Beginners** in the Library. Learn a new skill and liven up your life. No more dreary after-dinner chat about GM foods. Knock back a bacardi and coke then wriggle around your partner and friends! Women only.

SATURDAY. World Premiere. Hackney Council proudly presents the **Hackney Bin Dancers**. Six (later five, after redundancies) muscular men leap and prance around the new wheelie bins. Ankle bells and leather boots drum out a magical sound on the pavement outside your house. Black bags swirling around their bodies, these refuse operatives cut a dashing scene in the early morning. A 5-minute break will take place as they take part in a traditional 'withdrawal of labour'. Due to financial cuts, the time of performances will be announced, changed and then cancelled. This show is due for privatisation.

Just a Few Lines

Poets are everywhere in our parish, and the magazine is fortunate to have published work by two of the finest, John Hegley and Tim Wells. We begin this section with Gail Chester, whose Murder Mile *won a prize from BBC Radio 4.*

Murder Mile
By Gail Chester, Summer 2003 (18)

They call it Murder Mile, I call it home.
They call it Murder Mile, I call it
Waiting for the 253 bus which never seems to go beyond Hackney Central
Despite telling us they've improved the service.
They call it Murder Mile, I call it
The Sam and Annie Cohen Day Centre full of Afro-Caribbean elders
The Turkish bakery selling ackee and saltfish bagels, bacon bagels, croissants and pizzas
The Chinese Take Away selling kebabs, jamake patties, and fish and chips.
They call it Murder Mile, I call it
Marvin, trapped in his third floor flat
No longer able to visit his book-lined study, the British Library
Since the council took his Freedom Pass away
He wonders why his wasted body should condemn him to a wasted mind.
Yes, it's murder all right
When you're trying to raise your kids
And two of them have asthma from the cars
Racing through as they make their way to important other places that are not your street
And you've just heard they're shutting the local sorting office 'for economy reasons'
Like it's going to be very economical to get the bus to Leyton to collect a registered letter that arrived while you were out.
They call it Murder Mile,
Yet it throbs with the life of every continent
With the live and let live of every imaginable cultural variation
With the black and the white and the red and the green and the purple and the pink and the brown
Of a swirling kaleidoscope of life
They call it Murder Mile, I call it
Rabbi Grunbaum arguing with Mr Fawzi about whether we should support Bush over Iraq
Even though, or maybe because
They are both on the committee for Muslim Jewish understanding
Which, as everybody says, could teach the Middle East a thing or two about peaceful co-existence.
They call it Murder Mile, I call it
A heartbroken mother whose teenage son has just been given two years for possession and dealing
They've shattered her dreams, shattered her nerves
And all because a young boy wanted his own mixing table

Since they shut down the youth club and took his hopes away.
They call it Murder Mile, I call it
The road stretching between the shtetl on the Hill
Where the residents dwell, occasionally to excess, on matters of the soul
And the Town Hall Square, the so-called Heart of Hackney
Where the politicians meet, and the residents wonder if they have a heart at all.
They call it Murder Mile, I call it
Justin and Marie who moved to Clapton when their youngest was born and
they were priced out of Stoke Newington and are slightly nervous about what all these killings will do to the value of their house.
They call it Murder Mile, I call it
Despair, as yet another friend announces they are leaving
Because it's so dangerous in the city
Remember Soham, I say
Remember Dunblane
Remember Hungerford
Remember Telford
Remember that farmers have one of the highest suicide rates
Consider the pesticides and the sheep dips and the chemicals which deform growing foetuses
Remember being teased at school, and thinking you were the only gay kid on the planet
Remember going out of your mind with boredom in the small town where you grew up
Then tell me it's so dangerous in the city.
Wherever you live, the time comes to die
And Murder Mile is fuller of joyous life
Than all those places where alarmist headline writers pass their time when they're not at their desks giving us a bad name

Local poet John Hegley became N16 *Magazine's poet-in residence from Summer 2009. Following Richard's profile is a selection of his poems written for the mag.*

Local Laureate,
By Richard Boon, Spring 2008 (37)

There's a considerable interval between asking John Hegley whether he considers himself as foremost a poet or an entertainer and his reply. One during which he admits to being distracted (getting ready for a schoolkids' gig near Bedford in a few hours time); makes coffee; plays some 1950s South American pop from the British Library's collection; and encourages me to read some work by W S Graham from a dog-eared Faber anthology of verse. Admitting that I don't very often read poetry, he observes, 'Few people do. But, being a slow reader myself, the short form suits me.'

Though perhaps largely linked with Luton, where he was raised and whose football team he follows with

a mixture of chagrin and enthusiasm, John is yet a local lad. Born in 1953 in Newington Green, after all – before his family's relocation when he was 18 months old – he's been back in the 'hood for some time. Despite a digression into the demarcation of the old Stoke Newington borough boundary (he lives in a house on the borderlands), he still considers Clissold Park, for instance, as 'My Place' – with a poem to that effect in an anthology to be published in May, with other poets celebrating locations of fond memory. As he prepares for his performance, he fields calls about his contribution to a forthcoming benefit show for the Nicaraguan Solidarity Campaign at Chat's Palace and exactly which Bedford train he should catch.

He's a busy boy: Edinburgh Festival regular and (as he puts it) 'Radio 4 Hegular', his work has seen him take discarded NHS glasses to needy kids in Africa – a BBC documentary broadcast – (spectacles are one of his tropes, from his early band The Popticians to his 1990 volume of verse, 'Glad To Wear Glasses') and to what he describes as his most notable live engagement in a women's prison in Medellin, Columbia. And the rest – picking up an honorary Arts Doctorate from, naturally, Luton University in 2000 along the way – including these gigs in schools. 'Schoolkids get a 25-minute performance and up to an hour's workshop. I do one maybe every three weeks. Libraries, too.'

Oh yes, finally his answer to our initial question is, 'Foremost, an entertaining poet.' Indeed.

Differences between dogs and deckchairs
A deckchair doesn't beg
or cock its leg up.
Deckchairs don't sniff each other. Deckchairs can't swallow,

or swim, or growl.
Deckchairs aren't her or him.
Deckchairs don't join in games with sticks.
There are no prizes for well-trained deckchairs.
Deckchairs rarely have names (except 'deckchair').
People don't have trouble putting up a dog.
Dogs' legs don't have little notches in.
A deckchair's legs are much stiffer
with no knees.
A dog is better at running after Frisbees.
Deckchairs can be stacked quite neatly.
Dogs have more hairs.
Deckchairs have more letters.
Deckchairs don't sniff about in Autumn leaves.
A deckchair receives little praise.

(At the Edinburgh Festival 2004 while discovering the differences between dogs and deckchairs, a child in the audience pointed out that deckchairs can't fly.)

Frinton
From sea-sided Frinton I'm sent
a book which is not to be bent
and it's not to be sold
it's something to hold
and to look at when sat in my tent

A Turk Perk
In Aberdeen I see the work
of one who's name is Gavin Turk
"e's 'avin' a larf," I'm sure
Laid out upon the gallery floor
: a sleeping bag. A sleeping bag!
Why do people just lie down
and take this kind of guff?
"Stuff it," I say. Just say Nein! No, Non merci.
Then I turn and see the sign that makes me feel a
right bonzo "Sleeping bag - bronze".
Oh. It's not what it appears to me
Not just a bag to house the flea Not just an object
carelessly strewn and Cheap
It's time for me to change my tune
'Twas I who was asleep.

The Art of Teaching
My art teacher calls me to her table
She speaks to me as if I'm highly able. 'What do you
think of this?' she asks
showing me the painting of an un-named pupil
from another class.
I pass no genuine judgement,
unused to such genuine address.
She senses I am blessed with a talent
But I am tense at her attention
And when she mentions the 'texture'
and the 'wash of ochre'
it's just too much - too posh
and her efforts to reach me seem to come to nought
but nowadays I talk of texture
and the wash of ochre
without a fecund thought

And finally, his poem of praise to the Hackney Community Library Services Team.

If you find it a bind to get out and about
never you mind, you can give us a shout
and the library vibe can be brought to your home:
the large print, the average, the audio tome
we've huge cribbage boards; if your vision is blurred
we've jigsaws and scrabble just give us the word
and we'll make a selection around your idea
what seemed out of reach can be suddenly near.
If you are a dalek and can't get outdoors
and you live in Hackney – the service is yours.
If you want horror stories, we've horrible here
we've DVD, video, all of the gear
we will bring the horrific and have you some cheer.
Substantial the stock we can bring to your pad
as much as you'd get if you borrowed like mad,
our visits are monthly, our clients are glad.
No closed on a Wednesday, no frightening fine
some of our customers say it's a life-line
so get on the blower and we will start crating
and loading – yes Hackney your carriage is waiting.

John decided to pass on the mantle to another local poet, after much appreciated service to N16 for almost two years. Here is his last contribution, originally recorded for BBC radio on 21 October 21, to mark the BBC Electric Proms. Some matters of fact – if not punctuation and tense – have been corrected from the original performance.

Richard's Song
My local librarian is mates with Magazine,
they've played at Camden Roundhouse with The Doves,
from the same side of the Pennines,
who were seen
playing with a Bulgarian ensemble:
stretching out the goalposts, broadening the game;
that's what libraries are for.
You ask my local librarian
who knows that libraries are not dull,
his name is Richard.
Jethro Tull once wrote a song for Richard,
but, I think it was another Richard.
The pumpkins were all in the shops,
we headed for Hallowe'en.
My local librarian, just up the road from Newington Green,
where I was born,
is mates with Magazine:
they've played at The Roundhouse,
where Jimi Hendrix took the floor;
they've looked at life from both sides now
and that, my loves, is what libraries are for.
You ask Richard.
But,
      please,
          ask him quietly.

And the baton in the N16 poetry relay passed to Stoke Newington poet Tim Wells – as his business card (poets have business cards?) states: 'Tough on poetry. Tough on the causes of poetry'. As founding editor of the poetry magazine Rising, *Tim has published the work of such writers as Sean O'Brien, Roddy Lumsden, August Kleinzahler, Annie Freud, John Stammers and Matthew Sweeney. His work as a poet and performer has seen him touring the USA (a dozen times), translated into German and Chinese, working as a guest poet on Radio London and as Writer in Residence with Tighten Up, the East London reggae sound system. His* Boys' Night Out in the Afternoon *was shortlisted for the Forward Prize for Best First Collection in 2006. His most recent publication is* Rougher Yet.

Ben Sherman
In the 70s, people thought the future
would be flyless suits and hoverpacks.
I knew it would be no change really,
drunken yobs in Ben Shermans
kicking the shit out of each other.
Feels good to have backed a winner.

Heaven's Just a Sin Away
In a perfect world
on my way home from the pub
I would see:
a fight
a vomiting teenager
a stand up pair of shoes in the street
a blow job taking place
and a crying girl.
Of late
there's been a dearth of weeping women.
I live in Stoke Newington
which is far from perfect.
Even for one as easily pleased as I.

Steamy Windows
I've been sporting my bins a few months now and
they've not steamed up once. This concerns me. I
thought I lived a Carry On life, one with a fair dash of
sauce, but not once has a peek of cleavage or a peep
of arse caused any condensation at all. I feel cheated
– by opticians, by circumstance, by life.

In my boyhood it seemed that Charles Hawtrey's fogged like the inside of a Turkish Bath every time a winsome young thing bent over. I remark upon this to a bespectacled friend, one who has worn them for years rather than my paltry months. He says that walking into a warm pub from cold weather has done it for him. For several weeks of a 'tatoes spring I've walked into a variety of pubs, East End, West End, even across the river. Lunchtime, afternoon, night, nothing happens. I hunch face down over my usual lager top. I try brandy, whiskey and work my way across the top shelf. Nish. My girlfriend notes my frustration, as she is wont to do. She holds my hand and tells me reassuringly that'll it'll happen for me. It doesn't. Perhaps I've been looking in the wrong places?

I phone her from work and tell her I'm going to the Olde Axe. That's the best strip pub East London has to offer – best in my parlance, being the one where your shoes stick to the carpet, the girls have stretch marks, bruises and it's tears before bedtime. A couple of hours later, nothing: lager top, arses, salt and vinegar crisps, tits, bad jokes, pussies, a pickled egg and a girl who makes her arsehole wink just inches from my face, which, to be honest, I could have done without. Nothing.

My girlfriend can tell by my boat when I get home that I'm not best pleased, but asks hopefully how it went. I dejectedly shake my head. She tells me that she's sure the former Soviet girls tried their very best for me. She takes both my hands, leans into my face and haaaaahs a gentle breath into my face. There! The glasses mist with the fine dew of her whisper. She lifts her index finger and writes her initials onto the lenses – her first upon the left, the last onto the right in what, to her, must be mirror writing.

'What can you see', she asks.
'Oh yes, I love you and you love me.'

At the closing event of Stokey's literary Festival in 2011 – Ska and Reggae in Stoke Newington – featuring founder of the Four Aces club, Newton Dunbar, among others, local poet Tim Wells contributed these short pieces. Move your feet to the rocksteady beat.

A Quitter never Wins
A retort to critical theory
It's heartwarming;
my troublesome daughter
is tapping her foot to the triumphant soul choons
blaring from her iPod.

Even softened through ear-
phones this one's Okeh ...
'Oh yeah! Oh yeah!'

I picture myself

out on the floor:
spinning, twisting, turning.
The intricate steps of my feet,
the beat, the bass, the brass.
As a teenager I didn't
think about it,
just did it.

Wa do dem
Back in the early 80s I was a young pisher with a job. All the wedge in my bin went on lager-top, windowpane check and jamdown sound. At the same time, Eek A Mouse was the biggest DJ in the game – not only by virtue of the fact that his choons were massive, but 'cos he stood six foot six inches tall.

One Saturday, music pumping, I was bouncing round my room getting ready to go to one of his shows. I was so excited that I'd forgotten to pull the pins from the new Sherman I'd bought that morning. There I was, stepping round my carpet, blood dripping and Billy Whizzing.

We all met up early doors for a beer by Highbury and Islington tube. Them 2-Tone twins were there with their ghetto blaster blaring Barrington Levy. Later, walking up the Holloway Road, I spotted the Mouse outside the venue with some long-haired berk shoving a micro- phone in his face. Us skinheads legged it across the road, swerving around sherberts and yelling "Eek A Mouse! Eek A Mouse!" As we drew to the man, the longhair let out a faint "Oh my gawd," in a septic accent. The Mouse looked down at us...

"See it dere! Even de cockney dem a know we!" He stood a further foot taller with the pride.

Sound Man burial
They carried him box in like a bass bin.
Man, it had the dreadest thud of all.
We was all there, dressed for some
killer diller party night just one more time.
When they done laying him down
we supped the bottle and passed the draw.
Funny how it was youngsters there,
An' us here so, like it were east London
and south inna dance from time;
each group cupping spliff,
trying not to get caught by the other –
these sons truly sprung from these fathers!
By the time the bottles were emptying
the dance floor was raisin' up;
ska tunes from when we were rude,
rude once more. Prince Buster,
Lloyd Nibbs, Tommy McCook...
the horns blew a welcome.
'cos me hear that even in heaven
they have a sound but them can't get no Red Stripe
beer fe sell in a dance at night.

Letters

Browsing various websites on Saturday, I came across *N16*. As a person born and brought up in E5 it was great to see. I now live in Sunderland and I must admit I miss the excitement of living in a big city with all its good and bad points. Where I live is an ex-pit village, not bad but very introverted in nature – not many cafes to sit in (or out) and read the *Guardian*! Well, do your best to keep going and give my best to the pubs and clubs of Hackney.

Mark (ex-Brooke House pupil)

I could not believe my eyes when I read in your autumn edition, that someone had written a book about the Routemaster. Now when we were living in the middle of the road in a matchbox – that was a time for nostalgia. The 38 bus with open top deck – that was a work of art with all the comforts one could think of. Wooden slatted seats so that the rain would go through – canvas awnings that pulled out over your lap. If I remember rightly, they were designed to ensure that the rain collected and then came towards you. Consequently, nobody used them and were there until they died.

Stoke Newington likes to pose as being an interesting, perhaps the most interesting, part of north London. It may have been once, but in 2006, it most certainly isn't. I lived in Stoke Newington for five years, from 2000-2005. During this time, Church Street turned from being a heaven of laid-back, cheap, friendly bars, pubs, shops and restaurants to the expensive, Upper-Street-less-Starbucks strip of boredom that it is today, complete with its population of ultra-aloof yuppies, a frighteningly unfriendly generation of well-heeled young mothers with pricey looking prams (and husbands in city law firms / banks) along with many, many, more yukky posers, who it was once a relief to leave standing in Islington as a warm, crowded 73 Routemaster sped along Essex Road towards that little pocket of sanity east of Highbury. In those days, the friendly sound of jazz music echoed around the top of Church Street every evening, life in Stokey was still affordable and proud of its affordability I might add, and the High Street yet to be ruined by yet more trendy, shallow, dull bars and confusingly enormous numbers of ugly new buses and bus routes. Goodbye, Stokey of old, I miss you.

My name is Doris. I was brought up in Stokey (as you now call it). I was seven when we moved to Lordship Terrace in 1937. I loved living there, and used to go on the boats on the ponds, and look at the animals, deer etc. Is the mulberry tree still there? And the river by Green Lanes? There used to be trees down Queen Elizabeth Walk then but they had to be taken away when the war started. I went through the Blitz, and was an evacuee for a while. I went to St Mary's school in Edwards Lane. I had a teacher named Miss Phaff. I came across your website on my laptop (by the way, I am 76 now so was pleased to see all about Stokey). I have been inside the two churches as a child at school and heard the two bombs go off in the war. Thanks for the memories and look forward to hearing from you. Byeee.

Hi, it's me again, Doris, to continue about my life in Stokey when I was a child. I can remember when I lived in Victoria Road (I was, say, six at that time) a man on the corner playing an organ grinder with a monkey on his shoulder. I used to dance to the music then. Also this was the dying age of the knife grinder, the ice man, the cat meat man, the coalman, the milk that came on a cart and filled up a jug, a rag and bone man for old rags etc. It was all was horse and cart in those days. I used to play marbles on the kerb, flick cards, and do hopscotch and skipping. I was never bored in those times like they are these days, and at least we were safe to play out then. Oh dear, how times have changed. From seven years old we moved to the flats at Lordship Road. So I guess it's all for this time. Next time I will tell you about what I did after the 1939 War started.

(We never did hear from Doris again)

In response to Doris's letter in your last issue:

Dear Doris

Yes, the New River still flows through the park. And yes, the mulberry tree is still there, near the church. I was delighted to discover it last year – my son and I enjoyed scoffing some of the delicious fruits. Actually, it would be brilliant if there were more of these in the park. And maybe some Sweet Chestnuts, instead of those boring municipal Alders and London Planes.

'Do I get you? (*article on 'hoodies', issue 29*)' No, unfortunately I do not. Hoodies, young people, bad behaviour and general disrespect, I get that. But not an adult saying that our teenager's trends and attitudes are on the whole acceptable – not in inner London. I'd like to know where the reporter found her teenagers, because she certainly did not find them at my school (I am a secondary teacher in E1). I like kids very much, and I like the 'bad' ones. But I would not like to be a stranger passing them in their gangs at night, or even in the day really. Where were the two hoodie interviewees found? On their way home from a public school?

To say that the majority of kids nowadays, and I can only talk of inner London, are motivated, animated and sociable is a joke, if we're talking of the hoodie crews. And these qualities are the last thing they want to be. They want to be cool. As have all teenagers in the past. Saying that their styles are 'a rich expression' will only push these young people further from civilised society: they just want to be cool. In the comparison to the punk scene, there is the musical influence on dress sense; but the adults of that era didn't say, 'Oh yeah, I love that green spiky hair and those chains; think I'll get a few.' They said, 'You look bloody awful, son'. Today, the hoodie crew kids want to be gangstas, and rappers (of course not all, but lots of them), and rappers' wives. The popular music scene that shows the young people very rich people who have little or no education, but plenty of money, sex and power is the route many of kids are aspiring to. Fuck it, they can 'spit'. But they have to do something because everyone who they don't want to be is wearing a hoodie. So, up the attitude, stand out, be bad. There is no force to fight against because there are adults around them saying, 'yes, that's great, love; in fact I'll join you.'

I am being harsh, but goodness me, the teenagers do not run the country and should not be allowed to feel as if they do; and certainly should not be encouraged to stray further into anti-social behaviour – and gangs, and drugs. The glamourisation of this fantasy drug/rap/money-for-nothing world is a very bad influence, and the misconception of its coolness is a distressing route. Ride the buses around the East End after school, cover your ears and get off as quick as you can. We have to stop saying it's ok: it isn't. I am sad and afraid for these future generations. Take down your hoodie, pull up your trousers and shut up. Kids too. Incidentally, I woke up this morning to the news on my clock radio: a priest somewhere in Brixton is an advocate of hoodies, and he's wearing his up. God help us.

It's an ongoing argument between me and my other half. 'Stokey wouldn't be Stokey if we were on the tube map', he says. No tube means a 'village atmosphere', he says. Cycling and walking and

smiling at slightly unstable people on the bus to work is so much more civilised than all that faffing around with copies of *Metro* and getting intimate with the scent of a million strangers' underarms on the miserable old underground. But if, like me, you aren't blessed with a short morning stroll to your boutique business on Church Street, and must instead venture out of N16 to earn your crust – it isn't quite so beautiful. And for the truly damned and cursed among us, it is a living hell. Yes, I'm talking about those of us who rely on the 393 bus to take us to (what I insist is) the oasis of civilisation that is Highbury tube station. I have lived all over London, from Kilburn to Camberwell, and I have never experienced such a poor excuse for a bus service in my thirty years as a London resident. Waiting for the 393 at any hour, never mind the rush hour, is like waiting for Clissold Leisure Centre to re-open. Blind optimism means you never quite give up hope... but you know that the bookies would give you better odds if you put your money on Stokey traffic wardens putting away their ticket books and taking a tea break occasionally. The 393 bus is infrequent, unreliable, doesn't appear on any of the 'next bus due' monitors at bus stops and is, in short, rubbish. Why is Stoke Newington so under-served for transport? And who can tell me what is being done to address this?

393
TO HIGHBURY

Don't worry, it'll be along soon.

LONDON BUSES

Nicola Streeten

Home Thoughts

The continuing rise in house prices over the last few years in the Stoke Newington area is quite remarkable. Proximity to the City and the West End, the fact that building new properties is difficult, and the escalating prices in Islington and Shoreditch are driving cash-rich high-fliers into our trendy little paradise. Currently it's very much a sellers' market and rental prices are soaring. People who have lived here all their lives cannot afford the place anymore, their places taken by floods of wealthy incomers. It's been heading this way for the last ten years or so, as the following articles from the mag makes clear.

A Big Hello From Armani and Trotsky
(By Ken Worpole, Winter 2000 (8)

It's the way they sell them. Would-be buyers of apartments in the new development at the junction of Balls Pond Road with Southgate Road are promised an 'Islington lifestyle with Armani-suited concierges', whereas up in Stoke Newington, trading on the area's erstwhile cutting-edge political reputation, home-seekers are invited to 'Trot along to the Revolution'.

Hackney today is development crazy, and new refurbishments, conversions and wholly new apartment blocks are springing up on every street corner and down every back alley or derelict industrial mews. Stoke Newington seems ripe for the intensification of the new Richard Rogers' style inner city 'cappuccino culture', based on live-work developments where young entrepreneurs work from home via mobile phone and email, shop locally and network furiously in local cafes which become the centres of the new e-commerce industrial clusters.

Red Square is already famous (or infamous) for its tongue-in-cheek advertising blitz on billboards and in the property pages. It sells Stoke Newington as 'a bohemian quarter where diverse communities contribute to a rich cultural mix', a place where the new artisans of the e-revolution will work from home,

and in the evenings cruise Stoke Newington Church Street with '5,000 artists, 50 pubs, untold restaurants and the best Jazz joint in town'. It is designed by professional architects – the well-known practice of Campbell Zogolovitch Wilkinson and Gough – and it has a certain insouciant flair in its design. The extensive glossy literature says nothing, however, about local schools and council services, and one assumes that the apartments are aimed at young, childless couples who will not be settling in Stoke Newington for life, but passing through. Red Square offers 115 housing units with car parking for 90 cars, but there is no private gym, unlike the proposals for the former Defoe Road Depot comprising 45 residential and 10 live/work units with 33 car bays and a two-storey gym. Admittedly, cars are a part of everyday life, but the whole point of the government's urban renaissance was to discourage car use for these small inner city developments, and indeed even suggested that some should be built with no car parking provision at all.

And why a private gym at Defoe Road, when the nearby state-of-the-art Clissold Leisure Centre – finally due to open next year (*however, see page 108.*) – is within easy jogging distance? Is it because it is assumed that the people moving into these apartments don't really want to mix? The Defoe Road proposals suggest another disturbing trend about these new loft-style developments, which is that they are being built with little or no attention being paid to the impact upon the local infrastructure. In fact a number of them actually have replaced the historic civic infrastructure: Fleetwood is formerly Fleetwod Primary School, Scholar's Yard in Ayrsome Road was once Stoke Newington College, and Defoe Road is where the Council's refuse depot used to be.

If some of the new residents have children, where will they go to school? How are the new e-revolutionaries going to cope with uncollected rubbish, poorly managed and maintained parks, libraries and street repairs – or are they going to run away their worries on a private exercise machine? And what also of the government's – and one assumes Hackney's – commitment to halting social

polarisation and creating mixed communities? The new report from the Mayor's Commission on Housing for London has argued that inner London needs up to 50 per cent of all new housing to be 'affordable' to people who may be on benefits or without savings, as well as key workers such as nurses, teachers, hospital doctors and others who work and yet still don't earn enough to secure a mortgage.

The government's own planning legislation recommends that all new developments of more than 15 units should contain a significant element of affordable housing, and in London the Housing Commission has argued that this is now needed as a matter of urgency. But Red Square appears to contain no affordable housing, despite its revolutionary marketing rhetoric, although the development on the Wilmer Place site opposite William Patten School, does include a number of units for rent.

There's something fishy, too, about the sudden enthusiasm for live-work units, which suggests that these may have been imposed by Hackney's planning department as a means of trying to avoid Stoke Newington becoming wholly a restaurant district. Live-work developments were pioneered locally by arts and crafts workers in the early 1980s, but one suspects that there will be little monitoring by Hackney as to whether people really are working from home and sustaining some kind of local economy, or whether it is developers simply taking advantage of planning loopholes to get new private housing built with a veneer of social contribution.

Elsewhere in Stoke Newington the building frenzy is throwing up other examples of the good, the bad and the ugly. The new housing development for NHS workers at the junction of Brownswood Road and Green Lanes is as cheap and nasty as it can get, on a corner site where a bit of uplift was badly needed. Contrast this to the Peabody development at Newington Green, at the junction of Albion Road and Green Lanes, where a real landmark building has been designed and constructed. This is a fantastic building enhancing rather than destroying one of Stoke Newington's most treasured places, Newington Green.

However, one suspects that, given Hackney's parlous financial state, not too many arduous conditions are being imposed on developers, other than those which attract the maximum income for the Council. If Stoke Newington is to be a successful mixed urban quarter, retaining people rather than giving them a frisson of cosmopolitan café culture for a couple of years before they go off to raise their families in more propitious settings, then much more thought needs to be given to improving the basic infrastructure which, in the closing weeks of the second millennium looks distinctly close to meltdown.

Michael Naik Revisited
By Trevor Jones, Spring 2008 (37)

We interviewed Michael Naik in our first issue, so it's about time to chat to him again him to get his thoughts on changes in the local property scene. The first time round, Michael was a mere kid on the block, as he had only been working in Stokey for 17 years. Born and bred in Mauritius, Michael gained a degree in Business Studies in Wolverhampton and also has a Diploma in Estate Management from what was then North East London Polytechnic. In 1982, he worked for an estate agent in Stamford Hill and by 1985 he had opened the first Michael Naik office on Church Street. His business is one of the two oldest estate agents in Stokey. Michael assesses the current situation as follows: 'From the beginning of 2007 to the beginning of 2008 is the first time for some time I saw a few commercial properties come on the market in Stoke Newington Church Street. Some changes have occurred within the area for shops with an A3 licence. Some have turned to bigger premises. Yum Yum now has a 250-seat plus restaurant a stone's throw from where they used to be in Church Street... Stokey has been gentrified, but still has a village feel.'

What about the global credit crisis and rising local rents? 'I have witnessed rent rising appreciably over the last 8-10 years. Rents have almost doubled in the last ten years. Judging from the rent reviews in which I have been involved, an average unit, shop and basement in Church Street now commands a rent in the region of £18,000 per annum and £16,500 per annum on the High Street.' Pause for aspiring shopkeepers to take a deep breath. 'If you want to buy a shop with two flats, £800,000 to £1 million will do nicely.' Global credit crisis? 'With the slowdown of the residential housing market, I do not foresee any slump in commercial rent ... the reason being that there is very little similarity between the economic conditions today and the sad situation that precipitated the housing crash of the early 1990s ... the demand for good quality local shop units is still strong.' Other changes? 'Many businesses have been badly affected by the parking restrictions.' Essentially, parking on Church Street is a nightmare, and the Council should put more thought into the effect on local business.' The next ten years? 'The new hot area will be the expansion of Dalston.'

In Common

Stoke Newington Common, bounded by Rectory and Northwold Roads, has changed dramatically over the last few years. The influx of concerned, middle-class residents has made a significant difference to the scraggy old place, as it was, but its utilisation as a public space is constrained by the various modes of transport passing through it. Still, everyone has done everything possible to turn it into an attractive addition to the other green spaces in the area. But the one-way system really has to go.

Two Way Traffic
By Robert Lindsay, Spring 2006 (29)

Ever wondered what Stoke Newington Common would be like if they would just close the road that rips through the middle of it to traffic? I have, which is why I started a campaign to try to get Stoke Newington's one-way system scrapped and Rectory Road grassed over. The key traffic planner for Hackney, Dale McKenzie, wants to shut Rectory Road and restore the Common for residents. At a recent meeting, he said he was 'passionate' about closing Rectory Road over the Common, joining together the two parts that have been severed for 30 years. The closure of the road will form part of a feasibility study he is about to commission into scrapping the one-way system – known in the planners' jargon as a 'gyratory' – that I believe has blighted Stoke Newington High Street and the houses and lives of residents along Evering Road, Rectory Road, Manse Road and Northwold Road since the 1970s.

Atique Chouchury, who has recently formed the Stoke Newington Business Association, said: 'It's designed to get traffic going as quickly as possible through the area. It does nothing for the community or the traders.' Trevor Parsons, of the Hackney branch of the London Cycling campaign, and a key mover in getting rid off Shoreditch's one-way system three years ago, commented 'Good. We've been waiting for someone to do that for a while.' There was a similar reaction from three very active residents' groups – Northwold Area Residents, Cazenove Area Action Group and Listria Park/Martaban Road. Bringing a large chunk of the Common back to life is not the only benefit. Getting two-way traffic established again would make life safer and quieter for people. Drivers restricted to one lane cannot accelerate past each other in a race for the next traffic lights. Crossing to shops on the other side of the High Street would become easier because pedestrians would only have to deal with one lane of traffic at a time.

By the following issue (30), Robert had spoken to Jennette Arnold, Labour member of the Greater London Assembly, and representative of North East London, who promised to press the case for the

one-way system's removal with Ken Livingstone (then London's Mayor). Also, Hackney mayor Jules Pipe declared that he was '100 per cent behind' the campaign. Robert picks up the story.

So far, so good. There are two main objections that have been raised with me. One is from a few of the traders – not the majority – on the High Street who believe that their customers need the car parking spaces on the road. The fact is that shops do need places for their delivery vehicles to unload – outside working and commuting hours – and there should be room for time-restricted delivery bays, properly enforced, for all the shops that need them. But no high street should have to support customer parking. I firmly believe that shops would get more customers not less, if the High Street is made two way. Several surveys of the area in the past have shown that, despite what some traders think, their core, loyal customers get to the shops on foot. If the High Street was two way again, the noise and pollution from accelerating cars would be slashed, and more people would turn up to explore and enjoy the rich and diverse range of stores we have.

Another block, in the mind of some politicians at least, is the idea of grassing over Rectory Road, on the common. 'Why are you insisting on closing Rectory Road?' a former Hackney councillor asked me. 'The common is already divided in two by the railway line.'

A few weeks later Jennette Arnold told me: 'Grassing over Rectory Road is impractical. It's just too expensive – or that's what I'm told.' The need to revive Stoke Newington's forgotten green space seems a low priority. But for the thousands of people who live near the common, the lost opportunity stares them in the face every day. They see not only the potential in reuniting the two halves cut by Rectory Road but also in building a green bridge over the rail cutting. So I say, let's be ambitious. Money and political will can be found if enough pressure is applied.

Little further appears to have happened as a result of Robert's campaign, with TfL apparently obdurate in their insistence on maintaining the one-way system. But local residents are still applying the pressure.

A Common Treasury
By Rab MacWilliam, Autumn 2011 (49)

There are probably many people living in this parish, particularly those in the Church Street and High Street areas, who are only dimly aware of Stoke Newington Common. There is often a tendency to look south and west – towards Islington and Highbury – rather than consider the virtues of the eastern part of N16, particularly the Common. Admittedly, the transport links – the deep north-south rail cutting, the A10 gyratory system and the bus route which cuts through the middle – have diminished and trisected its attraction but, despite these obstacles, in recent years it has become one of the most pleasant and attractive green spaces in Stoke Newington.

Archaeological evidence has revealed that the Common was part of a plain, stretching to Kent, which was the location of the earliest human occupation of Britain. The space came under public ownership in 1872, and was known variously as Cockhanger Green and Shacklewell Common, until it acquired its present name in the early 20th century. The old Hackney Brook, which eventually turned into an open sewer, now runs under Northwold Road. Well-known residents included Marc Bolan, who was born and spent his teens at 25 Stoke Newington Common, and one of Karl Marx's sons-in-law lived nearby. The Common was largely derelict throughout most of the last century, and probably reached its nadir during the Binmen's Strike of 1979, when uncollected rubbish piled high on the open space and rats reportedly ran riot. However, over the last ten years or so, the Common has been transformed, largely due to the efforts of the Stoke Newington Common Users Group (SNUG) and the Tree Musketeers, who describe themselves as 'volunteers who plan, protect and help rescue trees in Hackney'. Berni Graham, chair of SNUG, commented 'We value this side of Stoke Newington. There's a lot happening round here.'

Having noticed that there are 21 schools and nurseries within 500 metres from the Common, and that no play facilities existed in the immediate area,

SNUG decided to create a play area for local children. A new playground in the eastern triangle of the Common was opened, after five years of hard work, in September 2006, using natural materials and colours. They have planted new trees and hedges, with the help of local volunteers, and provide care for the young trees. They have also planted a wild flower meadow, and have erected benches made by a local craftsman from recycled wood. Hackney Council are increasingly playing their part by regular mowing of the Common and generally making sure it's tidy and safe. The highlight of the year is the free SNUG-organised annual fun day in September, where hundreds of local residents and their children enjoy all types of activities, including food stalls, tug-of-war, face painting, organised games, arts participation, willow-weaving, music and so on.

As for the rest of the Common, well there's not much anyone can do about the railway line or about the bus route, but a recent consultation carried out by the Council found that 70% of the public want the removal of the gyratory system, part of which slices through the old Common, as do 50% of the businesses who responded. This magazine has long campaigned for the re-routing of the A10, so that the two western ends of the Common can be re-united. It's a forlorn feeling to walk along one of the paths, see it continue tantalisingly on the other side of the road, and have to wait until the cars scream past before you can cross with a degree of safety.

Stop the War
By Sue Jones, Spring 2003 (17)

As an activist in Hackney Stop the War Coalition, my life is currently never without a dull moment. I have been constantly amazed at the reception we have been getting from people in Hackney and the range of people who have been willing to get involved in the coalition. There have been vicars who have given over their church halls for Stop the War groups to meet, Kurdish and Turkish community centres who have let us use their facilities to put on teach-ins and meetings, printers who produced our publicity for free, the Arcola theatre who gave us the use of the theatre for a day and an evening, the shops and restaurants who display our posters but, even more overwhelmingly, the sheer numbers of ordinary people who have been prepared to give up almost all of their spare time to campaign.

Teachers, school kids, housing workers, clergy, socialists, anarchists, trade unions, have all been active in Hackney against the war. This movement has united black and white, gay and straight, men and women – an astonishing feat for Bush and Blair to have inadvertently pulled off. We have had parties for peace, pickets of petrol stations with placards saying 'No blood for oil', stalls at shopping centres, road blocks and leafleting jumble sales. A group of hardy and committed souls do a weekly cycle ride for peace around Hackney handing out leaflets and blowing whistles. There are inspirational figures, such as the 82-year-old pensioner who made an artistic arrangement of Stop the War posters forming a huge NO at Dalston Junction. Strangely, unlike most posters, which taken down immediately by the Council, the Stop the War posters seem to have a miraculously long life. I like to think that this is due to the active support of Council workers.

As I am writing this, Bush and Blair have given up on the UN and an illegal and horrific war is underway. Millions of people throughout this country have made it clear that this war is not in our name. School kids have already set us a fantastic example, with thousands across the country walking out of their schools to demonstrate against the war. On the day the war against Iraq began, around 1500 people demonstrated in Hackney at midday. These were people from community groups, workers and overwhelmingly school students who then marched from Hackney Town Hall to Parliament Square to join other demonstrators from all over London. Regime change could be starting a lot closer to home than Iraq.

Stokey Mini-March
By Saskia Little-Brown, Spring 2003 (17)

It was probably an innocent misunderstanding. But it was waiting to happen. Peter Kennard, long-established Stokey artist/ activist, was refurbishing his Cold War banner for the march against the War. Yes, of course, I'd be proud and happy to accompany it on

the big day. I just didn't realise it was 10 feet high. And that it wouldn't fit neatly – or legally – onto a 73 bus. And that, as a consequence, we'd have to walk all the way from Stokey to the centre of London, and join one of the most awesome gatherings seen in Britain for centuries.

We were late, of course. First, there was some technical stuff with the banner involving staple guns and duct tape (the very same stuff the American government is advising its people to use in the event of an attack by a weapon of mass destruction – how appropriate and how reassuring) then protracted and totally unsuccessful negotiations involving the use of public transport for (my) part of the delegation. Surrender, it appeared, was the only option. I was walking, It was going to hurt.

With a backpack stuffed with bottles of water, locally-sourced samosas, fresh fruit, a bog roll and Pete's partner Judy's dire warnings about frequent toilet stops ringing in our ears, we set off: the N16 Seven (if our two-year-old marching companion, who wisely opted for the buggy, counts).

Through the not-very-rolling hills of Dalston, via a faintly surprised Angel, and an undignified and very un-Ghandian spat over our mini-march route and our collective navigating skills half-way down the Pentonville Road, the Stokey faction – and what seemed like an even larger banner by now – finally collided with the rest of the millions in Gower Street. We'd encountered quizzical gawps along the way, but we'd also been greeted with smiles, waves, thumbs-up and cheers of support as we wound our unlikely way march-wards. The rest, as they say, is history. That's what I told my aching feet.

Ashtrays No More
By Rab MacWilliam, Spring 2007 (33)

It was like saying a final goodbye to one of my oldest friends, but it had to happen. After forty years, with the odd minor interruption, my intimate relationship with fags has come to an end. My buddies had seen me through all sorts of good and bad times, and to find myself bereft of their comfort and unconditional love has left me inconsolable but determined to end my reliance on their devious charms.

The health issue was partly to do with my decision, as was the fact that they now cost over a fiver a pack (at least £10 a day in my case). But the cruncher – the final nail in the coffin, so to speak – was the announcement that, come this July, smoking is to be banned in all public places in England. And that includes public houses, where I do tend to while away some of my spare time. All right, all of my spare time. I had no intention of standing in the rain outside the Rochester Castle, puffing away and revealing to all the pathetic nature of my addiction and my inability to function properly without the regular chemical hit from what I am increasingly beginning to perceive is a noxious, filthy and anti-social habit (or so I keep telling myself).

Having no willpower whatsoever in these matters, I threw myself into the hands of the National Health Service and joined one of their Stop Smoking programmes. The sessions were held once a week in the convenient Roman Road in Bow, two buses and over an hour each way. But the journey in itself, I figured, was part of the therapy. If I didn't really want to do it, would I give up four hours a week of my time? In situations like this you can convince yourself of anything.

There were six of us, in a converted church and under the guidance of a Health Worker from the Royal London Hospital. We ranged from a sweet old lady, who smoked two a day and clearly just wanted the company, to someone whose intake, incredibly, far exceeded mine. We were tested for the amount of carbon monoxide in our blood. Apparently, the normal non-smoker who lives and works in London has a reading of three. Mine was 27. This gave me a clue that things weren't perhaps as they should be, and my excuse that I'd been sucking on the exhaust pipe of a 73 bus for the previous hour did not impress the Health Worker.

We were advised that smoking is not exactly up there with press-ups and circuit training, and that one out of every two smokers dies from smoking-related diseases. Ah, good, that'll be the other one, I thought, in a brief moment of self-deception. We were encouraged to continue smoking for the first two weeks of the eight-week-long course, and then we had abruptly to stop after the third session, with the aid of nicotine replacements, if necessary. Naturally, I signed up for everything they had, except for anti-depressants, but I'll probably also start taking them the way things are going.

The previous time I stopped smoking I lasted nearly eighteen months (this, of course, does not include Tom Thumb cigars), and the initial three-month nicotine patch treatment seemed to have worked. But once an addict, always an addict. I was taking off in a 747 from Heathrow to Los Angeles and suffered a serious panic attack. I high-tailed it to the nearest stewardess, demanded a pack of fags (you could smoke on planes in those days), and finished it by the time we were over Ireland. The rest of the journey passed in a fug of smoke and several miniatures of whisky. I was happy and home again. My sense of wholeness had returned, and the previous eighteen months seemed, in retrospect, like a bereavement.

You people who have never smoked cannot possibly understand the ravenous, evil nature of the beast. Junkies can come off heroin in a few days (albeit often painfully) but nicotine addicts have to live with it forever. The drug itself is pretty much harmless, but the cravings, and the delivery system, are not. Nevertheless, I am now a resolute non-smoker assisted by the patches (which, incidentally, conjure up the most amazing psychedelic dreams). I threw away my last fags just before the Arsenal away European Cup game against PSV Eindhoven, although our dismal performance almost made me head straight back to the rubbish bin. I officially became a non-smoker on the following day, Ash Wednesday, which seemed to me an appropriately symbolic date.

'We provide the anorak – you go out in the rain and climb the hill', said the Health Worker, making me feel like a flawed but ultimately heroic Shakespearian figure. I intend to maintain this deluded self-image, but who knows? I'll report back on progress next issue, either dictating it piously from my exercise bike, or from the Rochester, coughing away like the rest of them.

Letters

I read with interest Victor Ardern's 'Press Watch' article in the last issue of N16. It concludes with 'the day when the sound of City lawyers discussing leveraged buy-outs over a Starbucks Caramel macchito (sic) may be upon us sooner than we fear'. Sorry, Vic – bad news, mate – us City lawyers are already here. However, this City lawyer (and – I would guess – most of the other City lawyers who live in Stokey) actually likes Church Street exactly as it is and has no desire for the big corporate names to take over (a la Upper Street). And as one of the 'fortunate few' I am happy to distribute some of my hard-earned to the local shopkeepers, bar owners and restaurateurs. I'm guessing that Victor's comments were tongue in cheek.

I do, however, know of a gym instructor working in Canary Wharf who was thinking of moving to this area. He came over one evening with a friend to check out Church Street and they went to a local bar for a beer. The gym instructor remarked to his friend that he liked the area but didn't think he would be able to stand the commute to Canary Wharf. One of the bar staff overheard and interjected 'we don't want your sort around here, anyway' – and he then clarified that by 'your sort' he meant 'City workers'. Nice and welcoming, then – and a comment that sums up a certain type of Stokeyite who seems to view anyone who works 'in the City' as being on a par with Satan. So, chaps – here are some facts for you.

1) A job can be just a job – it needn't necessarily define you as a person. Most people who work 'in the City' are not rabid, right-wing, money, power and status-obsessed Gordon Gekkos – and the few that are would be fairly unlikely to be living in Stokey.

2) The vast majority of people who work 'in the City' don't actually earn the outrageous sums that you read about in the papers.

3) As for being amongst the 'fortunate few' – true, there are still a few 'old school ties' around in certain areas, but the City is generally a meritocracy where intelligence and hard graft count for a lot. If you are a brainless, upper middle class twat, then you are unlikely to have a career 'in the City' because a) you wouldn't be able to hack it and b) if Mummy and Daddy have already bought you a nice flat in London to live in then you don't actually need to do a difficult, stressful (but relatively high-paid) job.

So the next time you see someone in the locality wearing 'their office uniform', rather than sneering at them why not try adopting the kind of liberal, open-minded attitude for which Stokey is justly famous – and give them a smile. They're probably pretty similar to you – just trying to earn a living.

With regard to the City-worker's friend (*Issue 31*), who didn't think they'd be able to stand the commute to Canary Wharf, and just in case this has put people off, I commuted to the Isle of Dogs for over a year, and it was quite easy. I worked near the London Arena, so from Stokey Station I'd either get a 106 and then a D6, or any bus to Dalston and then the 277, after which I'd take a pleasant walk over the Wilkinson Bridge to Crossharbour. On the way back, I'd quite often shop at Canary Wharf, or get off at Dalston and walk home, doing a bit of shopping along the way. Biking it along the Lee Valley, through Mile End Park is also pretty straight forward too. Hope this puts the record straight – getting to Canary Wharf is pretty easy from Stokey.

I always read the magazine and have a million raging comments about the same things, so it's time to put them down on paper.
1. I love the Controlled Parking Zone. There's too much traffic on all of London's roads, and especially those of Stoke Newington. You live in a city with a superb transport infrastructure (yes, with occasional minor annoyances), so you don't need to drive a car. Sometimes, N16 really is the epitome of the curse of 'me first' thinking that is overrunning this country. Do what's best for everyone, and leave the car at home when you go shopping. This is the area where you can't move for organic leeks, wooden bicycles and (I'm glad to say) Green Party candidates. So, put your legs where your money is, and get on the buses or walk. Show the kids the scum like me who have already made that choice, and you'll see they don't need protecting from us behind windscreens. If you can't be bothered, stop moaning and accept your place as those antisocials who should be inconvenienced and taxed to the skies.
2. In case you're thinking I'm a raging leftie, I also think Penny Rimbaud should wake up and realise it's 2006. He's one of those hard-left naifs who'd rather see dereliction and threatening men smoking weed in our public places than actual cultural activity. Would it please Penny if we all lived in the gutter as long as his beloved '70s institutions remained? A bit of subtlety, dear. Yes, Dalston Lane development, bad. Yes, Vortex eviction, bad (a fact *N16* magazine seems

to have conveniently forgotten now) (*Unfair, see back issues. Ed.*). But, Gillett Square is actually a good thing in an area where there's very few places to sit and have a nice quiet time. I bet it appalls him when he sees how much people like going into Peacocks too. Find the real things to moan about, Penny, you don't need to oppose everything that's new.

3. Does anyone in N16 actually support Spurs and Arsenal? Always seems to me the fans who watch them play in Stokey's pubs have been shipped in from the outer suburbs where their fans now live. More to the point, does anyone actually read those articles, months after they were relevant? Why not replace them with articles reflecting the area's diverse football-supporting fans? I always see more Galatasary and Besiktas shirts around here.

4. You're far, far, far too obsessed with restaurants. It's like a Sunday supplement once you get into the middle of the mag.

5. Who chooses your cover portraits? Stokey has a whole load of 'personalities' but you always forego them in favour of the most politically correct image. C'mon, go wild, show us those people we see on the street every day rather than those that'd win you a pat on the head from Jules and Ken.

Sorry to moan, I've got it out now, I'm okay.
Charlie

Like Charlie, I always read *N16*, but it's only since he has written to you that I've felt compelled to contribute to your Letters page.

1. Charlie loves the CPZ. He wants us all to use public transport, or walk. He imagines we never stopped to consider the environment before people painted red lines all over the road, making life still more difficult for Stokey's independent retailers. Only Charlie did, in his green underpants. And he's right – I'm so loaded and ignorant, I fly the 20 yards to my local store using an iceberg-powered jet-pack.

2. We're thinking that Charlie is a 'raging leftie', he worries. (Yes, Charlie, you just care too much.) And to prove the point, he disagrees with something that Penny Rimbaud said in the magazine. That's Penny Rimbaud who co-founded Crass, who practically squatted Thatcher's pocket.

3. Charlie asks, 'Does anyone in N16 actually support Spurs and Arsenal?' As the bloke who writes View from the Lane (for free, in case you think I'm trying to save my capitalist bacon), this cut to the quick. Charlie, believe me, as a Spurs fan – the bastard area is heaving with Gooners. 'I always see more Galatasary and Besiktas shirts

around here', he says. I was hoping to word a cogent riposte to that. But all I can think of is: you prat.

4. Charlie says the magazine is 'far, far, far too obsessed with restaurants'. It's barely worth the printer's ink, but: just check the ratio of features on restaurants to features on anything but in the last issue. One half-page food review in 44 pages. Just be glad you have a local magazine, supporting the area, for nothing. Some people have to pay to read a national publication, the *Guardian*, say, then lecture everyone on all they've learned while browsing organic leeks in Fresh & Wild.

5. Look, I'm bored now. Anyone who uses the phrase (with quote marks), 'Stokey has a whole load of 'personalities'' is stomping all over thin ice.

Charlie reckons that kids don't need protecting from him behind windscreens. I'd keep my son behind glass if Charlie were in the area, just in case talking sanctimonious drivel is catching.

Whilst the overall impact of the Olympics and the Thames Gateway plans could be pretty grim, Penny Rimbaud's disgruntled diatribe against Gillett Square (*issue 30*) is somewhat misplaced and peculiarly stand-offish. Perhaps he just had a bad night. Not only does he now romanticise the old car park (he certainly didn't when it was there) and, despite his support for the New Vortex Jazz Club, it seems he hasn't found out about the work that is going on to address his fears for the future of this new square in Dalston. Come off it, Penny: don't write us off. You know there is plenty else to play for and fight for here!
Adam Hart, Hackney Co-operative Developments Member
Gillett Square Partnership

N16 may be your opulent paradise now, but I remember when punk rockers and rastas roamed the streets – and as one of the aforementioned punk rockers, I remember when the whole of the Three Crowns pub turned out to hassle the cops when they stopped me on the street outside and started searching me for drugs. In 1979/80/81 approx my multi-coloured friends and I squatted all over Stoke Newington – Cazenove Road, Dumont Road, Bayston Road... oooo, lots of places. Your lovely little Abney Park graveyard was a hive of gay sex and drug-dealing – it was great! The black guy in the local grocer's would weigh us out a slab of dope on his big metal scales, then we'd go and smoke it down the shebeen in Cazenove Road where your pretty parade of shops is now – we were the only white folk allowed...

Digging for Victory

By Penny Rimbaud, Winter 2004 (24)

When the gas main is being dug up outside the front door to replace the one laid last month, the builder's radio on the roof opposite is almost tuned into Radio Essex, tree butchers are chain-sawing your favourite cherry tree in the park out back because they're worried someone might bump their head on the branches, the neighbours are having their fourth break-up this week and it's only Tuesday, a trio of car alarms are pointlessly calling for help from owners who are four miles away in the City and, to cap it all, there's a visit from the Jehovah's Witnesses, on that kind of day, when everything gets too much, there's always the oasis of the allotment.

Halfway out the door, you meet your neighbour going into hers. She's the one on the other side to the ones having the break-up. You tell her you are going to dig over the potato patch. She tells you that the Council have been testing all their allotments for contamination, and the news looks bad. You give up on the potatoes and decide to head for the pub. It's that kind of day.

But worse than that, you start becoming particularly sensitive to the slightest stomach pains. Lead? Arsenic? It's a slow, painful death that just now you're not ready for and, perhaps more to the point, neither are your children.

There's a meeting called a week later at Hackney Town Hall. The Council's going to clarify the situation. You go along with a portfolio of concerns: just how much of a genuine risk to health is your produce? The Council inform you that it isn't as bad as they'd first thought. The contamination is high, but you'd have to be eating it for fifty odd years for it to have serious effects. You find yourself wondering just what the effects are of the ten years you've been growing your own; and what about those who've been at it longer? In the meantime, you miss the next question. It was something to do with testing methods, asked by one of many allotmenteers who clearly suspect that the Council's real interest is in turning Hackney's few green and pleasant lands into development sites. He is assured that the tests were carried out to the highest scientific standards, and that the Council are committed to ensuring that the allotments remain as allotments. There's one or two doubting sighs from the assembled crowd, but generally the assurances are accepted in good faith.

A week later, you get a letter from the Council telling you that six of their nine allotments are seriously contaminated with lead and arsenic, and that if yours is one of the six, which of course it is, you should immediately stop eating any fruit and vegetables produced there, should not allow your children to play there, and should wear gloves to avoid contacting the soil whilst working there. But after that kind of news who in their right mind would go anywhere near the place. Not you. Suddenly your homegrown, organic dream of self-sufficiency turns horribly sour. The vine tomatoes that only yesterday you'd proudly hung above the sink take on a poisonous air. The marrows stored on top of the dresser now resemble timebombs.

Someone then wants to know how the soil has come to be so polluted, and is informed that the main causes appear to be a mixture of old industrial slag and lead paint, plus modern treated woods. But wasn't the soil tested ten or so years ago? Yes, but these are new EU standards. You're baffled, and so, it appears, is everyone else. Surely, old slag and lead paint were as poisonous then as they are now? But rather than risk the protracted, you decide to pursue the prosaic.

What about Clissold Park, it's only just over the road from your allotment, is that contaminated too? 'No', you're informed, 'it was private parkland for centuries.'

You wonder how it is that the wealthy always seem to get let off the hook, but you don't bother to ask. And then, at last, someone comes up with the million-dollar question: 'what are the Council going to do about it?' Why, replace the soil, of course'. 'And who's going to fund this massive exercise in earth moving?' 'The Council is looking to Government funding to make it possible.'

And the latest news? At this time, 'given that the Council will remediate the allotments shortly. the Health Protection Agency does not consider there to be a significant risk to human health from. consumption of vegetables and fruit, provided that the items are thoroughly washed and peeled. [or from] planting of flowers and shrubs.' However, they do recommend that you 'wear gloves when gardening, wash your hands after working in the allotment and before handling food, wash your children's hands after playing or working in the allotment and before handling food.'

It all seems somewhat toned down from the first devastating missive, but you're still worried about your tomatoes (the marrows having imploded several days ago). You haven't been near the allotment for weeks, and you find yourself worrying about all those other public and private places which might be similarly contaminated. What about your tiny back garden? Does that require protective clothing? What makes it all seem doubly bad is that they're still digging up the gas main outside the front door. You want to go out, but you hardly dare. In desperation, you reach for the phone. 'Hello? Is that the Contaminated Land Officer?'

And this is what you glean: in making the initial tests, the Council were fulfilling a legal obligation; equally, it is their responsibility to remedy the problem. They have taken further soil samples from the contaminated allotments so that appropriate 'robust' remedial action can be taken; this could vary from 'dig and dump' to the installation of raised beds, and will be decided over ongoing meetings with the Allotment Society. Once a contingency plan has been worked out, Government funding will be applied for, which the Council have been informed would take 'three to four weeks'. This should make it possible for the affected allotments to be put right 'over the winter months'.

Whatever the negative implications might be concerning the environmental health risks of city life (of which a book could, and should, be written), it would appear that Hackney Council, in seeing it as a 'showcase' issue, are taking the matter of the allotments very seriously.

One can only hope that the Government will be equally committed in releasing funds as soon as possible. Don't hold your breath.

KAC
By Sarah Dallas, Winter 2004 (24)

Asaf Rifat has run KAC with his wife Linda and son Grant for 17 years. It is Stoke Newington's leading DIY shop, and one of the oldest shops on Church Street.

What attracted you to Stoke Newington?
I started working at KAC when I was 17, as a van driver, earning £6 a week. In those days it was a builders' merchants. I used to get covered in cement and go to the bathhouse (today's Leisure Centre) to wash it all off. I met my wife Linda, who was working in a dry-cleaners opposite, where Oakwood Estate Agents is today. She was a true Stokey girl. We got married in what used to be the town hall.

Where does the name 'KAC' come from?
Mr Kac, a Polish Jew, opened the shop in the 1950s. I bought it from him 17 years ago. I kept the name. Changing it would have been like buying Harrods and changing the name – it wouldn't have been right.

Is there a typical KAC customer?
During the week, it's all women. They come in for everything: paint brushes, DIY stuff, plumbing equipment. There are lots of single women in this neighbourhood, and they like to do their own DIY. Some of them also seem to fancy my son, Grant.

What is your best-selling item?
Mouse traps. Not a day goes by without us selling one. The topseller is our standard wooden model, 'Little Nippers' (£1.15), but we also sell electronic ones for £42. All the restaurants around here leave rubbish on the pavements. So rats and mice are a problem. (During the interview, two customers do indeed come in to buy mouse traps).

Do you enjoy working so closely with your family?
We do have our fights, as our regular customers know. But I love my work. Every day I meet new people and have new challenges. Grant's been working here since he was 12. When I retire he'll take over. My daughters Aysha and Leyla have also worked here on and off.

What other shops and businesses would you like to see in Church Street?
I wish there were more ordinary, down-to-earth shops, like a butcher's or a greengrocer's. We don't need any more fancy bars or restaurants.

Where do you go to escape the shop?
I used to go to Clissold Park to watch people playing boules, but that doesn't happen anymore.

Where would we find you on a Saturday night after shutting up shop?
At home in Hertfordshire, relaxing. At the moment our first grandchild, Evie, is staying with us. It's a great chance for Linda and me to bond with her as grandparents.

Hopes and dreams for the future?
Next year I'm planning to revamp the shop-front, and build two flats upstairs. And Linda and I hope to build a property in northern Cyprus, where we can disappear to. We have some land there, and I'm Turkish, so it's a good place to escape to.

Nobody's Perfect

Life is not all sweetness and light here in Stoke Newington, and there are some disgruntled people at large. Strange as it may seem, they appear to dislike certain aspects of our little village. I know it's difficult to believe.

Letter from Stevie
Spring 2003 (18)

Here are thirty-three things I hate about Stoke Newington.

1. Three wheeled prams. 2. £2.50 a pint. 3. Streets full of shops and no jobs. 4. Career beggars. 5. Primary school that you can't get your kids into. 6. High school that I wouldn't send my kids to. 7. Stokie Police, Hackney's biggest and best ... gang. 8. No more Hackney homeless festival ... why not? 9. Shops full of expensive crap. 10. Bloody yuppies. 11. Estate agents. 12. Stokie Mafia (you know who you are). 13. One big new swimming pool ... instead of two big old swimming pools. 14. The wrong Mayor (again). 15. Street loonies. 16. Muggers. 17. Kids who wear hoods in the summer. 18. A graveyard with more action than Parliament Hill. 19. Local businesses who make big bucks and still pay their staff minimum wage. 20. MPs who think getting McDonalds into Hackney is great for local employment (do you want lies with that?). 21. Crackheads. 22. Junkies. 23. Prostitutes. 24. Shit on the streets. 25. A local council that's so incompetent it's not even funny. 26. Fresh and Wild. 27. Late night pubs that are so rough the bouncers have got bouncers. 28. The toerag(s) who nicked my last two bikes. 29. The loony who followed my girlfriend home singing 'I'm gonna sex you up'. 30. The Vortex for being too elitist for too long and then whining when they lose money. 31. The fact we can't get cable because we live on an estate in N16. 32. Competitions: People from Hackney never win competitions. 33. Myself, for still being here.

(The above observations drew the following response in Issue 19)

Anyone who calls the area 'Stokey' is too sad for words, especially when they spell it Stokie. Hoxton isn't Hoxtey and Clapton isn't referred to as Claptey so what is it with this tabloid press baby talk?

Anyone who hates everyone and everything from three-wheeled prams, Vortex and estate agents to prostitutes, junkies and crackheads (same thing, surely?) and loonies is at best a dreary bloody nimby and at worst a borderline fascist. What's your favourite fantasy, Stevie, a 'final solution' for the action seekers in the cemetery? Labour camps for the beggars and the kids in hoods? Anyone who hates the police is up their own arse, a plastic socialist trying to get some street cred.

Anyone who complains that the streets are full of shops selling expensive crap but that there are no jobs is so dumb that they don't realise that shops actually do create jobs (selling the expensive crap, geddit?). They are so dumb that even if they managed to discover what agency supplies the council with road sweepers and tried to get themselves a job cleaning the shit off the streets they'd be turned down. Anyone who thinks people from Hackney never win competitions is paranoid or no bloody good at competitions. Anyone who expressed a desire to watch cable TV needs to get out more. Anyone who thinks the bouncers need bouncers in any of the pubs around here is obviously too scared to get out more. Anyone in this position will be very confused. Anyone who hates him or herself for living here will be no loss. Bugger off.

PS. I was glad to read that your bikes got nicked. Couldn't happen to a more deserving person.

8 Things I Hate About Stokey
By Nick Griffiths, Winter 2007 (36)

It's very easy to bang on about how great Stokey is, and much of the hot air is true. But where's the fun in endless positivity? If we're not careful, we'll become Jacqui Smith. Or Geri Halliwell! And that would never do. It's time for me to play Devil's advocate.

1. The Gooners. Yes, I know – and the Gooners hate the Spurs fans, but then there are only three of us in N16, and one of them passed away last Tuesday. White Hart Lane isn't that far away! I can always spot the other living Spurs fan when I watch a North London derby on Church Street, because he's the only other prat in the boozer grimacing into his pint. I've watched sodding Spurs v Newcastle in the Auld Shillelagh – and we were outnumbered by Toon. Same for Villa. And Blackburn. Are we really that unfashionable? (Rhetorical.) I've seen small children

in Arsenal tops – so small that they could only fit on the HEN – wandering down Church Street, clutching an organic teddy, and I have wept. Alright, I didn't weep, I went 'Jesus' inside.

2. The Bendy Buses. It's a cliché because it's true. Bendy buses are as reasonable a solution to public transport around N16 as the average elephant herd, or Ken Livingstone with an armchair Velcro'd to his head. Not only are they ungainly, ugly and not manufactured in Aldenham, but they don't have an upstairs from which you used to be able to nose inside The Vortex. I never imagined I could feel nostalgic towards an old bus, but I do. I've hung off the back of a Routemaster up Albion Road, like Fred Astaire during a dance routine, sensed a monoxide rush in my nostrils and been shouted at to 'Oi! Get inside the bus!' and I have never felt more alive. Bendy buses make me feel more like Boris Karloff as he is today.

3. Three-wheel prams. I seem to recall a survey that suggested Stoke Newington houses more mothers than any other place on earth, including maternity wards in China. Why do they all gravitate here? 'Cluck-cluck-cluck', they go, while little Jonty/Arabella howls at the street lighting from inside a three-wheeler offering more safety features than the average Volvo. Have you seen how much those things cost? I've just found an Easylife Off Road Buggy on the net for over 300 quid! Who takes their baby off-roading?

4. The Noticeboard in Fresh & Wild. It's quite bewildering how seriously some people take their diets (and hence themselves). People on that noticeboard literally plead with F&W to stock the latest liver-friendly antacid minki beans from Peru. (Put the Blackberry down – I made them up.) The wife and I often nip inside the door, just to have a laugh at the po-faced lunacy. Yet the people who scrawl that high comedy fail to see it. Imagine being trapped in conversation with one of the fuckers!

5. The Islington Influx. There was a time, not so long ago, when the then-occupants of N16 thought I was a middle-class wanker (I know, I know). These days, I get to use inverse snobbery on the latest influx: the 20-something barristers and dentists priced out of N1, with their unapologetic halitosis and Cameron cheeks. Considering Bohemian Rhapsody to be a timeless classic does not make you bohemian! Here are some approximate figures. In 1990, a two-bed flat in N16 cost £3.64. Today, the same flat costs £1.2 billion. In fact, sod the Islington influx, we're on the verge of a Chelsea influx, and what a bunch of ***** that lot are.

6. The Ubiquitous Worthiness. Everything's so bloody organic, or recyclable, or sustainable, or dolphin-friendly. Don't get me wrong, I love dolphins as much as the next man (unless the next man's that bloke in Ireland), it's just: where's the spontaneity? Doesn't the self-righteousness ever get so stifling that you want to dig out a 1970s can of Elnett and – just the once – offload the entire tube into the goddamn ozone layer? A glaring example of that worthiness: small children on wooden cycles with no pedals, pushing them along like something out of the 1850s. Why not put the kid in tails and a top hat and be done with it? Children need pedals! How else are they going to skin their knees? Life lessons. Life lessons.

7. Gastropubs. No doubt a result of 5 (*see above*). Fine as pubs, for sure. But if I wanted to eat mille-feuille of hand-slivered, slow-roasted, oak-matured, Orkney-bred, slaughtered- while-listening-to-Enya lamb with daintily-picked, crinkle-cut, Mercedes-bonnet-fried pomme de terre au jus de Elizabeth II (or Harry, if the kitchen's out), at some bizarre price, I'd sod off to an actual restaurant. On the rare occasions that I enter a pub wanting to eat – surely missing the point – I want pub food! Doesn't everyone? Oh.

8. The Council. Actually, I love Hackney Council and think they do a really grand job.

The Neighbourhood

Over the years, N16 Magazine has focused on a variety of areas close to Stoke Newington, including Broadway Market, Highbury, Mare Street, Tottenham, Hackney Central, Lea Bridge Road, Whitechapel and other nearby parts of the world. For reasons of space we cannot include them all, and these can be found on our website. Here are four articles – on Columbia Road flower market, Lower Clapton, Dalston and Walthamstow Marshes – areas which are certainly worth a ramble around and can be reached in no time from the dizzy heights of Church Street.

Flower Power
By Avis Fenner, Spring 2001 (9)

It's 6.55 am on a cold, drizzly, Sunday morning. Oblivious to the weather, a group of late revellers wait for The Nelsons Head to open. Round the corner, trucks roll up. They have been coming in for an hour or so from places like Reading, Billericay, King's Lynn. Name anything to do with gardens and they are loaded with it: bedding plants, cut flowers, compost, fruit trees, herbs, house plants, shrubs, soil. The traders have long been resigned to a Saturday night in to be here for their most important trading day of the week at London's biggest flower and plant retail market, Columbia Road.

Columbia Road market was originally part of a development financed in the mid-nineteenth century by the wealthy philanthropist Baroness Angela Burdett-Coutts. The baroness financed the slum clearance east of Shoreditch church and erected Columbia Square Buildings to provide low rent accommodation for 183 families. She then turned her attention to the Cockney costermongers and stallholders who appalled her by their dishonesty. She believed the way to improve ethical standards was to provide a purpose-built, indoor market that would regulate trading.

The result, seven years later in 1869, was a huge mock-Gothic market building, decorated inside with moralistic aphorisms such as 'Speak everyman truth with his neighbour.' However, it was a complete failure and the small traders remained outside. The building was returned to the baroness within five years and subsequently let out as workshops.

Jim, who was born in Brick Lane, and now runs a cafe at the end of the Columbia Road, remembers its demolition and replacement by a block of flats in 1960. Today, the oldest trader is 87-year-old Fred Harnett who has been selling plants in Columbia Road since he came with his dad when he was ten. Like many of the stallholders, having a pitch in Columbia Road is a family affair. Fred still drives his own truck in every Sunday morning from Billericay, and flogs trays of

bedding plants with undiminished enthusiasm. For Fred and many of the other old timers the way of trading has changed profoundly.

What was once a market supplied by a cottage industry, where flowers and plants came from local nurseries on a seasonal basis, is now a year-round international business. Most of what you see on sale today in Columbia Road – and many other retail outlets – comes from the same source, the gigantic Dutch plant and flower emporium of Aalsmeer just outside of Amsterdam. Retailing shops may buy from wholesalers in New Covent Garden or Spitalfields but the traders in Columbia Road, keen to cut out the middleman, go once a week to Aalsmeer to buy for their Sunday trade.

And there's no doubt, compared to other retail outlets, buying in Columbia Road is good value but, as many stalls sell the same product sourced from the same place, variety in pure plant terms is limited and you will be hard pressed to find anything really unusual or rare. Traders say the market has survived because of the peripheral items; the decorated pots or the accessory knick-knacks in the bijou shops. It's these add-ons that have helped to keep it going all year round. Dennis, who's been trading here for 30 years, says people seem to be buying more plants than ever before and offers up the logical explanation that more people live in flats without gardens. Plus we no longer see flowers as a luxury item but as a interior design necessity.

At 10.30 the crowd, despite the weather, is thickening and Fred's vocal chords are finally warming up. 'Two boxes of lovely pansies for one!' Trading officially ceases at 2.00 pm. Those who want a bargain arrive for the last minute ditching of stock. I'm back at Dennis' stall and he has some beautiful red lilies for £6 a bunch. The punter says 'I'll give you £10 for two bunches.' 'You're robbing me, girl!' he replies, but he's smiling.

A Clapton Tour
By Nick MacWilliam, Winter 2007 (36)

When considering local places of historical and current interest, the stretch of tarmac that runs from Stamford Hill junction to the Lea Bridge Road roundabout is not usually the first place that comes to mind, yet Clapton Common/Upper Clapton Road has plenty to offer in terms of heritage, if you give it a little time.

Although its reputation has suffered over the years, thanks to its impoverished appearance allied to high crime rates and the notorious 'murder mile' tag, there are numerous aspects which make this a noteworthy area. A thoroughfare for a number of centuries, and known until the mid-19 century as Hackney Lane, Upper and Lower Clapton Roads once provided a main

access route from the north into the City of London. While nowadays Clapton Common/Upper Clapton Road may be largely ignored or avoided by people who have moved to the surrounding area in recent, relatively prosperous, years (it's not exactly bustling with cushy media jobs), there are still locations which provide insight into its past.

Clapton Common begins at Stamford Hill in typically drab fashion, with Netto followed by a row of large, charmless houses (double-glazed windows, bricked-over driveways), and it's not until you reach the Common itself that you reach the first point of interest, although unfortunately its dignity is rather obscured by a block of flats. The Catholic Church of the Good Shepherd overlooks the Common and the surrounding area, and it has a striking steeple guarded by four bronze statues of an angel, an eagle, a winged bull and a winged lion, while the main entrance is flanked by similar figures built into the stonework. The church was built in 1892 by the Agapemonites, a cult of somewhat dubious repute. *(To read about the Agapemonites in Clapton, read Anne Beech on page 19)*

The Common itself is an open patch of grass, complete with a pond that's home to swans, geese and ducks being bullied by invading seagulls, and public toilets in a (surprise, surprise) complete state of disrepair. The bordering main road and various council blocks detract from the tranquillity, and nearby Springfield Park is a better bet if you're looking for a picnic spot (which may not be for a while). On the opposite side of the road sits a grand terrace which dates from the 1790s, its grandeur emphasised by the mundane neighbouring blocks of flats. Next door is The Swan, nowadays a run-of-the-mill pub that sits on the site of what was once The Swan Inn, recorded by Charles Dickens in his Dictionary of London.

As you continue south-east, Clapton Common becomes Upper Clapton Road at the turn-off for Springfield. Quiet and pretty, with sports facilities, a nature reserve and good views over the River Lea and Walthamstow Marshes, the park makes an excellent choice for a relaxing stroll or any other form of open- aired malarkey. In addition, the park boasts another Dickensian connection: the now-demolished Springhill House, which stood just inside the park was once owned by Charles' eldest son, Charley.

Back on Upper Clapton Road and you soon reach a stretch of shops that is typical of Hackney and other parts of London: discount stores, fried chicken and takeaway pizza joints, Turkish mini-marts etc. The only sign of big business is the nauseous love-in between two multinationals which sees a mini-Sainsburys located in a Shell petrol station. Further along is Clapton station, for trains to Liverpool Street and Chingford, and The Crooked Billet, a pub reminiscent of those soulless places you see on suburban A-roads.

Brooke House College is on the corner of the Lea Bridge roundabout and today encourages 16-18 year olds with the motto 'aspire, study, achieve'. The original Brooke House, a royal property which stood on the same site, was built in the 15th century and was owned by the Earl of Northumberland, who supposedly had a thing for the unmarried Anne Boleyn and later hosted Henry VIII. After the Earl's death, the building passed between various nobles over the following decades, until it was converted to a private mental hospital in 1759, a purpose it served until 1940. During the Second World War, Brooke House, along with much of Hackney, suffered significant bomb damage and was subsequently torn down. Since then the site has been home to a number of educational institutions. Various local historians consider the demolition of Brooke House to be Hackney's greatest architectural loss.

And there you have it. The unremarkable facade of Upper Clapton Road masks a wealth of interest, and it's probable that there is much more that can be learnt by anyone with the inclination.

Duellin' Dalstons
By Richard Boon, Summer 2008 (42)

The recent media hype claiming that Dalston is 'cool' finds local librarian Richard Boon searching for his bullshit detector.

I'm sure I had it here, somewhere. Funny how you can't find anything just when you need it. Like 'Cool Dalston'. I mean, all these other people have found it: The Guardian kicked off this 'find' in April; Italian Vogue, Evening Standard and the London Paper in pursuit in May, with even more from the Standard's ES mag, June 19. Steps may have to be taken.

I'm even having trouble, lately, with the notion of 'cool' itself. I'd so gotten used to 'bad' meaning 'good' over the years of domestic yoofspeak, but what terms do today's teens use for 'cool' I began to wonder? For clarification, I asked one I'd previously prepared...

'Adam?' 'Wot, dad?' 'I just wondered what your cohort said for "cool"?' 'Why?' 'I'm doing this thing about Dalston being cool, but thought there might be a new term.' 'Well, "sick" could be good.' 'Evil?' 'Dark?" 'Dad, that's sad. We don't think Dalston is cool, anyway. Though there's this place, Sweeping Clouds, or something, I dunno. Look for Motherskank on YouTube.'

Never trust a teenager. It's actually Passing Clouds Art Club, 440 Kingsland Road, live music sometimes, and based in the 19th century building that once housed the Hackney Gazette (whose more than a century of back copies are held by Hackney Archives, of whom, more, later). So, that's cool, to start with. 'It's a very exciting underground scene,' director Eleanor Wilson is quoted as saying. Celebrated Sunday night jam sessions with internationally renowned musicians, already. Time to locate my psychogeographic miners' lamp and put on my Vans and take those steps – down to Dalston.

Well, down the A10, Roman Ermine Street. You don't have to be a Feng Shui practioner to expect such an ancient North- South route crossing an East- West one (Balls Pond Road/ Dalston Lane) to have so much chi you could levitate a megalith. But most of the junction is missing, a spectacular absence anticipating the new rail lines and station, while opening up the aspect of the Reeves + Son building (The Print House) to better view.

Going South, passing everything that's longer established and so well-renowned that 'cool' doesn't count any more, it's given (Arcola Theatre; Rio Cinema; Nandos; Bardens Boudoir; Centreprise; Ridley Road Market; the desolate Stasi-planned Gillett Square – location of jazz institution The Vortex, but little else except SIM-card off-sale booths and the like, of which, more, later), you'll notice (well, I did) lots of closed shops, dead pubs and lots of pound shops – some of which are themselves closed. And sales everywhere. Even in nail bars. Pawnbrokers, money transfer sheds, SIM-card shacks – oh, that was the 'more, later' wasn't it?

There are, however, other institutions of note. Draper J Hull + Co, by Tesco/Argos, on the corner, established 127 years ago, and the oldest shop in the UK selling only curtains. That's what I call cool. As, naturally, is the interior of Shanghai Restaurant, listed, preserved old pie-and-mash caff tiling to die for. What claims to be London's only Peruvian restaurant, El Aguajal, sometimes with music. Peacocks. Oxfam. East Garden Noodle Bar, huge fast food canteen my adolescent advisor used to like (me too), on the junction. Peace mural, on the Lane, designed by Ray Walker (1945-84) – disrespect – fully tagged by aerosol trippers, sadly, but also available as one of the designs on Hackney Libraries' membership cards). Arthur's Café (1935). Oh, yes, the Job Centre Plus. Always useful.

I'm sure there's much more fun to be had than rehearsing Patrick Wright's Journey Though the Ruins – an astute take on Dalston Lane on the 70/80s cusp – which plenty of folk seem to enjoy doing. Hackney was so much better when it was broke(n), right? Of course, down past the new-build marking the 4 Aces Club, there is the levitation: rapid, midrise flats, soon to house a library and the blessed Hackney Archives opposite the new station. And the ruins: Wright's beloved shops, burnt out, waiting for some settlement claim on what was the real scandal of Dalston's regeneration history.

Now, I get the whole deal that as Shoreditch got hip, its progenitors, artists and fashionistas were priced out (in my time, same deal for Wapping and Butler's Wharf) and so have moved North. But wouldn't they be better off keeping quiet about that (good East London Designers map on http://blog.mawi.co.uk, BTW – yes, they really are all over the place and the map is in proportion – unlike that in the ES), rather than gossiping loudly in achingly hip bar Dalston Superstore, : 'Oh, I found a cool place!'

It may have good media going (I suspect to sell the new housing developments) and there are places to eat beyond numbering – many good, as you'd expect from the area's ethnic mix – but this is not a tourist guide, here, just a ramble. As usual. But cool? Word is, actually: Deptford.

Walthamstow Marshes
By Rab MacWilliam, Autumn 2011 (49)

As you gaze down the steep slope of Springfield Park towards the River Lea and the haphazard jumble of boats on the marina, you cannot but observe the eerily flat land on the other side of the river, an area uninhabited by humans and

In the summer you can see old breed longhorn cattle, brought in to graze down the more aggressive plant life, and you have to do a double-take when you stumble out of the Anchor and Hope Fullers' pub on the river to remind yourself that you are not in Arizona. The bird life includes reed bunting, reed, sedge, marsh and willow warblers, finches, woodpeckers, kestrels, herons, wagtails, grebes, teal and much more. Some of the plant life, in particular the internationally rare creeping marshwort, are unusual in the city, and include sedge marsh, sallow scrub, bee orchid and tall herb vegetation, through which flitter such insects as skipper butterfly, dragontails and pyralid moths. You can also hear the constant chirping of crickets in the summer, and there is a growing number of water voles, blinking at you as they scuttle back to their places of safety. The Marshes are truly a paradise for all nature lovers. They are also much used by walkers, cyclists, dog owners, joggers and athletes, no doubt in training for the coming Olympics down the road. The area is on National Cycle Route One, which wends its way between Greenwich and Cheshunt, and the Lea Valley Walk meanders along the towpath. The Marshes can also claim its place in aeronautical history, as in July 1909 one Alliott Vernon Rowe, who went on to found AVRO, flew his triplane over the land, making the first all-British powered flight.

untouched by development. What you are looking at is Walthamstow Marshes, 90 acres of land owned by the Lee Valley Park and a designated site of Special Scientific Interest. Lying within the borough of Waltham Forest, the Marshes were once lammas land – strips of meadow used for growing crops and grazing cattle – until 1934 when the land came under public ownership.

They are now a refuge for all sorts of wildlife, not often found elsewhere in London. One of the last remaining examples of semi-natural wetlands in the capital, the area is crossed by the railway line to Stansted, the only visual evidence of human interference in the Marshes.

For those of you on less of a peaceful nature kick, just on the southern end of the Marshes on the Lea Bridge Road, you'll find a splendid ice rink and, further along, they've done up the old, scruffy 9-hole golf course. There's also a riding school on the edge of the Marshes. Just look east.

Letters

I grew up in **Stoke Newington**, with working class parents. My dad was a London bus driver, my mum an office clerk. We were the original 'Latch Key Kids' – you let yourself indoors when school finished. The four of us turned out fine. We had a few scrapes in Stoke Newington but nothing worth reporting. I remember my dad saying to me and my brothers: 'don't go up to Church Street, it's too rough up there'. I lived in Queen Elizabeth's Walk then, going to Woodberry Down School which had a great reputation; not that I was one of its greatest pupils, but I felt I had a chance to work and improve.

In Stoke Newington now we have 'the rich and famous'. That's good, but there are still many of us who have lived here 50 years or more, watching the changes, seeing each new culture as it arrives. But what about the knife culture? My brother was part of a gang in the late 1960s, in what they called 'The Highbury Mob'. They fought other local gangs. Some of them carried razors, my brother had his face cut, and two associates were stabbed, thankfully not fatally. They carried different kinds of weapons, and used them. But I never once saw it reported in local papers, on TV or even spoken about in the street. One of the big differences today is the media. We all know what happens all over the world, and I believe that our memory just stores up all these bad images the media report over and over again. We then become overwhelmed and frightened. The knife culture is real, it has touched lots of people and needs urgent government and social attention, but whilst we know that these crimes are happening in all areas, because they are reported on TV, radio, papers, or texted to all our mates if we hear of something.

I still believe most of our teenagers are great, who look up to footballers, actors and musicians, and we know some of them are leading the way in setting bad examples. But it looks so glamorous, and many are teenagers who haven't got much to look forward to with the growing credit crunch, jobs paying minimum wage, and worst of all teenagers being tarred with the same brush as those committing the crimes. I know young boys who feel that they have no chance at all of achieving what you and I might have. And it can be depressing for them, but not one of them belongs to the 'knife culture', but sadly so many of them think the way to make 'It', is to be famous. Lives have been lost unnecessarily. But if knife culture is a teenager trend, who's set the examples? The middle-aged thugs who are filling our prisons, the non-stop violent TV programs, computer games, or is it plain and simple lack of parental control?

We have to stop these crimes. I don't know the answer. I'm relying on the police and parents, but if we really think about it we've been trying to sort this out since man became civilized! So let's hope the few that are involved are dealt with and are taught. Crime does not pay in the long run. Perhaps they won't know that until they are a parent or grandparent. Let's hope it's sooner rather than later.

Three things I hate about Stokey

1) The Lack of Gluten. Stoke Newington seems to be suffering from an acute gluten shortage. Everything's gluten-free as a consequence, which is a shame. Who stole all our gluten? It gets worse. I've seen a notice advertising bread that's gluten-free, wheat-free, yeast-free. I'm not sure how it qualifies as bread, frankly – surely that's just stiff dust? – but what do I know? Really, what is wrong with people? Imagine going into a baker's and asking for gluten-free, wheat-free, yeast-free bread. If I did that and the bastard took an axe to me, I'd be hard-pressed to protest. It's no wonder everyone's suddenly allergic to everything, if people on – adopt whiny, nasal internal voice for the next two words – specialist diets are driving high-street (or at least Church Street) consuming habits. "My body's a temple!" they cry. No it's not, it's a rabbit hutch with some lettuce-free lettuce and pellet-sized poop. Get a grip. I reckon that one day the people who stole all the gluten are going to hire a Hercules and drop the lot on Church Street, and we'll all drown in sodding gluten. And that'll show us.

2) All Other Traffic on Bouverie Road. As someone who has passed The Driving Test and thus understood The Highway Code, I take pride in driving on the left (my side) of the white dotted line. Which puts me in a minority of one on Bouverie Road, where every fucker in a vehicle blatantly straddles said line until they are a millisecond from crushing me, before veering back to their actual own side of the road like Doyle (plus perm) in 'The Professionals'. It Does My Head In.

There are three reasons for their actions:
a) The parked cars on either side mean that Chelsea Tractors – the usual offenders – are too wide for the available space. The cocks.
b) The road bumps are sited centrally, and to straddle them requires driving plumb down the middle of the road.

c) They are arrogant shits who think they own the place.

So I have a plan. I'm going to build a long section of road nearby and divert each vehicle onto it, one by one, so they can happily zip down it whilst literally being the only person on the road. Hurrah for them! But – here's the catch – at the end of it I'm going to dig a big pit and cover it with a road-coloured rug. In which I'm going to put Jim Davidson in a talkative mood, some children from Britain's Got Talent and all of the royal family's fecal output since 1973. And I'm going to sit beside it in a deckchair with a peg on my nose.

3) Some People. I was at the Stokey Farmers Market recently, a pleasant concept, though the sparseness of the stalls only highlights the lack of farmland in the area. I'm at a pig caravan, a sort of mini-butcher's, selling tasty-looking pork stuff, about to purchase some smoked back – indeed my mouth is open, inhaling in preparation for speech – when an older gentleman gets there first. 'Do you have any pancetta?' he asks. I have two immediate problems with this.
a) It's only a sodding caravan – have a look yourself!
b) Hang on, I'll don my Guessing Hat and – oh, 0.0138 seconds later – hazard that, No, he bloody doesn't! I've been in a few normal-sized butcher's shops and am usually pleasantly underwhelmed by their range of meat cuts for toffs. I raise my eyes in a 'What a twot!' gesture. The vendor spots this but fails to return it, perhaps in a nod towards customer relations with the other bloke. Not done yet, the older gentleman compounds his error. He says this: 'You slice it very finely', while making a very-fine-slicing motion with his hands, in case the verbal output isn't already patronising enough. As if the guy is such a wurzel, he has no idea what the average N16 resident considers to be the apogee of porcine sophistication. The vendor merely nods. If I were him, I'd have reached over the counter, minced the bloke and flogged him off as Free Range Black Pudding.

I think it was Spring of 1991. I was living in Grazebrook Road and working at Gillespie School, over near the old Arsenal ground. Walking through Clissold Park one morning on my way to work, there was a chap sitting on a bench by the ponds who looked the absolute spit of my dad. I walked past him, but after about ten yards stopped and came back. I said something to the effect of, 'I'm sorry to bother you, but you look just like my dad, who died nearly 20 years ago. Would you mind if I stared at your face for a little while?' This kind chap just sat perfectly calm while I drank in the sight of that dear face which I thought I would never see again in this life. The likeness was uncanny, the only difference being in the eye colour. My dad's eyes were tawny brown and this man's blue. After not too long (I hope!) I thanked him and went on my way. A week or two later I saw him again. The resemblance was still there, but not so strongly – the distinction was clear between one person and another.

In February this year it was the 40th anniversary of my mother's death, and I was hurrying along Church Street to play my violin in church as a little thank-offering for her life, when, just outside the Spence, there was this chap again. I said, 'Oh hello! You're the man who looked like my dad!' He said, 'That was a long time ago! Is it still true?' I'd kept on walking, really, because I was running out of time, but I looked at him over my shoulder and said that it was. I thought how wonderful it had been to see him in the first place, how very kind it was of him just to let me stare at his face without being weird or impatient and then how extraordinary it was that I should see him again on that particular day after so long a gap. I wish I hadn't been in such a rush, but then, if I hadn't been - if I'd been punctual - I might've missed him entirely!

Far, far away

Parochialism is not a concept generally understood or practised by Stoke Newington residents. In the magazine, we have printed articles concerning Cuba, Palestine, Uganda, Zambia, India, USA, Tunisia, Lapland and other places just outside the boundary of the N16 postcode, written by residents who have travelled or worked there. Here is a selection of a few others.

Beer Over The Ocean
By Pete Brown, Spring 2008 (37)

However much you love London, it doesn't automatically mean one is tired of life if one wants to get away for a little while. But sitting in the middle of the Indian Ocean on a container ship with sixteen Filipino sailors, a Ukrainian electrician and two German officers, one of them the double of an adult Stewie Griffin, with the lights off and doors and portholes bolted against the threat of Somali pirates, I couldn't help thinking I'd taken things a bit too far. A nice weekend in Norfolk would probably have been a much better idea. But I was on a quest, and I couldn't help myself.

I write books about beer, and just before Christmas 2007, I was challenged by a friend to write about a famous beer journey. I replied that there weren't any, not really, as beer was always expensive and bulky to carry, and would spoil on long journeys. Beer has always been more local than other products – just try getting a London Pride drinker to accept a pint of Yorkshire bitter served with its characteristic inch of thick, creamy head, and you'll see what I mean. And then I remembered one very famous journey. And as soon as it reared up in my mind, I was lost to it.

'IPA' is a term any pub-goer will be familiar with. A few may even be aware that it stands for India Pale Ale. But most people believe that, along with acronyms like ESB or XXX, it's merely another piece of trad ale bar adornment, nomenclature that harks back to a more artisanal age with no real contemporary meaning. The truth is that India Pale Ale was created specifically for export to the subcontinent. In the 1780s, when you couldn't even get beer to the next town in good condition, the ships of the East India Company took on barrels in the Thames, and sailed through the Canaries, across the Equator, round the Cape of Good Hope and across the Indian Ocean to Calcutta. After passing harbour-side inspection, it was drunk by the civil servants of the Company and by thirsty troops whose only other option was arak – a fiery, locally brewed spirit that could kill you in one binge.

It was a long, gruelling journey with extreme temperature variations. Ordinary beers often turned to malt vinegar by the time they got to Calcutta. But a brewer not far south of Stokie – George Hodgson in Bow – perfected a light, hoppy, strong beer that not

only survived the journey, but thrived on it. Hodgson's pale ale arrived in India bright and sparkling, and soon cornered the market.

When Hodgson got greedy, the East India Company went to Burton, home of strong export ales, and persuaded the brewers there to enter the Indian market. It was a brilliant stroke of luck: Burton's unique spring water created a version of Hodgson's beer that far surpassed the original. Burton beers such as Bass and Allsopp were soon drunk in every corner of the English-speaking world, the first-ever global brands. The beers came down through the Midlands by canal, along the Regent's Canal through Hackney, out to Limehouse docks and away to India. Later, after the railways came, the vast arches under St Pancras Station that now house London's fanciest new shopping mall were originally built to hold thousands of hogsheads of beer at time. This was the journey I wanted to recreate. The trouble is, since the Suez Canal was built nearly 140 years ago, no one goes around the Cape to get to India. Why would you?

There are travel firms on the web who specialise in booking passages on container ships for people who are scared of flying, or want to get away from the world for a few weeks with a pile of books and an empty journal. These firms told me my journey was impossible. The problem was, by this time I'd already sold the idea to my publisher, told all my friends and arranged for a recreated 19th century IPA to be brewed at the White Shield Brewery in Burton-on-Trent. I had to do it somehow.

After six months of making enquiries, an obscure

Following encounters with gun-wielding Iranian guards and venal, corrupt Indian customs officials, I finally made it to India. The experiment worked. The beer tasted amazing, more complex, rounded and ripened than before we set off, somewhere between a beer and a wine. I'm currently trying to persuade the brewery they'd have a market both here and in India if they were to brew it full time.

And what about London? After a sleepless, nerve-shredding week in Delhi, I flew back into Heathrow (look, I deserved it, alright?), and was in a cab coming along the Euston Road. And for the first and possibly last time, I thought, 'Isn't London nice and quiet and peaceful?' This is just as well: I've a book to write, and after my adventures on the high seas, there's no way I can afford to hire the cottage in Norfolk.

Chance of a Lifetime
By Cleo Houghton, Autumn 2008 (39)

When I finally returned to Stoke Newington, I felt it had all been a dream. It began when I earned an archery certificate and won a gold medal from the Hampstead Bowmen Club in August 2007. I wanted to go to Mongolia and learn how to do archery on horseback. I found out about the Fourth International Horseback Archery Competition 2008 in Korea, and I wrote to the Grand Master Kim about going to the competition. He wrote back and asked me to enter. I couldn't say no, even though I had no sponsorship and marginal backing.

Before that, in December 2007, I contacted Seded Batkhyag, who is the Honoured President of the National Mongolian Archery Association. He said he did not did not know where the Horseback Archers, being nomadic, were at that time. I had to go and find them myself. I took up the offer of shooting archery with Batkhyag, and went to Mongolia to find them in July. Meanwhile, I had six months to jump back in the saddle, practise archery and become as fit as possible.

Finally, I arrived in Mongolia, and Bathkyag greeted me at the airport. He introduced me to a man called Munkhjargal, the President of the Mongolian National Horseback Archery Association. I needed horseback archery lessons and I was running out of time. Meanwhile, I wrote to the Master in Korea and asked very nicely, if I could bring some 'Mongolian friends' with me, but the flights were so expensive, because of the Olympics and the Total Solar Eclipse, with the line of totality straight over Mongolia, in early August. He wrote back telling me to invite all the Mongolian Horseback Archers and that he would give us free accommodation, food and we did not have to pay competition fees. The horseback archery lessons started the next day.

I trained four days a week for three weeks in the Mongolian Steppes, where they had 500 wild horses. I drank fermented mares' milk, ate the freshest yogurt

shipping company based in landlocked Switzerland came up trumps, in a way I'd never dared dream of. And so on September 11, I left Burton on a canal boat, got as far as Rugby, switched to the train and brought my alarmingly heavy beer barrel back to London. A few days later I boarded the P&O cruise ship Oceana for the 'Canaries Carousel', and jumped ship in Tenerife.

A week later, I boarded *Europa*, a three-mast barque that made hard-bitten sailors and seedy customs men gasp whenever she entered port. I helped sail her across the Atlantic to Brazil (the trade winds mean that if you're under sail, you often have to go across the Atlantic in order to get to South Africa), and for three weeks my life was governed by sunrise, sunset, the cycles of the moon and the occasional visits of dolphins. I took the helm of the ship through the night, hoisted sails, was ducked when we crossed the equator, and finished the journey with the sea in my blood.

In Rio I boarded the container ship Caribbean and sailed down the coast of Brazil, where we socialised (and nothing else) with prostitutes and drug dealers in seedy dockside bars, then set off back across the South Atlantic. I realised I knew the answer to the question, 'how would I cope without communications technology?' when, passing the Cape of Good Hope, I found myself standing on the bridge, holding my Blackberry and mobile phone to the heavens, praying for just one bar of signal. From there it was up the East Coast of Africa. Somalia is lawless, and pirates frequent its coastline. They might be funny at the cinema or on Facebook, but not when they're speeding towards you in a launch armed with AK-47s.

you can imagine, and the stars at night were so bright it seemed like they fell on me. While the wolves sang into the night, I felt freer than I'd ever been in my life. I was the only foreigner and my Mongolian was not so good. Even so, I was included as part of a family on a nomadic farm.

There was one small problem. I no longer had a bow because I had given it away, and I needed a horseback archery bow. The Mongolian bows were too big and strong for me. The master in Korea said if I bring a Mongolian bow to Korea, he would exchange it for a Korean horseback archery bow and arrows. On the 11th of August I arrived in Korea with the Mongolian Horseback Archery Team and a Mongolian bow for the Grand Master Young Kim Sup. He said 'you are the bridge between Mongolian and Korean horseback archery'.

The teams competing there were from Germany, England, Korea, Mongolia, and Japan. In the first round I beat the English and the German men and a few of the Koreans. I won a certificate and a gold award. After that I went to the first European Horseback Archery Competition Germany 2008. I fell off the horse playing Mogu, a moving target game. I had no medical assistance in Germany, even though I had asked for this. Since then, I have been to the British School of Osteopathy and they said no riding for at least three months, I have a fractured foot and a sore arm left muscle, which was holding the bow, and I have a common riders' back injury and it will heal, which is lucky. So I did not complete the event. However, I still won another certificate.

I have been asked to prepare my kit and wear my Mongolian Horseback Archer costume for an event soon to be held in the UK. Also, next year I have been invited to Seoul, in Korea, to race in chariots and shoot crossbows. The best present I had was Seded Batkhyag saying 'you will always be like a daughter to me'.

Mau Mau Memories
By Tim Webb, Summer 2011 (48)

Switching on the television and seeing four elderly Kenyans – three men and a woman – standing in front of the high Court steps while their lawyer explained that they were claiming compensation from the British government for castration, beatings and, in the case of the woman, rape, brought back quite a few half-forgotten memories.

On 9 August 1958, the SS Dunera docked at Mombasa in Kenya. On board was the 1st Battalion Royal Fusiliers who were mostly cockneys, many of them dockers' sons from London's East End, plus a few odds and sods, including me. I had signed on for three years for the regimental band in order to learn to play the tenor sax but had fallen out with the bandmaster and had been expelled. I became a radio operator, as unlike many of my comrades in arms, I was able to read and write.

After landing at Mombasa and spending a day on a special train to Nairobi, we heaved ourselves into army trucks to be driven to Gilgil in the Rift Valley, or 'Happy Valley', as it was called, due to the rampant adultery and drinking prevalent among its white settlers. The camp was a ramshackle sort of place plagued by mosquitoes – which had been used 10 years earlier as an internment centre for members of Irgun, the militant Jewish insurgents who were fighting the British to establish the state of Israel.

Many of the British troops in Kenya regarded Africans as servants and paid the young men small amounts of money to polish their boots and arrange 'jigajig' with their sisters. That was hardly surprising, as an official Army handbook said: 'The African is simple, not very intelligent, but very willing if treated in the right way. Do not regard him as a slave or as an equal. You will find that most Africans have an innate respect for the white man.' We understood little about the Mau Mau as we marched, patrolled and generally did nothing much, except provide reassurance for the white farmers who were desperate to hang on to the prime agricultural land they had seized from the Kikuyu people and a lifestyle that owed more to the English Home Counties than poverty-stricken Kenya. For extra security they would invite a squaddie to stay with them for the weekend, provided he brought his rifle and some ammunition. The army encouraged this. At first it was regarded by the troops as a good number with the possibility of plenty to drink and perhaps a chance to get up close to a settler's daughter. It didn't quite work out like that. The braying accents of rural Surrey ordering a young east Londoner to sleep in a hut on the fringe of the farm didn't go down too well, especially as the long grass contained all sorts of venomous creepy-crawlies that were rarely found on the streets of Aldgate and Whitechapel.

I stayed with a family whose name I have forgotten. We didn't get on. They were obviously expecting a battle-hardened sniper, ready for action. What they got was a skinny young soldier, uncomfortably carrying a heavy rifle and who was more interested in reading the just-published *On the Road,* by Jack Kerouac, a chronicle of the beat generation with its jazz, drugs and poetry. Those were subjects that were not fully appreciated by my hosts. Drink however was – mostly huge gin and tonics – which they downed from morning until late at night. Some of the farmers complained that their expensive silverware went missing after weekend visits from the troops. The goods often appeared in the local shops a few days later.

We were stationed some distance from the Hola Detention Centre, which was one of a number of labour camps that the British set up in Kenya, after most of the military action against the insurgents was over. Soldiers who had delivered prisoners there told us that it that it was a 'shit-hole'. Troops had swept through the areas of rebellion and the RAF had strafed and bombed to the extent that most Kikuyu people were cowed into submission.

Eliud Mutonyi, a Nairobi-based businessman was chairman of the Mau Mau Central Committee. He was captured and sent to Hola in 1958. He describes his experiences: 'On the awful morning of March 3 1959, the detainees at Hola were divided into three groups. The first was sent to the kitchen. The second, of whom I was a member, was sent to the dispensary for treatment. The third, comprising 88 young and reasonably healthy men, was taken for a work assignment. Each man was given a spade, a basin and a hoe, and then ordered to dig the soil. We had refused all along to perform this task, and the young men refused on that morning as well. Broken down into groups of five, the men were whipped and beaten up, whipped and whipped, until at least 11 of them died.' The Governor-General of Kenya, Sir Evelyn Baring, said later that the men had died from accidentally drinking poisoned water.

The event at Hola left 11 dead and 60 seriously wounded, but it was not an isolated incident. A witness in another camp told the author of a study on the atrocities: 'By the time we cut his balls off he had no ears, and his eyeball, the right one, I think, was hanging out of its socket. Too bad, he died before we got much out of him'. Dogs were used to terrify the captives and then attack them. African troops carried out much of the torture but the British military and the civil administration directly controlled their actions.

The King's African Rifles, a colonial regiment commanded by white officers, was known for its brutality. Idi Amin, later President of Uganda and responsible for the ethnic cleansing of Asians from that country, served in the regiment and learned his trade in the Kenyan camps. The Colonial Secretary at the time was Alan Lennox-Boyd. The man was a nasty piece of work – he'd had fascist connections when at Oxford – who claimed that his sympathies lay with 'martial races' and 'traditional' rulers. He was immune to all the reports of torture and murder that emanated from the camps.

The state of emergency ended in 1960. During that period Mau Mau supporters killed around 2,000 African civilians whom they accused of supporting the occupiers and inflicted 200 casualties on the army. The British hanged more than 1,000 Kikuyu without proper trials, and at least 150,000 were detained, including President Obama's grandfather. Despite reports in the British press of widespread massacres, only 32 white settlers, the people at the heart of the problem, were killed in the rebellion.

When the truth about Hola became known, investigations were carried out, reports were produced and debates were held in the House of Commons. For a brief period, it became something of a scandal but a blanket of indifference was soon drawn over it and, in the usual British way, things returned to normal. A Conservative government was re-elected, Alan Lennox-Boyd became the First Viscount Boyd of Merton, Sir Evelyn Baring received a peerage, the initiator of forced labour, J.B. Cowan, the Commissioner of Prisons, got an MBE, the camp commandant was retired from the service without loss of pension and charges against his deputy were dropped. Hola was renamed Galole and is now touted as an upmarket tourist attraction with no mention of its past history.

It was believed that the colonial administration had destroyed all the incriminating documents, but they have recently been discovered and are providing crucial evidence in the current legal test case. Our coalition government is fighting the claim, with the bizarre argument that says that any responsibility lies with the present government of Kenya, as the country is now an independent state. This attitude reflects only too clearly the failure of successive British governments, and historians, to record accurately and publicly the atrocities committed in the name of the monarch and empire. The myth is peddled that the colonies were administered in a mainly benign manner, that our withdrawal was voluntary and not through long, often armed, struggles for independence.

The blank refusal to admit that torture, imprisonment without trial and brutal military crackdowns were an integral part of official government policy still continues. The crimes committed by both sides in Northern Ireland have received a great deal of attention. Perhaps the testimonies of four frail Africans might encourage us to demand that the true story about British colonial rule in other parts of the world should also be told.

In Brief

Four members of an IRA Active Service Unit who waged a 14-month bombing campaign in the mid-1970s, leaving in their wake 40 explosions and 35 dead, lived in what was described as a 'bomb factory' in Stoke Newington's Milton Grove. In information released recently in a confidential Downing Street file, by the National Archive, it was revealed that a death list and names of potential targets – including the British Museum, National Gallery, Tate Museum, Somerset House and several others – were found in the flat, but the information was suppressed by order of the Home Office and Prime Minister Harold Wilson, who considered it 'low grade and out of date' and neither wished to alarm the intended targets. Perhaps also it was not released at the time as it may have been considered circumstantial (apparently it was not particularly well organised and may not have survived judicial scrutiny). Nevertheless, the 'Balcombe Street Gang', as they became known following their surrender in December 1975 after a six-day siege, holding two hostages, by the police in Balcombe Street, Marylebone, received 23-year jail sentences. Four years earlier, at 395 Amhurst Road, the 'Stoke Newington Four' (soon to become eight and become known as the Angry Brigade) were arrested for possession of gelignite, sten gun, detonators etc. Four of them were eventually found guilty and sentenced for up to fifteen years for conspiracy to engage in bombing and possession of explosives.

We appear to be witnessing a corporate takeover of Stoke Newington. First, we had Tesco, Sainsbury's, Halford's and Nando's, none of which appear to be doing as much damage to the local economy as was predicted and, it could be argued, have made other retailers sharpen their acts a bit. Another recent development is the arrival of the *Daily Mail*, whose strident, middle England views and political stance are pretty much the antithesis of what Stoke Newington represents, in the shape of a new website, stokenewingtonpeople. co.uk. Giving the appearance of a cuddly, local site, it is actually a template which Associated Newspapers have spread across over sixty areas in southern England (Yeovil, Surbiton, Berkhampstead etc) in order to colonise middle-class, wealthy areas such as ours (well, bits of it) and eliminate the competition. The competition, in this case, is n16mag.com (locally owned and in operation for eleven years but without access to the funding which the *Daily Mail* can provide) and several other blogs and websites, including stereostokey.com, who have at heart the interests of the area, rather than the Associated Newspapers balance sheet. Now we have the arrival of the *Stoke Newington Gazette*, owned by Archant Publishing who describe themselves as 'the UK's largest independently-owned regional media business' and who are responsible for, among many other periodicals, the *Hackney Gazette* and *Angel*. We make no comment on the layout or content of this new tabloid, as we would prefer to leave this to our readers and advertisers (without advertising we would not exist – Archant have no such constraints). Large companies now obviously have the Stokey pound in their sights, and market share is all. They want to drive out local competition so they can have it all to themselves, a familiar tactic. Please resist all this and support your local magazines, websites and businesses. This is not sour grapes, rather an appeal to continue to support local businesses in the spirit of our radical, dissenting history.

On our way in early March to the Vortex to see the magnificent folk musician and N16 Fringe regular, Martin Carthy, we had to pass through the much-trumpeted Gillett Square in Dalston, designed by the architects and Hackney Council to be a beacon of enlightened and joyful community spirit in the surrounding urban desert along the lines of the bustling squares of Barcelona, Paris, Rome and the like. The reality is a bleak, badly-lit, dingy and depressing space, deserted aside from a couple of kids desultorily clacking around on their skateboards. What a waste. Where are the cafes, restaurants, street musicians, jugglers and local folk milling around enjoying the spectacle of our would-be city cultural oasis? There are probably, like many other things in Hackney, planning regulations which prohibit people enjoying themselves. The depression lifted as Martin began his set, and his singing and guitar playing were as uplifting and joyful as ever. But we still had to look over Gillett Square.

Do we really need a one-way gyratory traffic system in Stoke Newington? *N16* has been proposing for years now that Stoke Newington Common, at least, should revert to an open, public space without A10 traffic hurtling through it. Hackney Council has now decided to do something about it. Basically, Transport for London (TfL) is the main public agency responsible for changing the current road layout or operations. Hackney Council is responsible for minor alterations that can improve road safety, amenity or traffic conditions in all local roads. The one-way system was originally introduced approximately forty years ago to reduce congestion through and on the approaches to Stoke Newington High Street which, by having restricted space, created a traffic bottleneck. However, there has been increasing local opposition to the one-way system, which causes congestion and speeding, creates severance between local areas and promotes 'rat running' along parallel streets. It is also seen to adversely affect the shopping environment on Stoke Newington High Street.

In an article in the *Evening Standard* entitled 'The slumming of our great city has gone too far', the ubiquitous journo Simon Jenkins states that our little parish, along with Camden Town, Brixton and Peckham, falls into the category of 'virtual no-go areas for law and order'. Eh? So it must be down to the yummy mummies, then, and the café latte drinkers on Church Street. Dodge City, London N16. One of our magazine contributors recently left her handbag containing all her credit cards and a lot of money on the 73 bus. Panic ensued, naturally, when she realized she'd left it in this 'no-go area' and she headed off to the Arriva terminus in Tottenham with little hope that she'd find it. Meanwhile, the doorbell rang at her home in Brooke Road and a young woman handed the bag to her partner, saying she'd found it on the bus. 'Can I borrow your phone to phone my mum? I'm now over half an hour late,' she said. Darling, you can have what you want. Occasions like this remind one that very few people are thieves and most are generally pleasant, socially concerned human beings, despite our supposedly crime-ridden streets and 'no-go areas'.

Standing outside the Post Office at Brooke Road the other morning, we noticed a gentleman with a strange machine and determined attitude. 'Is this the queue?' we asked. "No, mate, just carrying out a traffic survey for Transport for London', he replied. What, speeding, needlessly hitting the horn, timing the Old Bill sirens, watching old ladies being terrified by smart-ass drivers in initialized number-plated, black-windowed speed machines, Dutch artics full of flowers and intent on mowing down pedestrians crossing the road quite legitimately, cyclists sailing through red lights, cars parked on double-red lines?' 'No, mate, just counting the cars'. One, two, three...

These days smoked salmon is available in every supermarket and corner shop. Most of it is farmed salmon produced by large commercial smokeries. Most of it is rather salty and tasteless. In the old days, there used to be a difference between Scotch and London smoked salmon. The curers in the North, used to dealing with kippers and haddock, were too heavy-handed with the smoke for the more delicate wild salmon. So Jewish fishmongers in London started producing it in their own smokehouses, but the clean air acts closed them down. Imagine our surprise when we heard of Ole-Martin Hansen from Norway who has a smoker in a side street off Church Street. The smokehouse is at the back designed by Ole's grandfather. The salmon hanging on tenterhooks – smoked in the true Norwegian way – above a smouldering blend of juniper and beech wood chips. The result is some of the finest smoked salmon you dream of eating.

Gathered in a Stoke Newington flat one recent Saturday: a Scot, American, French and a Serbian. Two weeks later, the aforementioned Yank and Scot, Uruguyan and a Chinese lady at the same household. The next day, the Scot had extended conversations in the street with a couple of Turks, a Jamaican guy, a local Pakistani Muslim leader and a leading ultra-orthodox rabbi, followed by discussions with an Egyptian and a Libyan about recent turbulent events in the north of Africa. This is as well as the stunningly attired West African ladies who emerge from the churches on Sunday lunchtimes (check out these hats!), and the Spanish, Brazilian, Italian, Somali and French kids who wander around the place. Although English people are obviously in the majority, including the scary influx of Hoxditch types who seem to be edging up the High Street with their skinny trousers, pork-pie hats and Hank Marvin specs, we really don't need your views about multiculturalism, Mr Cameron.

Acknowledgments

I would like to thank Tim Webb and Trevor Jones, the two other co-founders of N16 Magazine, and also Zoran Jevtic of local design company Audiografix. Without all their efforts in the early days of our publication, the magazine would not have survived. Tim was the first editor, Trevor was in charge of advertising, and Zoran was our designer, both on the printed copies and the website. Tim and Trevor remain regular contributors to the magazine and Zoran continues to make design sense of the articles, ads and photos. He regularly turns out exciting and innovative work, for which the magazine has been rightly praised. Also, my thanks go to Alex Smith, Publisher of N16 Magazine, whose enthusiasm for the book has been an invaluable source of encouragement.

This book would never have seen the light of day had it not been for Atique Choudhury, whose local range of restaurants began with Yum Yum, and Lawrence Albonico, owner of Next Move estate agents in Stoke Newington and Islington. Their generous sponsorship has gone a long way to help with the printing, writing and design of the book. They have both been regular and valued advertisers since the very early issues, have subscribed to the magazine's ethos, and have also been enthusiastic and generous sponsors of the N16 Fringe, which was originated and promoted by N16 Magazine. Many thanks, gentlemen.

I would like to express my appreciation to all the article contributors, letter writers, columnists and everyone else whose assistance has ensured the remarkable durability of the magazine. To name them all would require a book in itself, but they know who they are and many are mentioned throughout the text of this book. The photographers and illustrators in this book include Pete Bennett, David X Green, Hackney Archives, Knife, Steve Pinhay, Mike Roberts, Martin Rowson and Nick Smith.

Also, our gratitude goes to everyone who has advertised in the magazine, thereby providing us with the funds to keep the magazine afloat and triumphantly to reach its 50th issue.

Finally, without a loyal readership, there is little point in producing the magazine. Thanks to you all for reading it and for your feedback and comments. We all hope you enjoy the next fifty issues.

For all sales please go to www.clissoldbooks.net

For other information contact us on info@clissoldbooks.net

www.clissoldbooks.com

www.n16mag.com